CHURCH
CHAT

CHURCH CHAT

Snapshots of a Changing Catholic Church

TOM SMITH

CHURCH CHAT
Snapshots of a Changing Catholic Church

iUniverse books may be ordered through booksellers or by contacting:

iUniverse
1663 Liberty Drive
Bloomington, IN 47403
www.iuniverse.com
1-800-Authors (1-800-288-4677)

ISBN: 978-1-4917-5057-5 (sc)
ISBN: 978-1-4917-5058-2 (hc)
ISBN: 978-1-4917-5056-8 (e)

Library of Congress Control Number: 2014918569

Printed in the United States of America.

iUniverse rev. date: 12/16/2014

To our small Christian community,
which began a decade ago as a renew group
and continues as a community of friends
who not only share our faith
but who also share our lives,
thanks!

CONTENTS

Part 3: You Gotta Be Kidding

Part 4: Culture Versus Catholic

Part 5: Spiritual Tidbits

Part 6: Holydays or Holidays?

Part 7: The Francis Factor and Other Signs of Hope

Part 8: Bishop Schneider's Dilemma

INTRODUCTION

The chapters in this book were born as columns. I wrote them originally for about fifty friends who have similar views of the Catholic Church and for myself because writing helps me clarify what I am thinking and feeling. Before long, people on my list forwarded the columns to other people, some of whom did the same. The life of the columns grew. It got to a point where I had no idea how many people were getting them, but I do know that some people read them because they emailed me or my friends. Most reactions were encouraging so I kept writing. And I still needed self-clarification on many topics.

I wrote a column about twice a month. I had no deadlines, but after five years, I have quite a collection and some of my friends suggested I turn them into a book. While I liked the idea of extending the life of the columns, I also know that turning these columns into a book is dangerous.

First of all, columns are dated. They often deal with events that were current at the time they were written but outdated by the time they slipped into a book. That's certainly true of some of the chapters in this book.

Secondly, my columns are usually around 700 to 750 words. This is not enough space to get deeply into any topic, many of which have significant nuances. When someone reads a book, they usually expect more details.

Thirdly, this book is about the Catholic Church, and on March 13, 2013, the Catholic Church changed dramatically when Pope Francis I was elected. At least, the part of the church that I usually write about changed. Why would anyone want to read about the way things were before Francis? And he hasn't been pope long enough for us to know what his impact on the church will be in the long run. So why try to catalogue the beginning of something when we really don't know how it will end?

However, here is why I am putting these columns together now:

First of all, these chapters are history as it happens. They start in 2009 and go into 2014, a period that witnessed the end of one papal era and the inauguration of a completely different one. Ten, twenty, fifty years from now, historians will try to record what happened in these five years. It may not feel like it while we live it, but these are remarkable times. I submit that these brief chapters, snapshots, describe some of the emotion, frustration, and anger, as well as the excitement and joy of being a progressive Catholic at this time. I doubt if future historians will see it the same way. Looking back, these five years will always be seen through the prism of the changes championed by Francis. Much of this book records the frustration of a Vatican II layperson before the happy appearance of Francis I.

Many of the incidents, personalities, and complaints described in these pages will not make the history books. But I contend that these stories and these candid, caught-in-the-moment snapshots are the stuff of real history as it is lived. Gathering these impulses, emotions, and observations into a book provides a collage of insights, examples, and pictures of being Catholic in the United States during this historic period.

Secondly, this book is titled *Church Chat* for a reason. We are chatting, not studying, analyzing, researching, or even learning. We chat. Well, at least, I chat and I hope you have your chatting ears on when you read.

So, why chat about the church? The church is serious, holy stuff with afterlife consequences, and to chat about that sounds somehow sacrilegious and superficial. If I want to write about the church, shouldn't the writing be serious and holy too?

Not necessarily. People do chat about the church: the latest gossip about church leaders, a statement from the pope or a bishop, a fight over various moral issues, last Sunday's homily, something someone read or a TV show they saw. There is a lot of conversation about church, some by people with significant theological backgrounds and some by folks who know very little about church history or doctrinal teachings. But we all chat. I simply want to put some of my chat on paper.

Thirdly, I do not present these chats in chronological order. I have organized them under seven broad categories in an effort to help readers stay with one general topic at a time. As a result, one chapter may be from 2010 and the next chapter may record something from 2012. I dated each chapter to help orient you to the time frame. Some chapters could fit into a number of the broad categories, but I put them where I put them.

Part 8 offers something different. I asked myself: who doesn't like Pope Francis? I answered that probably some bishops don't like him. So part 8 describes my version of a bishop who is having a hard time with Francis.

Fourthly, I believe this is a great time for a book like this. It is a glimpse, in real time, of the end of John Paul II and Benedict XVI's era and the transition into Francis I's very different pontificate. If another pope had been selected on March 13, 2013, one more like John Paul II or Benedict XVI, this book would be much less interesting and perhaps not needed.

But transition times stir things up, cause unusual hopes and fears, bring stuff at the bottom to the top, and take one set of priorities and replace them with another. Things move quickly during major transitions, what was standard at one time is replaced by a new approach. Besides, just the personality of Francis is such a contrast with John Paul and Benedict that the world has taken notice.

Since this new period is just beginning, we don't know how it will turn out or what those future historians will catalogue as significant. The practical impact of this fluid time on this book is that some of the comments, observations, and predictions in these chapters may be totally wrong. I don't pretend to have accurate knowledge of fast-moving events, inspired insights, unique powers of observation, or uncommon clarity of what's going on and why it is happening. I'm just chatting.

What I do promise is an honest recording of how I see things as they happen. I view these chats as snapshots because they capture moments, highlight them, and move on to the next moment or event. It is like a picture album arranged thematically.

Occasionally, at the end of a chapter, I will add a brief comment that updates the theme of that chapter. I call this section: Francis Follow-Up. What was true when I wrote the original chat may no longer be true at the time of this book. That's how history works—messy but interesting and sometimes surprising. I did not include the Francis Follow-Up comments in the main body of the column because I want to retain the integrity and perspective of the original version. The follow-ups identify specific changes in tone or action that highlight the differences between the two previous popes and Francis, which is a major theme of this book. At times, these comments will quote *The*

Joy of the Gospel, the book Francis published in December 2013 that outlines his vision of the missionary thrust of Christianity. If you haven't read it yet, I encourage you to do so.

For the sake of full disclosure (well, not totally full!), I am clearly, proudly, and correctly labeled a progressive Catholic. I try to be fair to differing points of view, and some people say I am balanced but there is no doubt where my convictions lie. I was also ordained a priest for the diocese of Belleville, Illinois, in 1966, laicized in 1973, married in 1974, fathered twins in 1976, and worked in various lay ministry positions all my life, except for the ten years I was with American Airlines. I discovered some years ago that my vocation had always been to lay ministry. I am now retired and spend most of my time with our family foundation, the Karla Smith Foundation (www. KarlaSmithFoundation.org).

I have also written seven other books, numerous articles, and over six hundred columns on various church-related topics.

Enough of that. I want to chat about the church, not myself. There is a lot to talk about. But it's hard to chat with myself. Chatting implies a conversation. If you want to join in, email me at tom.smith@karlasmithfoundation.org. I will continue to write these columns even after this book is published, and I enjoy suggestions, criticisms, and reactions to the chats.

These are historic times. I am glad I wrote the before-Francis chapters so that I have a record of what it was like during that period. But I am much happier to write about the Francis era because it feels like the vision and teaching of Vatican II is growing some flesh. Finally.

PART 1

Yes, Your Eminence

This cluster of chapters deals directly with the hierarchy. From my perspective, the hierarchy is the cause of many of the problems facing Catholicism. The current structure of the hierarchy and some individual bishops, cardinals, and popes advertently or inadvertently create unnecessary conflicts, hardships, and pain for the people of God.

Expect some criticism of the hierarchy in this section.

However, Pope Francis, in the early stages of his time as bishop of Rome, demonstrates a clear alternative to the recent past and a gospel simplicity that captures the spirit of Jesus and the Second Vatican Council.

CHAPTER 1

Two Hierarchies

June 2011

Two hierarchies? Isn't one more than enough?

Actually, two may be better than one.

In practice, there are two discernible, distinct, yet overlapping hierarchies in the Catholic Church. One is a structural hierarchy and the other, a service hierarchy. Though related, these two hierarchies are different and at times in opposition with each other.

The structural hierarchy is the one we all know. It is still a pyramid, despite the efforts of Vatican II to make it circular, or at least a little rounded off, with some softer lines and not so stark. But recent decades have sharpened the top of the design and have reinforced the middle of the pyramid with rebar that solidifies the upper half of the structure. The three sides of the pyramid all look the same, black with a little white collar in the middle, and as you gaze up the sides, they turn episcopal red, then cardinal crimson, and the very top is papal white. Colorful, but still a pyramid.

The structural hierarchy has really just one central concern: doctrine. Other issues pale in comparison. Whether it is HIV/AIDS versus condoms, a so-called abortion in an Arizona hospital versus the life of a mother, Bishop Morris in Australia versus a reference to ordination of women, etc., the pattern is clear: doctrine trumps everything. Faith must be expressed in clearly delineated creedal formulas, and morals are determined by preset rules that allow no deviations.

The lay base of the pyramid shows signs of wear and has not been reinforced, which seems ominous if you look at the structure from a distance. It appears that the people in the middle of the structure keep looking up, toward the top, so they miss the view of the bottom. Since the pyramid has lasted a long time, their assumption is that it will last forever or at least another very long time.

But will the crumbling base continue to support the weight of the reinforced top?

Not a chance. In a time of an Arab Spring, a China that is interwoven with democratic countries, and an Internet world delivering global awareness, a pyramid will not survive in the long run. People who live in pyramids will be ignored, shrunken to a quaint miniature, and quietly entered into a museum along with plaques of the Roman Empire, King Tut, and some very intriguing Neanderthal bones.

Service hierarchy refers to pastoral ministry, all those services that make direct contact with people. Parishes, hospitals, schools, relief agencies, social services, etc. are all included. They remain a hierarchy because they are governed, for the most part, by the clergy, usually, the "lower" clergy. The service hierarchy is driven more by the needs of people than by doctrine, though that is not always the case.

The tendency of some of the service hierarchs is to ignore the structural hierarchs when doctrinal issues interfere with service needs. By the same token, the structural hierarchs impose the doctrine regardless of the service needs.

For example, the Eucharist. The structural guys (there are no women) insist that a celibate male is necessary to consecrate and to transubstantiate (their word) the bread and wine into the body and blood of Jesus. The doctrine crushes all other considerations. The service hierarchs focus on the needs of the people and believe that Eucharist is a crucial source of faith, hope, and love so they see the value of including married men and women as celebrants of the Eucharist. Maybe even add a temporary priesthood. Doing so would simply provide better service to the people. The doctrine interferes with needed service, so change the doctrine. Jesus clearly agrees with the service-first model.

The advantage of making the distinction between a structural hierarchy and a service hierarchy is that both groups remain a part of the hierarchy. It isn't the hierarchy versus the nonhierarchy. The hierarchy remains with the structural guys emphasizing doctrine while the service proponents put service as the highest priority.

You can't put a round peg into a square hole or a pyramid. On second thought, you can put a pyramid into a circle; you just have to make sure the circle is big enough to surround the pyramid. I like circles.

And two hierarchies are definitely better than one.

CHAPTER 2

Institution Versus Community

October 2009

Avery Dulles, SJ, said it so well in his little book *Models of the Church*. He outlines five models of the church, which taken together provide a limited but valuable description of the church. His models are: institution, community, sacrament, herald, and servant. The church is each and all of these, and to eliminate one of them would be to deny an essential aspect of the mystery of the church.

But let's not be naive. As helpful as this analysis is, to experience these five aspects of church as a balanced reality is rarely, if ever, achieved. Dulles calls for a creative tension among these five competing impulses, but experience shows that the tension can be destructive and mean-spirited as well as creative. Church as sacrament, herald, and servant get along together pretty well. But the miter meets the pew in the clash between church as institution and church as community. And a mighty clash it is.

The institutional church refers to its hierarchical structure, its decision-making process, its policies, and the teachings that support its structures and policies. The church as community includes the fellowship of its members, love, faith, hope, spiritual journey, and the elusive but indomitable presence of the Holy Spirit. Dulles summarizes these two opposing models by pointing to external factors in describing the institution and internal (spiritual) factors for the community. He, of course, insists that we need both.

That's a nice, valuable intellectual distinction. In real life, however, it's a struggle between control and freedom, conformity and diversity, obedience and intuition, rules and conscience. The problem is that most people are unable to juggle these two, paradoxical dimensions of church in a way that gives value and provides limits to both of them. As a result, most people lean one way or the other and in practice, give much more credence and behavior to whichever way they lean.

This conflict between institution and community is not surprising, and it is not new. Institutions and the people who run them tend to protect themselves and the institution. Any dictator illustrates the political use of this self-protective principle, and within the church, the sex-abuse cover-up is just one example of the church institution protecting itself.

I am and will remain a Catholic. I know enough church history and doctrine to insist that the current church would be a much better church with less institution and more community, and that there have been times and places in history when community was predominant.

Fortunately, people in the pews are basically ignoring many of the exhortations of the hierarchy. This casual dismissal of the teachings of the pope and bishops is not a denial of a hierarchical church but a simple wisdom that in many cases the pope and the bishops just don't know what they are talking about. The days of blind belief in the hierarchy are over. Leadership is now required but clearly lacking. The birth control encyclical in 1968 gave great impetus to this attitude in modern times, but a whole series of statements and papal/episcopal pronouncements since then have reinforced it. The people of God aren't buying it, and we're forcing more community on the institutional church, whether they like it or not.

The people know the institutional church is way out of balance, and we are gradually taking care of it by ignoring much of the institutional self-serving nonsense and developing faith community experiences in our parishes and on our own. History will thank us.

CHAPTER 3
The Vatican Catholic Church

June 2012

This is a side issue. With the recent attack on the Leadership Conference of Women Religious; the ongoing, simmering resentment of the unnecessary, forced imposition of the liturgical changes last fall; and the persistent, damaging reality of the clergy sex abuse/cover-up disaster, this issue is very minor.

Here it is: I suggest we no longer refer to the universal church as the Roman Catholic Church, but we call it the Vatican Catholic Church. The Vatican is not part of Rome anymore, so why taint the unique, beautiful city of Rome with the machinations of the Vatican? Let's at least be honest enough to keep the Romans out of it.

I told you it was a minor issue. So, end of chat?

Well, let's see. What difference would it make if many of us started using Vatican Catholic Church instead of Roman Catholic Church? Many of us just say Catholic Church anyway. In that case, what would happen if we added the Vatican label in our chatting about church?

First of all, and this is a side issue to a side issue, just how catholic are we? *Catholic* means universal, and I get the part about Catholics in all parts of the world. But in terms of how and what we believe and how we express those beliefs, it seems the Vatican Church is becoming less and less universal.

I agree that we need some parameters on what we believe. Being Catholic must have some definable content to it. But those boundaries can be broad or narrow. Catholics in previous ages who believed in heretical superstitions were still considered Catholics. But today the tendency is to narrow those parameters if you are a pre-Vatican II conservative and to widen them if you are a progressive.

How catholic is that?

Anyway, back to the primary side issue: the Vatican Catholic Church. When we use "Roman" as the adjective describing the church, we attach the history, power, and prestige of the Roman Empire, ultimately the Holy Roman Empire, to the church. By association, the church absorbs the unearned *gravitas,* the respected accomplishments of a dominant, political government and culture.

The only reason we are identified as the Roman Catholic Church is because the Roman Empire was there first. Sure, it made sense that we would headquarter there during those early centuries. But Italy is not a world power these days, not by any standard. Do we need to remain there today because we have some famous buildings in the neighborhood?

Maybe the Avignon popes had a good idea: get out of Rome. Remember that the popes were in Avignon, France, for about seventy years during the fourteenth century? How about a papacy today that headquartered in different parts of the world every ten years? It could be done with digital technology and rapid communication. Now, that would be a symbol of universality. Besides, it would break the Italian stranglehold on the Vatican (despite the two recent popes being non-Italian. Check the ratio of Italian cardinals compared to any other nationality. Once again, how catholic is that?)

The least we can do is to name our church correctly. When we refer to our headquarters by where it is, we must say Vatican City. Vatican City is about 110 acres with a population of a little over nine hundred people, and it is the smallest independent state in the world. Sounds much humbler than "Roman," doesn't it? Sounds a lot more like Jesus of Nazareth, doesn't it?

When we insist on being Roman, we assimilate the baggage of the Roman legacy: the drive to political power and control over nations. We mimic Roman organizational structures. We freeze the times and customs of the early Middle Ages and transport them into the twenty-first century, even to the point of petrifying something as transitional as fashion (vestments and clerical dress). Being Roman means being domineering, institutional, ponderous, and downright stubborn.

As far as I know, the Romans of today do not have aspirations of becoming the Romans of old. It is only the Vaticanistas of today who want to become the Romans of old. What a shame! Being humble and insignificant in the presence of world powers is precisely what the church needs and the gospel commands. That posture is not likely when we are Roman. It is possible when we are Vatican.

Maybe this side issue is more central than I thought.

Francis Follow-Up: Amazingly, Pope Francis seems headed in this Vatican-better-than-Roman direction. While he would never change the official designation of the Roman Catholic Church to the Vatican Catholic Church, he is living the lifestyle and giving witness to the humility, simplicity, and compassion of a Jesus born in Bethlehem and who grew up in Nazareth. He is de-Romanizing the Catholic Church as I had hoped when writing this chat.

CHAPTER 4

Dictators

February 2011

The dominoes keep falling. First, it was Tunisia, then Egypt, and Libya. Whom did I miss? Oh yes, Bahrain. Who's next? Revolutions in countries with dictators headline the news around the world. Add Facebook and Twitter and we have instant, eyewitness testimony to the streets of change.

I am not smart enough or informed enough to chat about the causes and consequences of this revolution. But I do encourage you to watch the news for the latest on this world-changing series of events.

My simple observation is that tyrannical regimes are being rejected after decades of strongman rule. Millions of people are shouting their aspirations for freedom and getting results. At this point, these revolutions have Arab names, but the antiauthoritarian yearnings of subjugated throngs around the world are just one Facebook entry away from sparking more revolt.

How it will all turn out remains to be seen. Will there be various forms of democracy, or will new dictators, as ruthless as the past ones, capture control of their countries? The stakes are high for our interconnected, global civilization.

Wikipedia describes a "dictator" as a "leader who holds and/or abuses an extraordinary amount of personal power, especially the power to make laws without effective restraint by a legislative assembly."

Here's my question: to what extent is the pope a dictator? I must immediately qualify the question. I am not asking if Pope Benedict XVI and Pope John Paul II are the ecclesiastical equivalents to Hosni Mubarak or Muammar Gadhafi. I am asking if our hierarchical model of leadership lends itself to characteristics similar to a dictatorship, depending on who sits in the seat of power. History resounds with a thunderous "yes."

The church is not a democracy: that principle has been drummed into me since childhood. And I support the principle. There are nuances, but the apostles had a unique relationship with Jesus. Some early church leadership appropriately fell to them. But then there was Paul whose leadership had a different origin and followed a different model. And undoubtedly, others, some recorded, some obviously, not.

If the governance of the church and the determination of orthodox teaching are not based on democratic principles, then what are they based on? Scripture and tradition. Plus a hierarchical model.

While democracies can be messy and contentious, the advantage is that there is a checks-and-balances dynamic that, in theory and for the most part in practice, prevent domination. A hierarchical model offers efficiency and compliance, but there are no checks and balances.

It is a short leap to see that a hierarchical model, whether it is in politics, business, or religion, is closer to a dictatorship than the multiple forms of democracy. Any hierarchical leader in any of these arenas can become a "leader who holds and/or abuses an extraordinary amount of personal power, especially the power to make laws without effective restraint by a legislative assembly."

Does this description of a dictator fit the papacy as currently exercised? Well, the pope certainly holds an extraordinary amount of personal power. His personal theology, devotional preferences, priorities, personality, and convictions move a billion-member religion in a particular direction. The fact that all billion members don't immediately point in the same direction doesn't change that direction. That capability clearly demonstrates extraordinary personal power, regardless of the degree to which the Holy Spirit influences the pope.

The Second Vatican Council reintroduced measures to balance some of this extraordinary power with some collegial responsibilities. The council outlined structures to facilitate the exercise of the collective governing powers of bishops and their responsibilities not only within their dioceses but for the universal church. National episcopal conferences, synods, priest councils, diocesan pastoral councils, and parish councils all followed this collegial model. The hierarchy remained, but the people of God engaged in the process. We felt like we were the church as opposed to belonging to a religion owned by the hierarchy with the pope sitting at the top of the pyramid of power.

To quote the Pete Seeger song: "Where have all the flowers gone?"

CHAPTER 5

Efficient Hierarchy?

April 2011

A few chats ago, the one titled "Dictators," I slipped in a phrase that I knew was troublesome, not nuanced enough, but I used it anyway. And, as it should be, one of you caught me. That's what I get for having perceptive readers, some of whom take the time to email me. Thanks; that's what happily happens when we chat.

The offending phrase was: "A hierarchical model offers efficiency..." In the chat, I was asking to what extent the pope fits the definition of a dictator, and one of you correctly commented that hierarchical forms of governance are not automatically efficient.

Hierarchy in theory is one thing; in practice, it is quite another. In theory, a wise, benevolent leader can run an efficient government, company, organization, or church. It is efficient because the policies are reasonable; the implementation is just; the relationships are based on integrity, mutual trust, and respect; and the goals emerge from the common good. Nice arrangement.

Does the Catholic Church fit this description? You know, it probably does in some parishes and perhaps in some dioceses. Pastors, in many ways, have a great deal of freedom to do or not do whatever they want, or don't want, in their parish. Technically, they are accountable to the bishop, but that accountability has no teeth. As long as he says Mass on Sunday, a pastor can quietly ignore the bishop and the parish, for that matter. There are no practical consequences to him. On the other hand, wonderful pastors can function quite freely as well.

A bishop can mismanage the diocese, belittle the people, disregard his advisors, intimidate many of the priests, insist on his privileges, judge others based on his own personal theological and psychological prejudices, and govern for years without any effective checks and balances. But, once again, another bishop can be exemplary as the diocesan leader.

Any form of government that spawns such contradictory styles of leadership as benevolent, collegial leaders on one hand and lazy or arrogant despots on the other hand is not efficient. When I worked for American Airlines, managers would be fired or demoted when they didn't perform according to minimum standards. Not so in the church.

One factor that undermines the church's hierarchical governance model is that most of the policies and practices are rooted in medieval Europe and a feudal society. From what I know of the first few centuries of the church, I doubt if we can even use the word "hierarchy" to describe leadership during that period. Apostles, and others, were leaders but not "hierarchs" as we understand the term that was pulverized by the medieval sausage factory called feudalism.

The hierarchical model that we know does not come from the scriptures or the early church but from this medieval period in Europe. Our current governance structure is frozen in that period with the erroneous assumption that there is something divinely inspired about that European style of society.

I hate to burst too many balloons, but God is not a feudal lord or emperor of our souls. Jesus taught us that. The feudal system died as a governance model for society but lives on in the Catholic Church because it benefits the few clerics who continue to control it.

Vatican II tried to break this thousand-year stranglehold on the church but was only moderately successful. The *Constitution on the Church* introduced a people-of-God view of the church more closely aligned with the early church and what we have experienced in recent centuries with various forms of democratic societies. The problem with the constitution is that it also has paragraphs reflecting the hierarchical model. One paragraph envisions a collegial form of governance, and the next paragraph repeats the hierarchical theme. Today's conservatives simply quote the passages they like and maintain the flawed, antiquated status quo.

The resulting inefficiencies are inevitable. Priests are selected as bishops based on their proven allegiance to the system. The reputation of the institutional church is the misguided but highest priority. The laity remains second class to the privileged, elite clerics. These are the principles that guide the decisions that lead to inefficient management of finances, personnel, and priorities. The people of God know this system makes no sense today.

So, for the record, the hierarchical model of governing the Catholic Church is anything but efficient. It is a medieval disaster rolling downhill.

Francis Follow-Up: Now, in 2014, Pope Francis has initiated many more collegial elements to this hierarchical model and the vision of Vatican II gets clearer as it becomes reality. Here are just two examples of his collegial style:

He created an advisory council of eight cardinals, chosen from around the world and not tied to the curia. That group initiated a worldwide survey to gather the opinions of Catholics in preparation for a "Synod on the Family" to be held in October 2014. He speaks often about consensus building. There's a long way to go, but he has turned the corner and left the superhighway to monarchical control. What a delightful surprise!

CHAPTER 6

Much Ado...

December 2010

I wasn't going to chat about Archbishop (not-yet Cardinal) Dolan's election to the presidency of the USCCB because people smarter and more informed than I have already made the most significant comments. Actually, now that the dust has settled, it strikes me that the whole thing is much ado about little. But it is worth one chat.

The differences among those two hundred plus mitered men are so small that it doesn't really matter who is president. It's like a tea party where the polite repartee is about whether Bigelow's raspberry decaf tea is better than Lipton's unsweetened regular tea steeped slowly in hot, but not boiling, distilled water. Where are the bishops who drink strong, black, caffeinated coffee and who consistently and loudly proclaim the gospel of social justice, peace, love, joy, inclusion, sexual sanity, and the preferential option for the poor?

Maybe I am out of the loop. I believe that some of those stalwart bishops still exist, and I actually worked for a few of them. I am not a diehard bishop-basher; I respect the office and many of the men who carried and carry a crosier. But at this point, I don't know who they are. I knew Bishop Gerry Kicanas from Tucson in the seminary because he was in the class behind me at Mundelein. I didn't know him well, but I thought he was smart and a nice guy, and from what I heard, he would have made a fine president of the conference. Then the bishops voted in Dolan instead of Kicanas. Is that a good choice or not? Since I am out of the bishop loop, I really don't know. But I am guessing that Kicanas would be better than Dolan.

How about this? If you know a bishop who seems holy, has integrity, credibly reflects the spirit of the gospel and the Second Vatican Council, and has a pleasant personality, send me his name. If I get enough names, I will chat about them. If you think my criteria are too tough, let me know that too.

In any case, what is most significant about the American bishops these days is that most people, including Catholics, don't pay much attention to them. What is worse than much ado about nothing is little ado about little. It is a far cry from the time when a bishop would express an opinion or give an order and hordes of loyal followers would immediately obey and scurry to implement his wish. That was then; this is now.

I don't do polls so I don't know what Catholics think about their bishops, but my suspicion is that they don't think about them much at all. They are not relevant to the joys and struggles of daily life. People who are part of a Catholic faith community look to the pastor and staff of that community for spiritual nourishment and guidance. The local bishop, and by extension the bishops as a group, simply are not a significant part of the equation.

I am not looking for rival groups among the bishops, like Democrats and Republicans, or Tea Partiers versus Progressives. But some lively, healthy debates and some varying opinions would be nice. Like during Vatican II.

In the recent comments by the pope regarding male prostitutes and condoms, the American bishops responded by referring the matter to the Vatican. One article on this ongoing issue indicated that the pope introduced the topic to invite discussion and debate about it. What a great idea. One of the clearest teachings of the Second Vatican Council is that the bishops, in union with the pope, have "supreme and full authority over the universal Church" (*The Church*, chapter 3, paragraph 22). Discussion and debate among the bishops is one proper forum for exploring the meaning and implications of the pope's comments.

You don't discuss and debate when you immediately refer the topic to the Vatican.

Over the last few decades, the Anglicans/Episcopalians have discussed and argued over issues like ordination of women, gay rights, and episcopal ordination of gay priests. There has been division, loss of membership, ruptures in the church community, and antagonism. But, to their credit, they have dealt with these very difficult issues directly and openly. These same issues face Catholics, but all we do is refer these topics to the Vatican.

That's why it doesn't really matter who is president of the United States Conference Catholic Bishops.

CHAPTER 7

Vatican Splendors

August 2010

I am not a Vatican art basher. I do not advocate selling the art and using the money for the poor. Well, not all the art, anyway. They could sell some of it, like some of those ornate chalices and lesser known paintings. On the other hand, while it may not technically be sacrilegious, I do have difficulty visualizing the Sistine Chapel as an upscale Olive Garden, serving expensive wine with their house salad.

The reason I am even thinking of Vatican art is that I recently visited the St. Louis Historical Museum where they are featuring an exhibit called "Vatican Splendors." The exhibit was packed with people viewing and listening to the audio descriptions of original paintings and artifacts along with replicas of priceless masterpieces like Michelangelo's Pieta.

Since I am more intrigued by history than by art, I was drawn to the two-century-long design and construction of St. Peter's Basilica, plaza, and colonnade and the 1100-year-old history of the previous basilica initiated by Constantine in the fourth century. Pretty fascinating stuff, if you ask me.

The idea, of course, is for religious art to inspire viewers to increased faith. That effect clearly happens for some believers. Art, including Vatican art, instructs and inspires many people. But (and you knew there was a "but" coming, didn't you?), enough is enough and too much is too much. The basic problem is that all that Vatican splendor washes away the human service inspired by the gospel, ignores the experience of the genuine faith community, and enshrines the institutional church. The splendor of the art obliterates the splendor of a humble, lived faith.

It is no wonder that pope after pope comes across more as a regal lord than a humble servant. It is no wonder that those golden thrones, massive monuments, outdated vestments, and priceless paintings obscure the simple faith, hope, and love of popes, priests, and the people of God. Those stones speak louder than faith-filled hearts.

The only person I can recall who broke through this stifling splendor was

Pope John XXIII, whose grandpa smile was backed up by his Vatican Council II. Unfortunately, during the past forty years, the Vatican once again reinforced the oppressive splendor.

The tragedy of the art, the Basilica, and the Vatican itself is that it is an icon of the Vatican Catholic Church. It is the image that represents the church. All around the world, the picture of St. Peter's is the symbol of Catholicism. How many times does it show up in movies, pictures, TV? The crucifix may be the universal icon for Christianity, but St. Peter's is the sign identifying Catholicism. It is how we are branded.

It doesn't matter that millions of Catholics around the world are deeply spiritual, loving God and other people, courageously faith-filled, inspiring, and joyful. It makes no difference that our institutions of service (hospitals, schools, agencies for the poor) are monumentally successful. Never mind the vast diversity of people from every continent, each culture, thousands of languages, and all ethnic groups who call themselves Catholic. Our logo remains St. Peter's Basilica.

It isn't that some New York public relations firm, after millions of dollars, months of closed-door, late-night brainstorming sessions, and long lists of suggestions finally emerged with St. Peter's Basilica as our proposed logo. No, we did it ourselves. We thought and bought Roman, pope, hierarchy, splendor, and centralization as the way we wanted to be identified. And so it is.

It is ironic that, in actuality, we are no longer the Roman Catholic Church anyway. Not since 1929 when the treaty with Italy created Vatican City as the smallest country in the world. More accurately, we then became the Vatican Catholic Church. But, of course, the Roman label outlasted the reality.

It is also ironic that Roman Catholic is a contradiction in terms. What is catholic (universal) is identified by what is minutely specific (one city). Does that really make sense? This kind of labeling surely wasn't Jesus' idea. We need a logo and a language that truly represents both the unity and the diversity of the Catholic experience.

Not surprisingly, the splendors of the Vatican, regardless of their value and beauty as art, do not measure up as the appropriate symbol of Catholicism. So … what does?

Francis Follow-Up: Delightfully, Pope Francis has turned splendor into simplicity, grandeur into graciousness, and pompous aloofness into accessible mercy. In word and deed, he separates himself from the splendor that surrounds him.

CHAPTER 8

Appointing Bishops

September 2009

I never could figure it out, but then again, I guess I never was supposed to know. Who really selects bishops, and how are they appointed? What makes one priest "bishop material," and how does a name make its way through the hierarchical system until the pope supposedly signs off on someone?

At one time, I thought I knew part of the process. A current bishop submits the name of a priest to the metropolitan bishop (the one who heads a region or group of dioceses). These names are discussed among the bishops of the region, and some of these names are eventually forwarded to a congregation in Rome who culls the list down to just those who are recommended to the pope. In some cases, surveys and opinions are sought from dioceses without a current bishop for the kind of bishop a diocese feels it needs. That's an outline of what I think happens sometimes.

If this summary is basically accurate, it certainly doesn't happen all the time. In any case, much of the process is still very secret. What criteria are used to determine whether a priest is bishop material? Is it better to have chancery office experience or pastoral experience as a priest? What kind of forum is used locally, nationally, and in Rome to decide the selection? Who has the most impact on the final selection? The pope obviously relies on the recommendations of some group. Who makes up that group? What are their credentials? Realistically, what part does the pope actually play in the selection? The bishop of my diocese was appointed two weeks before John Paul II died. Since the pope was very sick at the time, who actually transferred my bishop to the diocese of Belleville? And why? The questions go on and on.

It is a process that is ripe for backroom favoritism. Closed-door proceedings are required, and secrecy is demanded to protect the manipulations. Since the pope officially makes the appointment, there is no recourse. The "good, ole boys with miters" keep feeding the pope names of priests who think and feel like they do.

There are so many obvious flaws in this system that even *Church Chat* can't chat that long. But one question just overwhelms me. Why does it take so long to name a new bishop for a diocese? Months and sometimes years go by before a new bishop is appointed. If it takes that long, who needs a bishop anyway? If it is a matter of Vatican inefficiency, then get people who are more efficient, or get more people to do the necessary research. If it is a matter of policy, then explain the policy.

I can't think of any reasonable explanation why it takes so long. Simply identify the priests who are eligible for ordination to the episcopacy. Keep a list. Appoint them shortly after a vacancy occurs in a diocese. Adjust the list. What's so hard about that? Even if they survey the priests and laypeople of the diocese, it doesn't have to take as long as they generally take to fill a vacancy. What's the point? If a company or government agency operated like the Catholic Church does in this area, they would be bankrupt or most middle management positions would be eliminated.

Since I want a church with a different emphasis, this outmoded and manipulative system of appointing bishops must change. Sometimes, I wish that such a declaration would actually make something happen. Did it change yet?

CHAPTER 9

The Selection of Bishops

September 2010

In his *Essays in Theology* column of September 13 titled "The Selection of Bishops," Rev. Richard McBrien focused on Cardinal Marc Ouellet, the new head of the Vatican's Congregation of Bishops. McBrien predicted that Cardinal Ouellet would not change the pattern of selecting and appointing bishops established by Pope John Paul II and continued by Benedict XVI.

I have admired McBrien for many years and consider him one of the best theologians in our country. His body of work is amazing, and his ability to communicate theology on a popular level is unequalled. Many of the things I merely chat about can be traced to his thinking.

So, I might as well chat about the selection of bishops. In general, they select priests who look to the past and not to the future. It's appalling, and all of you know it because it's likely that you too have asked the question: why did they make *him* bishop?

I have worked directly for four bishops, and I am a classmate of another one. In my opinion, of the five, two are exceptional church leaders whom I continue to admire. The other three force me to wonder why and how they were selected as bishops.

As I see it, none of the other three should have been made a bishop. Just to keep this opinion from being purely subjective, many other people agree with me. How do I know? We chatted about it, and the consensus is overwhelming: none of the three should be or should have been bishops. When I expand the discussion to include bishops I don't know personally, many more bishops are added to my list of three to the point that the list would be much shorter if we ask which bishops *should* be bishops.

The current system for selecting bishops is clearly flawed and downright destructive. Some form of consultation with the people in the pews is required because it is clear that for over thirty years the intent in making bishops is to shore up the church as an institution. Other aspects of the church, such as community, sacrament, servant, and herald (remember Fr. Dulles's models of the church?) are neglected as qualities for consideration.

The result is that many of the men who are bishops simply are not qualified to lead a diocese today or at any time. Even if some of them are well-intentioned, they are ill-suited for the role. They don't have now and never did have the talent, personal characteristics, and sense of mission to cultivate within themselves and within their ministry what it takes to juggle those five aspects of the church successfully. The result is that they are one-dimensional and incapable of leading the people of God into a genuine, balanced journey of faith worthy of the gospel. They are company men with little creativity, courage, or compassion. They lack easily identifiable personality traits that appeal to the human spirit. They are incapable of honest, respectful relationships with the people they govern. Some are so ego-centered that they scuttle the heart of the gospel. Others are weak, obsessed with superficial issues, but capable of bullying and misusing their authority and power. Then again, there are some who have a clinical mental illness.

I am not making this up; I can name names, but I won't. Besides, I bet you can name your own names. And it isn't that many of these bishops suddenly developed these destructive traits when they were selected bishops. They were known and identified long before they greedily grabbed their first crosier. Talk to other priests, guys they grew up with in the seminary and priesthood, and they will tell you what kind of persons they were before they became bishops. The clerical club knows who is bucking for bishop, who toes the line in an effort to get noticed, who desperately wants to be a bishop, and who will do whatever it takes to wear a miter.

What is it about the whole system that promotes priests who have never demonstrated basic qualities that clearly are required to lead the church? The stock answer to those kinds of questions is: absolute doctrinal loyalty and unwavering hierarchical obedience. Unless those criteria are eliminated and replaced with successful, practical pastoral experience confirmed by the people they serve, the institutional church will never genuinely proclaim the gospel. Right now, too many lightweights with rigid personalities are bishops.

My guess is that Fr. McBrien agrees with me.

CHAPTER 10

The Selection of Bishops II

September 2010

This is a chat about my previous chat. I'm not foolish enough to think that my last effort was all that memorable, so here's a quick summary: the process for selecting bishops is destructively flawed.

Many of you sent encouraging email responses. So, thus encouraged, I will add a little more. First, a word of caution: we have to be careful when we call out individual bishops. There is a danger in accusing anyone of anything publically. Lawsuits aside, to judge someone as ineffective, self-serving, obstructionist, irrelevant, or mean-spirited, whether it is a politician, CEO, bureaucrat, neighbor, cleric, or celebrity, can easily be unfair, unchristian, and/ or unkind. Allegations must be based in reality.

Granting those cautions, it still seems to me that our current process for selecting bishops guarantees a high percentage of ill-equipped men to lead the church in the twenty-first century. I'm not just referring to different theological perspectives; I'm also talking about personality traits, political preferences, lifestyle longings, and pastoral skills. Today's method of choosing bishops ensures mediocrity and compliance.

How can I make this claim without personally knowing thousands of bishops? By the results. For example, if there were greater diversity among bishops, there would be lively, public, episcopal debates about optional celibacy, ordination of women, liturgical practices, collegiality, and a host of other issues. These are hot-button concerns among millions of Catholics worldwide. If even fifty bishops would publically take a united position contrary to official policy on optional celibacy, for example, it would be headline news in multiple languages around the globe.

But this kind of break with the party line doesn't happen even though poll after poll across the world indicates that hundreds of millions of Catholics, generally the distinct majority of the laity as well as parish priests, favor optional celibacy. And yet the bishops are not even "allowed" to discuss the issue publically. Why would they all obey such an obvious power play? Because, for the most part, they have been thoroughly prescreened to be compliant. Courage and creativity are left at the cathedral doorsteps.

All organizations, companies, governments, and associations ask their members or employees to be loyal and compliant. Shouldn't the church expect the same? Isn't it reasonable to demand similar submissive behavior from bishops when the Vatican speaks? No, the church is different. The church's mission is to proclaim the gospel, not sell a product, govern a citizenry, or promote a specific cause. Actually, even in companies and governments, there are "whistleblower" laws to protect employees when they have issues with official policy or procedures. There are occasional, lone, whistleblowing bishops (Bishop Kevin Dowling, CSSR, in Cape Town, South Africa, on June 1 is the most recent example I know of), but, as usual, other bishops have not rallied to his message about using condoms to prevent the spread of HIV. Nothing significant or long-lasting will come from his courage. Bishops as a group are chosen based on their high probability of conforming to Vatican policy.

Actually, the screening process begins long before potential bishops don their first cassock. Initial requirements for priesthood eliminate most of the human race. Even though being male and celibate have absolutely nothing to do with priestly service, they are used to narrow down the episcopal candidate pool to a manageable few. Years of seminary training and priesthood provide ongoing monitoring so that by the time someone is identified as "bishop material," he is known to be appropriately compliant. That's how a small handful of cardinals and the pope can control a church of over a billion people.

It's not that hard, really, and totalitarian governments, companies, and organizations have done pretty much the same thing for centuries. Fear is the primary motivator, so it makes sense to choose fearful people as surrogate leaders. Machiavelli would be proud.

The problem is that the church is not a government; it is the people of God (as Vatican II insisted) humbly trying to follow the way of Jesus as outlined in our tradition and the scriptures. There is an inherent, necessary, inevitable, self-critical feature to the church because we will never get the gospel completely right as an institution. We are an institution in search of a gospel community.

And our current process for selecting bishops guarantees a very, very long search.

Francis Follow-Up: It appears in 2014 that Pope Francis is aware of and addressing this issue of the selection of bishops. Recent appointments reflect a greater emphasis on pastoral experience and a humble personal lifestyle. This is encouraging, but we have to wait and see if he can initiate significant, long-term change to the recent protective and defensive system of selecting bishops. Throughout *The Joy of the Gospel*, Pope Francis insists that the church needs to be self-critical, a necessary attitude to create the atmosphere for changing the process and criteria for selecting bishops. In particular, read the section titled "An Ecclesial Renewal which Cannot Be Deferred" (paragraphs 27–33).

CHAPTER 11

My Bishops

August 2011

I know from experience what I don't want in a bishop. But what *do* I want?

I'm not talking about idealized bishops, living in perfect world cathedrals, presiding over loyal flocks of smiling sheep in a secular society turned sacred. No, I am talking about bishops in this Benedict XVI–led church, during an Arab spring/summer, in this recession-prone, conflict-producing collection of civilizations we call the early twenty-first century. Realistically, what would my bishops be like in this current world of ours?

Here is a brief, partial list, in no particular order, of the qualities I want in my bishops:

- Holiness—My holy bishops value the body-spirit interaction, embracing the material world as a companion to the spiritual world. They accept their personal, individual responsibility for their spiritual growth but only in conjunction with their unshakeable commitment to community. They cultivate a personal relationship with Jesus, spending considerable time each day in prayer and meditation coupled with a loving familiarity with current scriptural scholarship. With these qualities, not every brand of holiness fits my bishops (e.g., a holiness that is too individualistic or one that is based on nonscriptural devotionalism doesn't comply with my standards). Their spirituality is genuine, not a contrived, professional piety engineered for public, ritual display. People know that they are authentically holy.

- Leadership—My bishops are leaders not because of their position but because of their character. They look you in the eye and speak directly and clearly, with a calm confidence. After consulting with a variety of people with various opinions, they make decisions. They humbly admit when they are wrong and give others credit when they are right. They are courageous, willing to confront other church and civic leaders on policies they believe are wrong and harmful. They are exceptional public speakers, in liturgical and nonliturgical settings. People look forward to hearing what they have to say, and their words and opinions have influence. They earn the respect of others, even those who disagree with them. They do not insist on deferential treatment, places of honor, titles, or public attention.

- Intelligence—My bishops are smart, comfortably exhibiting a wide range of knowledge, creative thinking, and lively, broad-based curiosity. They read current books and keep up with the news and significant trends in the world and the church. Their intelligence helps fuel their leadership. They lead by service, listening to pastors and parish councils, promoting an active and informed diocesan pastoral council, visiting parishes to dialogue with the people. They hire a diocesan staff that reflects their vision, and they challenge us to deeper spiritual lives, which includes outreach to the poor. When in school, they distinguished themselves academically, particularly in the theology of Vatican II. They do not simply parrot the "party line" or immediately follow predesignated priorities set by the Vatican. They are proud to be Catholic but refuse to be puppets or "branch managers" of the central Vatican office.

- Pastoral—My bishops put people before policies and dogmas. Their primary concern is not teaching but service. They focus on the people in front of them, accepting them, supporting them, and doing what they can for them. They are, in a word, compassionate, and people feel this understanding. These bishops are pastoral more than doctrinal. They have warm, welcoming personalities and are able to be relaxed and enjoy people in multiple settings.

That's a brief outline, but you get the point. Is it too much to expect these qualities in our bishops today? No, it is not too much to expect these kinds of bishops. In fact, history has already delivered many bishops who lived these virtues. I, frankly, don't see too many of them today, but there are people who could meet and exceed these standards.

And, by the way, my bishops could be male or female, married or single, gay or straight. Oh, that's right; I said "realistic" at the beginning of this chat. So I will rephrase: tomorrow morning, my bishops would be male, presumably celibate, and gay or straight. Regardless, my expectations remain. Someday … someday …

Francis Follow-Up: As it turns out, Pope Francis is a perfect example of the kind of bishop I described in August of 2011, though I knew nothing about him and he certainly didn't know anything about me. When I wrote that this kind of bishop was out there somewhere, I wasn't sure where I could find him. Now, of course, I can. I also suspect that some like-minded bishops around the world will now surface and take leadership roles. And I predict that future bishops will fit the model I outlined here much more so than in the past forty years. It will be intriguing to see how the Francis bishops collide with their predecessors.

CHAPTER 12

The Diocese of Penn State

November 2011

The firings of Joe Paterno, head football coach at Penn State, and Graham Spanier, president of the university, again demonstrate an essential flaw in the Catholic Church. I assume you already know the broad outline, if not many of the details, of the story. But if you don't, here is one link that will bring you somewhat up-to-date: http://news.yahoo.com/paterno-gone-questions-penn-state-remain-011614817.html.

My comparison with the Catholic Church is this: if Penn State were a diocese and Paterno a monsignor with Spanier as his bishop, no one would be fired. If the Penn State diocese were like some dioceses (Kansas City-St. Joseph, for example), Sandusky, as a priest, would be removed from active ministry (if the sexual abuse were public) or transferred to another parish (if the abuse were not public).

The difference between Penn State and a diocese is that Penn State has a governing board of trustees with the power to fire. The pope is the only authority with the power to hire and fire a bishop in the current Catholic system.

In 2009, there were 5,065 bishops in the world, each one directly reporting to the pope. Other people also report to the pope, but let's just count the bishops for now. The only other organizations that have similar power concentrated in one person are brutal dictatorships. Even benign dictatorships split up the hiring and firing authority among more people.

No management company in the world would support a ratio of 5,065 to 1 as direct reports. It is patently and obviously ridiculous. And don't tell me that Vatican congregations and national episcopal conferences monitor and control errant bishops. Isn't so. The pope alone has the power to hire and fire bishops. And, of course, he can't monitor 5,065 bishops.

The system itself is not only outmoded; it is inherently and inevitably defective, with predictable destructive outcomes.

Here's the real irony: there is no evidence that Jesus was that stupid.

His management style was personal, creating relationships, not structures modeled on the Roman Empire. When His core message was misunderstood by the crowds, He formed a small faith group of apostles who would get to know Him personally and ultimately absorb His radical principles regarding life and death. He and His followers did not have 5,065 direct reports; He clearly was not that dumb of a manager.

The current state of affairs with the governance model of the Catholic Church is so flawed that it resembles the famous quote of Lord Acton in 1887: "Power corrupts; absolute power corrupts absolutely." It is nowhere near the initial, gospel mandate: "You know how among the Gentiles those who seem to exercise authority lord it over them ... It cannot be like that among you ... serve the needs of all" (Mark 10:43–44).

I do not advocate the abolition of the hierarchical governance of the Catholic Church. But history plainly demonstrates that church hierarchy can be expressed in various ways. The first three centuries were light years away from our system of the last three centuries.

Vatican Council II introduced collegial styles of governance: synods of bishops, national episcopal conferences, subsidiarity, all with the potential of evolving into genuine decision-making authority, including some possibilities for reorganizing those 5,065 bishops. Those Spirit-filled, promising impulses of Vatican II were deliberately smothered by a minority of some powerful, inside-traders who protected their personal authority.

The pope could delegate the power to hire and fire bishops to local leaders (some early bishops were chosen by a mixture of local clergy and laypeople) and still remain Supreme Pontiff. It isn't God-ordained that the pope must select all bishops. It is a chosen system, not a divine imperative. And, once again, Jesus was not a naive and power-hungry cult leader who would have insisted on the governance system we currently have. That approach is precisely what He fought against—to His death.

Our current hierarchical system is a choice, not a mandate. Other hierarchical models are possible, and it is high time we pick up the impulses of Vatican II and find a new structure. Maybe even the Penn State system can teach us something.

CHAPTER 13

Restructuring

August 2013

It's clear that Pope Francis is in the process of restructuring the organization of the church in some way. At this point, it is unclear how that reform will look, and it may take years.

But at the diocesan and parish levels, reorganization is happening right now. Not because of Francis, but because of forces that have been brewing for decades: demographic changes, Catholics leaving the church, fewer priests, younger generations simply not interested, etc. Many dioceses, forced to address these issues, closed parishes, merged faith communities, and lost membership.

My own diocese of Belleville, Illinois, is in the middle of this kind of major restructuring. Despite the risk of becoming too local for my non-Belleville readers, I believe our experience represents many other dioceses. So, it is worth a chat.

The heart of this "Pastoral Plan for Parish Renewal and Restructuring" is the formation of "partnerships." These partnerships comprise two or more parishes, and each unit has the task to develop a plan by which this partnership will be able to be served by only one priest. But not all groupings have the same configuration: some include the closing of a parish as soon as possible but no later than next spring. Some have no time line on when there will be just one priest available. But all partnerships must have their plan by the end of 2013.

Despite the obvious cynical euphemism of calling this plan a "renewal" (it is destruction, not renewal) and the constant reference to partnerships (way too corporate—sounds like fast-food franchises merging), the plan is reasonable enough given our current status.

The premise is that our diocese will have just fifty pastors at some point, not counting international priests or retired priests. Therefore, there are fifty partnerships. I have been asked to be part of my parish partnership meetings and to facilitate the process in two other partnerships. I see the impact up close and personal. It is heart-wrenching, demoralizing, unnecessary, and, frankly, sinful.

There will always be parish and school closings due to demographic changes: people move to other areas, leaving a once-thriving parish unable to survive. That is painful but understandable. But what is happening now is completely different. One thriving parish is asked to share a pastor with another thriving parish, each parish with its own one-hundred-year history and identity. A few examples:

- A smaller parish led by a parish life coordinator is connecting with one of the largest parishes in the diocese and feels like they will be assumed into the bigger faith community. Despite assurances that this consolidation is not the plan, this feeling of frightening vulnerability pervades the smaller parish.

- Creating workable weekend Mass schedules is impossible. Many parishes report that, with a Saturday Mass and two Sunday masses, their church building is completely full now. When they lose a mass because their joint pastor is shared with a similar parish, there is physically no room to fit people into the building with fewer masses. People will simply leave in frustration.

- A woman reporting on how they might combine some of the administrative tasks cried when she spoke of the long-term history and personal identity of her parish.

- Pastors stoically lament the loss of the "personal ministry" they have with parishioners and doubt they will be able to create that experience when they pastor two or more parishes.

And why do we put the people of God through this kind of agony? Because we insist on ordaining only celibate males. Our stubborn, blind adherence to this one, outmoded, church-made policy is destroying our church experience as we know it. It's not the loss of faith, a secular society, an irrelevant message, not even a heavy-handed, authoritarian structure that is undermining the church. It is a celibate, male priesthood that can easily be changed with one or two decisions.

It's not a consolation to say that, in the third world, many pastors serve large, diverse communities. We are a first-world country and deserve first-world pastoral leadership. It is gravely sinful that our church allows, indeed causes, faith communities to lose reasonable access to the Eucharist and personal pastoral ministry because we refuse to open ordination to married men and women. That sin trumps all other considerations. Repent, and sin no more.

CHAPTER 14

Pope Francis and the Bishops

November 2013

This is conjecture because we will probably never know what the bishops worldwide really think of Pope Francis. They may not even share those private thoughts and feelings among themselves. But the hierarchical ground they walk on is now shaky. Before Francis, they knew what was acceptable talk and behavior and could navigate through the unwritten expectations of episcopal chatter, expectations, and behavior. With Francis, those ground rules have changed.

One quick example: the Vatican created a questionnaire intended to poll the people of God on issues related to family life, the topic for an episcopal synod in Rome in October of 2014. The cover letter for the questionnaire was clear: poll the people. But when some other Vatican official talked about the questionnaire, he didn't use the exact same language that the cover letter used but the intent was the same. In some reports I saw, some American church officials got all confused and wanted clearer directions from Rome on how to proceed.

What? Just poll the people. Just figure out the logistics, and do it.

My conjecture is that they can't handle this kind of openness and certainly not the implication that the people might have something to say about family life. Plus, the survey includes hot-button topics like outreach to divorced and separated persons as well as same-sex couples and gay persons. Asking the people for their opinions on those issues? Why would a bishop do that since he already knows the approved answers? It's no wonder they wanted "clarification."

The USA bishops hold their annual meeting starting on November 11. The published agenda is rather dull, but my guess is that it will not be business as usual and the public response will be telling. They will also elect a new president. My suggestion: go back to Bishop Gerald Kicanas, whom they dumped when they selected Dolan three years ago. Kicanas would fit the Francis style much better than Dolan does.

While I am conjecturing, here's another guess: in short order, the bishops will fall in line with Francis. That speculation runs contrary to what many other progressive Catholics predict, so I better try to explain myself.

There will be some pushback to Francis, but that will come from a minority. The majority of bishops will rather quickly fall in line behind Francis, once they are confident of his direction. I have already noticed that Cardinal Dolan, for example, has not "spoken for the American bishops" from his episcopal hip pocket since Francis became pope. Remember how cavalierly, wittily, and confidently he would meet the press and make pronouncements about the church's response to, say, health insurance coverage for Catholic hospital employees? Looks like he has backed off recently. Thank goodness.

Here's the core reason why the bishops will follow Francis: it's all they know. Their personalities will not allow anything other than that. Most of the bishops appointed in the last thirty years were chosen for their loyalty. That loyalty is not to a set of doctrines; it is loyalty to the pope and to the office of the papacy. They are not principled people, like people who are committed to social justice and who spend their lives fighting for a cause or a group of people. No, these bishops are loyal to the hierarchy, the offices they hold, and the offices of the people "higher" than they are, ultimately the pope.

In my supposition, most bishops are conservative theologically and culturally because the pope and the Vatican were conservative. They are not ecclesiastical Tea Partiers and will not "go to the wall" for their conservative positions. They are loyalists. So, changing their spots to fit a more progressive pope and Vatican is no problem.

Not all priests are like that. Many of them are more principled, committed to a set of values that anchor their personal and ministerial lives. But my guess is that many of the priests chosen to be bishops were selected because they demonstrated their foundational loyalty to the upper layers of the hierarchy.

It's like the military. The president, the commander in chief, changes from a Democrat to a Republican, and the military gets in line with the new policies and approach of the new commander. So too the bishops.

Anyway, that's my current conjecture. Who knows? I might be right.

Francis Follow-Up: A number of dioceses, including mine, did invite parish councils to answer the papal survey. There are many versions of the survey, and organizations are scrambling to get as many people as possible to complete the questionnaire. It is a research nightmare with all those open-ended questions, but it is the first time the people of God have been asked their opinion in my lifetime. And that fact may be the best feature of the survey. More to come on this story. We will have to wait and see how the synod proceeds in October 2014.

PART 2

Can You Believe It?

This section deals with some examples of church teaching. These chats certainly are not intended to describe or even comment on many or all of the church's teachings. They are simply observations about some of the teachings and the role that doctrine seems to have in modern-day Catholicism.

One theme that appears in these chats frequently is the apparent disconnect between magisterial teaching and the lived faith of the people of God. The role of Catholic doctrine in the daily lives of Catholics does not seem as significant as some of the hierarchy thinks it is.

This is an area that Pope Francis is minimizing while he emphasizes living the faith in concrete service to others. The contrast between his approach and the recent past is reflected in many of these chats.

CHAPTER 15

The Male God

August, 2010

Fortunately the dust has not settled on the worldwide outrage generated by the Vatican because they included women's ordination on the same list of the most serious crimes as pedophiles. Actually, the dust that has settled has turned to mud. And, by the way, who are "they," besides the pope? I want name, rank, email, home address, and private phone number to be distributed to the universe. Personal harassment is not only justified but demanded.

Much has been said, screamed, written, and broadcasted about this destructive debacle, and I certainly don't want to repeat what has already been said better by others. My question is: what can cause people to list women's ordination with pedophilia? My question remains, even though "they" say the two crimes are in different categories.

My guess is that one part of the answer emerges from an unlikely source: our image of God. How do I get from pedophilia, crusty old men in the Vatican, and women's ordination to an image of God? Do those dots really connect? I think they do.

In Judeo-Islamic-Christian tradition, the image of God is male. Not just a little masculine, overwhelmingly, undeniably, pervasively, unquestionably male. In scriptures, dogmas, doctrines, catechisms, pulpits, classrooms, conversations, rituals, prayers, art, thoughts, words, and actions, the image of God is male. It's the religious air we breathe. Recent attempts by some people to get beyond the image of a masculine God have not changed official teachings or most preaching. Our God is a guy.

It is easy to show that the real God is beyond our gender categories. By definition, God is bigger than our thoughts and descriptions. Not a little bigger, like just beyond our reach—we are talking about a completely *Other Being*, for whom we have no categories or descriptions.

We know something about this God through revelation. Christians believe that we learned about this God primarily through the life, death, and resurrection of Jesus. The fact that Jesus is a male is not proof that God is a male. The fact that we use Father, Son, Creator, Savior, and Lord in our scriptures, dogmas, rituals, and prayers does not make God a male. Those titles are our culturally conditioned ways to refer to God. Don't be fooled into thinking that those titles indicate a masculine God. The real God is much more and essentially different than all those titles.

The problem is that a lifelong, insistent, pervasive exposure to this supposedly male God leads some people to believe that maleness is better than femaleness. Add a culture that elevates men over women to this perception of a superior, male God, and we get people who conclude some bizarre things about themselves, the world, and God. So bizarre, in fact, that some little minds housed in rigid personalities can list pedophilia with women's ordination.

Since we need some pronoun to refer to God, I proposed over thirty years ago that the best we can do is to refer to God as "They." That eliminates the sexism and goes to the heart of the Christian belief about God: Trinity. We can point to God as Three Divine Persons just as accurately as One Supreme Being. I admit, however, that my campaign for "They" isn't going too well.

However we do it, we have to free God from our fixation on divine maleness. If I am even partially correct in my analysis of how anyone can even remotely put ordained women with pedophiles, this obsession with a man-God is one cause that has serious consequences. Males are not better than females, and God is genderless, despite our references to Father, Son, and Holy Spirit. I am not denying the Trinity; I am simply saying that our titles for the Divine Mystery are woefully inadequate and sometimes destructive. And my guess is that They are not happy about it.

I agree with anyone and everyone who believes that listing ordained women with pedophiles is outrageous, ridiculous, primitive, sexist, and just downright stupid. But as we rail and wail against this pompous garbage, we do need to ask how this connection can happen.

My two cents: be wary of male gods; they can cause despicable nonsense.

CHAPTER 16
The Teaching Church

February 2010

Jesus teaches. The church teaches. Why do those two realities feel so different?

Read the gospels, and then read church documents. What went wrong between then and now? Obviously, a lot. More learned people than I need to analyze and clarify that drastic change, but I do have two observations.

1. Jesus taught people using parables. The church teaches doctrine using theology. Enough said? Probably, but here's a little more: Jesus also taught doctrine (His identity, relationship with His Father, multiple lessons on and about life, the reign of God, etc.) but this "content" was always in the context of his relationship with people. He connected with a person or a crowd first and then mingled in some appropriate and often challenging teaching. Person first. Very effective way to teach and to learn.

    On the other hand, the church emphasizes doctrine. Believe this; memorize that; do this; don't do that. It is not person first; it is doctrine first. The RCIA (Rite of Christian Initiation for Adults) is a modern-day revival of the original "person first" approach, but it must counteract centuries of the doctrine-first, regardless of the person, approach. The jury is still out on whether the RCIA will survive the relentless onslaught of the doctrine-first (and only?) attacks. With our present crop of bishops, pope, and Vatican insiders, it's unlikely that person first has much of a chance in the long run.

    The problem is that people are not saved, converted, and only minimally persuaded by doctrine. People respond to whole-person, person-first stirrings of faith, trust, hope, and love. Information and knowledge alone do not move people to a level of personal commitment included in a genuine faith response.

    Head trips are short journeys to the mind, bypassing the heart. For centuries, catechisms, doctrinal statements, intimidation, superstition, and fear spawned mental and sometimes verbal adherence to faith statements. But the gospel experience of faith demands more than a head response; it includes mind, heart, emotions, and spirit—a personal response. Few people get to the heart through the head. Intellectual persuasion may win debates but not hearts.

Effective ministers are person first, not doctrine first. Like Jesus.

2. We have it backward again. We impart information before we have the experience to use that information. Doctrine has a place: to clarify a faith experience. We clarify, explain, pronounce, and clarify again before we experience. Our pastor is fond of saying: "Jesus played with children and taught adults. We teach children and play with adults." Good observation.

Faith is caught more than taught. Children may catch it from their family and/or friends. Adults may catch it from other adults. Faith is like a good virus; it spreads through personal contact. We spend way too much time and money on teaching children doctrine before their level of faith experience raises appropriate questions about the meaning of their faith.

Confirmation for fifth- through eighth-graders, even high school students, is a prime example of too much doctrine before the experience of faith. Either confirm at baptism or during adulthood when people really want to confirm their faith. What is the result of people not being confirmed? Honesty. What is the point of confirming people in their faith, even if they know answers to doctrinal questions, when they are not really "confirmed" in their hearts? Makes no sense, and it reaffirms the doctrine-first approach to faith. It's that ole head-trip again, another journey to the mind and ignoring the heart.

A bishop once asked me: "What can be more important for a bishop than to assure that correct church teaching takes place in his diocese?"

I replied: "The formation of community." A person-first approach. He either didn't get it or didn't agree because he didn't respond and changed the topic. My answer remains.

Francis Follow-Up: Francis is clearly person first. In his writing (just read almost any section of *The Joy of the Gospel*), his focus on people is evident. In his actions, he always puts any person or any group of persons as his obvious primary concern. This personal ministry preceded his papacy as millions of people in Argentina will attest. This trait puts him closer to Jesus, and as time goes on, this commitment to people will mark his papacy even more.

CHAPTER 17

God Speaks Latin

February 2010

Well, now we know. I suspected it for some time, but it is now confirmed. Think how this discovery will unify civilization, resolve all religious conflict, and move us all to the next level of evolutionary consciousness.

We now know the language God thinks in and speaks most naturally—or, oops, most supernaturally: Latin. When the Trinity communicates among themselves (How do they do that anyway? Mental telepathy? The Father thinks something, and somehow, the Son and the Holy Spirit are automatically tuned in?), They clearly use Latin. I always thought They communicated in a unique language like Godese, Trinitish, or something like that—a language that only They knew.

But now that we know it is Latin, we can all be at ease, learn Latin, and converse with God in His/Her/Their own language. God doesn't have to translate into all these languages anymore in order to communicate with us. The Tower of Babel is reversed. Everything will be so much better when we all learn God's Latin.

The proof that God speaks Latin comes from the new English translation for the Roman Catholic missal. This new translation isn't law yet (2011, if I have it correctly), but it is on its way. Fr. Michael Ryan from Seattle started a movement called "What If We Just Said Wait?" (http://www.whatifwejustsaidwait.org/), which invites people to sign a petition to delay the implementation of the new missal until some pilot areas could assess the impact on people. I signed the petition and support the effort. But frankly, I don't think the people who are forcing this translation on us are interested in waiting or grassroots opinions. They simply don't care.

How can they be so righteous? Because they discovered that God speaks Latin.

The primary language criterion for the new translation is to make our English reflect the Latin most literally. A third-grader would ask: why Latin? Our polished, pedantic, pompous pundits would say condescendingly: because at one time in our history, many people spoke Latin and our official documents and prayers were in Latin. We kept the Latin even after people no longer spoke Latin because the language made things uniform, and we didn't have all the messiness that comes from trying to translate stuff into all those languages. The third-grader says: "Huh? Whatever."

I will give them this much credit: they are not yet forcing us back to Latin itself for our liturgy. If I believed in "Then, next ..." arguments, I would certainly make that case here. You think the folks making this change really want a Latinized English? They want it all: Latin everywhere. I'm old enough to remember those days, and it's ugly.

Am I being too frivolous? Maybe. This is a serious issue. And there are many pieces to it, some of which I'm sure we will chat about in the future. But at the heart of it is this insistence that Latin is somehow a sacred language, the measuring stick for orthodoxy. That unwarranted assumption strikes me as being just downright silly. It looks like a handful of people who love Latin are able to force their linguistic obsession on the rest of us. And we let them do it. That's ridiculous.

I am not anti-Latin because I don't know Latin, or, more accurately, knew it. I learned it, spoke it, and read textbooks in it when I was in the seminary. I forgot almost all of it because I am not a linguist. Never could think in Latin. But I do know that it isn't any more sacred than any other language. The fact that the church used it (presumably with good reason) for some formative centuries does not qualify it as the normative language for all time and in all cultures. Period.

On the other hand, if there is more conclusive evidence that God does, in fact, think in Latin, uses it as a native tongue, and prefers it, then I will get out my Latin language books and try again to learn it. Otherwise, give me recognizable, comfortable, sometimes poetic, understandable, reasonable English for my prayer and liturgy. The Lord be with you ... and also with *you*, all of you, not just your spirit.

CHAPTER 18

God's Will

July 2009

Do God's will. Everything is supposed to fall into place when we do God's will. Fine and dandy, but who in the world really knows what God's will is?

There are those people who say they know God's will. There was the time when a man we knew years ago was pacing up and down in our living room claiming that it was God's will that his wife should come home to him. His wife, by the way, was in another room in our house crying her contacts out because he had just beaten her. He was quoting scripture, chapter and verse, about how his wife belongs at home with him. And she was showing us the bald spot on her head where he had pulled her hair out. He insisted that he knew God's will. I insisted that he was not going to get near his wife, God's will or no God's will. In fact, at that moment, I thought it might be God's will that I bust the guy (he is smaller than I am) right in the chops. But I didn't, not because it wasn't God's will but because I was chicken. Then, I wanted to call the police, but she wouldn't press charges. We got her to a safe house. Later they divorced and he wound up in a mental health-care facility. Now *that* was finally God's will. I think.

Hitler claimed God was on his side too.

Then there was the pastor who prayed and "discerned" that a particular fellow should be on the pastoral council. And so it was. Before long, the pastor prayed again and "discerned" again that this fellow should be president of the council. And so it was. A month later this new president disagreed with the pastor over some parish procedure. Guess what? The pastor got back on his knees and "discerned" that this guy should not be on the pastoral council. And, once again, so it was. Who's discerning whom?

Knowing God's will can be tricky business. It's a pretty safe bet that loving God and loving your neighbor is God's will. Sticking with the Ten Commandments and the eight beatitudes also looks reliable. But how to love God and love your neighbor is not always clear. When is tough love and not-so-tough love required? And the Ten Commandments look simple on paper but are often complex in practice. And those beatitudes? Name five people who really live the beatitudes.

Does God want you to take this job or that job? Wear your hair this way or that way? Marry this person or that person? Join this church or that church? Turn left or turn right? Vote for Harry or Mary? How do you know? Does God have a will for us in little things? Or, is God's will reserved for only the big things? How specific is God's will, anyway? How do we find God's will, whether in small or large things?

And the answer is …! I don't really know. What I do know is that I pray to know God's will, seek some advice from people I trust, make a decision, and hope for the best. That's as good as it gets. I think.

CHAPTER 19

Protecting Jesus

July 2011

Do we really need to protect Jesus? We believe that Jesus is fully human and fully divine: two natures in one divine person. It would be most arrogant and foolhardy to contend that we need to protect the divine Jesus. Surely, God doesn't need—and my guess is that God doesn't want—our "protection." You will not find me in that procession.

So, presumably, we feel we need to protect the human Jesus. This protectionist policy is most evident in our official teaching about who can receive the Body and Blood of Christ in the Eucharist.

Recently, I was part of a group of twenty-five faithful, active Catholics who met for an hour after Mass on Corpus Christi Sunday to discuss the scripture readings. During that lively discussion, not one person spoke in defense of the church's teaching that excludes non-Catholics, divorced and remarried (with no annulment) Catholics, and other categories of "unworthies" from reception of the Eucharist. That negative reaction to excluding people from Communion is not surprising since nationwide polls consistently reflect the same response.

Then I took the discussion a step further by outlining the church's teaching on transubstantiation. You remember transubstantiation, don't you? That's the official doctrine of the Council of Trent, which describes the mystery of the Eucharist by borrowing from the philosophy of Aristotle who taught that reality is composed of "substances and accidents." The substance of bread and wine becomes the substance of Christ, while retaining the accidents of the bread and wine. Thus, transubstantiation.

Well, the response to this brief description ranged from a nostalgic "Oh yeah, I kinda remember that from the Baltimore Catechism days" to "Why do we follow a Greek philosopher anyway?" to "I don't believe in a 'real presence' since real to me is something physical." Everyone had just received the Body and Blood of Christ an hour earlier.

Needless to say, there is a significant disconnect between church teaching and church practice on this point. What it comes down to is that Jesus was amazingly, thoroughly, uncompromisingly inclusive in His ministry, message, and mission while church teaching is amazingly, thoroughly, and uncompromisingly exclusive, trying to protect Jesus from the same people that He deliberately and warmly welcomed. Go figure!

The common sense of the people of God has outrun the declarations of the Council of Trent. Trent was conditioned by the Protestant Reformation and the turbulent times of the sixteenth century. It isn't that Trent is "wrong." It's just that the mystery of the Eucharist demands continual forms of expression; ways to describe the mystery that fit different times and cultures. Trent's correct way to state the mystery doesn't mean that there aren't other correct ways to state the same mystery. That's the nature of mystery; it is ultimately unexplainable, but it still seeks expression.

I often hear that people remain Catholic because of the Eucharist. It is a core feature of the Catholic experience, and when the Eucharistic liturgy is celebrated well, the reception of Communion is a powerful spiritual and devotional encounter with the divine. It is a central ritual act and a deeply personal manifestation of faith for millions of Catholics.

Why exclude people from this possible experience because their thoughts and statements about the Eucharist do not align perfectly with the words of Trent? Jesus can handle it; He isn't so fragile a divine personality that He can't accept the hearts and history of people who don't fit the presumed perfect profile of a worthy believer.

I suspect that the core faith life of many people who are now excluded from the reception of the Eucharist is a lot stronger, deeper, and more personal than some of those who legitimately receive Communion regularly.

Let Jesus judge the internal and external lives of those who receive Him in Communion. He doesn't need us to protect Him.

The Body of Christ … Amen.

CHAPTER 20
Doctrine Versus Mission

November 2011

This past summer, the State of Illinois passed a civil union law that, among other things, made it discriminatory for a group to refuse to work with unmarried couples, gay or straight, in providing foster care and adoptions.

Catholic dioceses all over the state scrambled for a way to protect their foster-care and adoption programs. Most of those programs get most of their money for these services from the state, so the law now says that they must consider gay and/or unmarried couples as potential foster or adoptive parents.

Guess what that did. After some legal protests, the church pulled out of the state-supported foster-care and adoption business because the new law recognizes the legitimacy of civil unions and official church teaching says that's a no-no.

In other words, doctrine trumped mission.

My home diocese, Belleville, added another wrinkle. Since foster care and adoptions are the major services offered by our Catholic Social Services, dropping them to comply with state law would truncate the department. They would have to lay off most of the staff and, more important, abandon about six hundred children in foster care or adopted homes.

So, guess what Catholic Social Services did. They severed ties with the diocese, formed their own organization, changed their name to Christian Social Services, kept the contracts with the state, and continued the foster-care and adoption programs.

In other words, mission trumped doctrine.

There are multiple dimensions to this whole issue: the relationship between church and state; what values take priority; when to compromise and when to maintain principles; when to ignore a situation and when to highlight that same situation; and some things I can't think of right now.

But here's a minor one that I can think of immediately: apparently, it's not okay to accept qualified gay or unmarried couples as foster or adoptive parents if you are Catholic, but it is okay if you are Christian.

Help me out here. Since I lived for over twenty years in Tulsa, Oklahoma, the hometown of Oral Roberts University and many other fundamentalist churches, I spent a lot of time insisting that Catholics are Christians. Looks like I was wrong again!

It's not that I find fault with the fine folks at Catholic (woops, Christian) Social Services (I know many of them). It's just that the name change raises lots of confusing issues. For example, being Catholic now includes being against gay and unmarried couples *plus* being willing to abandon six hundred kids who need foster care or adoption. Being Christian now includes accepting qualified gay and unmarried couples as possible foster-care and adoptive parents *and* provides continuing service to all those kids.

It's getting harder and harder being a Catholic Christian.

This is not just a local, Illinois dilemma. The core issues are worldwide. What takes precedence, dogma or service? When it gets down to the bottom line, what determines the final, practical decision, doctrine or mission?

In this case, I side with mission. Loving gay and unmarried couples can provide a more nurturing family environment than many married, heterosexual couples. Besides, civil union partners who volunteer as foster or adoptive parents show some desire for what could be a very difficult commitment. Obviously, all these parents need to meet appropriate criteria before they are accepted, but no one should be excluded simply because he or she is in a civil union.

How does this position square with my Catholicism? Not very well, I'm afraid. Actually, this situation is one of many that create a tension between doctrine and mission. My goal is to experience these tensions as creative rather than destructive.

I wish my diocese would continue its support of Catholic Social Services officially. It was an agency that made me proud to be Catholic. The mingling of church and state is inherently problematic; in this case, it is worth the dogmatic complications. It will be interesting to see how well Catholics donate to the new agency compared to how well they contribute to the diocese.

Someone could argue that the state could find some other way to continue their foster-care and adoptive services rather than outsourcing them to Catholic Social Services. But since nothing is in place for that approach immediately, a severe interruption of services seems inevitable. Those kids deserve better.

I applaud Christian Social Services for continuing their mission. They are still Catholic to me.

Francis Follow-Up: Now, in 2014, Christian Social Services has changed its name again to Caritas Family Solutions and extended their services beyond the boundaries of the Belleville diocese to other parts of Illinois. Simultaneously, the state just passed a law allowing same-sex marriage. CSS or Caritas remains Catholic to me. I have no idea where Francis stands on an issue like this, but my guess is that he would leave this decision up to local leaders. I suspect, however, that his top priority would be those six hundred kids who need a home.

CHAPTER 21

Creed, Code, Cult

August 2013

In 1958, Huston Smith wrote *The Religions of Man* (revised in 1991 and retitled *The World's Religions: Our Great Wisdom Traditions*). Along with over two million other people, I bought a copy and still have the original version.

Smith maintains that a helpful way to understand various religions is to ask three questions: What does a religious group believe (their creed)? How are they supposed to act (their code)? And what do they do when they get together (their worship or cult)?

Those three questions have been invaluable to me in assessing the world religious terrain and my own personal faith for decades. They are also a convenient way to chat about the ongoing changes ushered in by Pope Francis.

1. There are 2,865 paragraphs in the *Catechism of the Catholic Church*. Obviously, not all of those teachings are of the same value or importance. Some concern the existence and nature of God; others are commentaries on familiar prayers. Some reflect Catholic dogma articulated by ecumenical councils; others reflect the theological opinion of a particular school of thought. Clearly, a compendium like this calls for an ordering, a hierarchy, of importance. Which teachings are of the highest order? Which are more peripheral?

   What Francis seems to be doing is rearranging this hierarchy, not denying the truth of them, but putting them in a different sequence. His criticism about "overintellectualizing" our faith, about Christianity not being an "ideology," etc., signals a new emphasis. He follows that break with the recent past by stressing the gospel centrality of simplicity, humility, and an insistent identification with the poor.

   To put it in terms of Huston Smith's first question, Francis wants to change the usual, popularized answer to: What do Catholics believe? Our instinctive response has been to focus on how we differ from other Christians, which leads us to answers about papal authority, hierarchy, infallibility, and organizational structure. Francis wants us to respond—and wants the world to identify us—as the humble followers of the biblical Jesus, even though other Christian denominations may claim the same response.

We believe, proclaim, and witness to the basic message long before we focus on the less important issues of authority and organizational structure.

2. How are Catholics supposed to act? Once again, there seems to be a major shift in emphasis. Our core code of conduct seems to be changing from a concentration on sexual matters (birth control, homosexuality, etc.) to a much broader focus on the virtues that motivate us to think positively about and reach out to the poor, marginalized, and underserved members of our society.

    Outreach to the poor often gets mired down in politics, conflicting ideologies, and cumbersome programs. There are many ways to help the poor: direct service, creating and constantly adjusting policies and programs that address structural problems, or education to help people think positively about how to help marginalized populations.

    No one can do it all. But the gospel challenges us, and Francis reminds us, that to be Catholic, each of us must do something along these lines. It is a matter of conscience to find your niche and determine how much you will do for the "least of us."

3. What do Catholics do when they get together (cult)? This change at the top was crystal clear within weeks of Francis's selection. Holy Week in the Vatican included minimal pomp, shorter services, washing the feet of prisoners (including a Muslim woman), and a pastoral homily instead of a theological treatise. Subsequent papal liturgical celebrations followed this same simplified pattern.

    But there is more to this question than vestments, incense, and liturgical pomp. When Catholics get together, who has what role not only in the sanctuary but also in the meeting rooms and parish halls of the world? Among other issues, the gender inequality is obvious and must be changed, including ordination of women.

At this point, it is hard to say how far Francis will go or how much power he really has to make substantive changes in restructuring the hierarchy. After thirty years of neglect and outright punishment, the word *collegiality* has reentered the Catholic lexicon. If we had pursued that concept aggressively after Vatican II, we would know by now what it means in Catholic practice. But, alas, we must begin again. We can only hope that Francis starts a renewed collegial process.

Three handy questions: Creed? Code? Cult? What are your answers?

CHAPTER 22

Catholic Identity

March 2010

Are you Catholic? If you are, how do you know? Whether you were baptized Catholic and then also chose it as your adult religion or whether you "joined the church" as an adult, what is it that makes you Catholic?

Can you simply declare yourself Catholic, and therefore, you are? Do you think there are at least some minimal beliefs and behaviors that qualify you as a Catholic? If so, what are they? Millions of people self-select out of Catholicism. They call themselves former Catholics. Other millions are inactive Catholics. If they are inactive, what is it that makes someone active?

Maybe all of these questions are irrelevant. Who really cares? Do we all decide for ourselves whether we are Catholic or not? A friend of mine, raised Catholic, rarely goes to church, disagrees with some official positions, but always identifies himself as Catholic when asked. Another friend seldom misses weekend Mass, attends daily Mass regularly, serves on the pastoral council, sent his kids to Catholic School, is progressive in his theology, and insists he will die Catholic. Are both of these friends Catholic? How wide is the Catholic spectrum?

I don't ask these questions in order to try to answer them. Personally, I don't care very much about the "right answer." I ask them because I attended a lecture by John Allen.

Allen is the Vatican correspondent for CNN, a columnist for the *National Catholic Reporter*, author of multiple books, and a dynamic, informed, and intelligent presenter. In the lecture I attended, he raised the question of Catholic identity and the importance this issue has on Vatican policy. His talk was based on his recent book *The Future Church* (Doubleday, 2009), in which he describes ten trends which he believes will shape the future of Catholicism.

What Allen said, if I understood correctly, is that Vatican policy makers are determined to clarify what it means to be a Catholic. In marketing terms, they want to brand Catholicism, make it clearly identifiable, and distinguish it from other Christian and, of course, non-Christian religions. They emphasize the Catholic part of Catholic Christianity, not to deny our Christian base, but to underline our uniqueness. If Allen is right and if I am right about what Allen said, this analysis explains the motive behind much of what is coming out of Vatican City and most dioceses these days.

My question is: why? Why is the identity question so important? Catholicism is unique because of the combination of our understanding of sacramentality and our authority structure. At least that's how it seems to me. But is it so crucial to brand ourselves as distinctive and different from other religions?

Just exactly how do we do that anyway? We had all the clearly distinctive Catholic features before Vatican II: no meat on Friday, Mass every Sunday, uniform teaching on multiple issues like birth control, homosexuality, proper dress (hats for women in church), authority of the pastor in the parish, pope in charge with bishops enforcing papal directives, bingo, genuflecting, sign of the cross, and I'm sure some of you can name some more.

Catholics were easily identified, honored or vilified, but identified. Is that where the Vatican wants to take us again? If so, why? Because we are then more easily led? We are then more committed to their agenda? We are superior to other religions? We eliminate the deadweight of those who are former and inactive Catholics? The remaining active, loyal Catholics feel better about themselves? So there is just one face of Catholicism that confronts a secular world and other religions? And all of this is somehow better than a more diversified expression of Jesus, the gospel, and the church?

This chat certainly has a lot of questions. More questions than answers. At some point, answers are very helpful and desirable. But right now this call for a clearer Catholic identity raises more questions than answers. And the questions must be addressed before the answers are given. Unfortunately, that is not always the case; sometimes we are given answers before we have a chance to ask the questions.

Francis Follow-Up: This is an area where Francis seems to be taking a very different stance than the one I outlined in this chat. Francis seems to be saying that following Jesus in terms of forgiveness, mercy, and compassion is much more important than determining what specifically makes a person a Catholic. He is not denying any of the previous attempts to emphasize the uniqueness of Catholicism, but those issues don't appear to be too important to him. Makes a lot of sense to me.

CHAPTER 23

Once a Priest

April 2010

A friend of mine emailed me an article that appeared in his parish bulletin that raised some critical questions about the sexual abuse of children and the subsequent and widespread cover-up by church authorities. His pastor wrote this:

> To be sure, the bishops have taken major steps to right this great wrong. But something more fundamental is needed, I believe. We need to understand better the source of attitudes and presumptions about Church and priesthood that led many bishops to conclude that the good of the Church is best served by concealing the sins of its leaders. Why are these attitudes and presumptions so widespread? What have bishops and priests been taught that would lead them to identify the good of the Church with the interests of bishops and priests? What sort of theology leads them to divinize the Church to the extent that it is practically impossible to admit the possibility of a sinful clergy, or that priesthood is anything but humble service to and care of the People of God? How does a culture of privilege, secrecy, power, and exclusiveness flourish among clergy? More importantly, are we still teaching these theologies in our seminaries, and are we still forming priests in these attitudes and presumptions?

This pastor then invites his parishioners to read *A Report on the Crisis in the Catholic Church in the United States*, published in 2003 by the National Review Board (NRB) (www.usccb.org/ocyp/reports.shtml.) for perspective on these questions.

He asks very good questions.

In my opinion, the "once a priest, always a priest" theology contributes to the attitude of priestly protectionism. There are many other factors, but if the church believes in "once a priest, always a priest," then it seems logical that the institutional church is always responsible for each priest, regardless of behavior, beliefs, or even the priest's own decision that he no longer wants to remain a priest. Does that make sense?

If doctors, lawyers, or plumbers act contrary to the ethics expected in their profession, they are censured or expelled from that profession and cannot continue to work in that field. Why doesn't the same reasonable standard apply to priests? Because the Church believes that once a priest, always a priest.

It is time to reexamine this aspect (and many others) of the theology of priesthood. Actually, for a period of about ten years (approximately 1968 through 1978) the process of laicization (an ordained priest is considered a layperson once again) was more easily available. I know because I was voluntarily and wisely laicized in 1973. But as soon as Pope John Paul II became pope, he stopped the process and reverted to the previous policy of making priests who desired laicization wait for twenty or thirty years before they even got a response from the Vatican. What is the point of that? Once a priest, always a priest! There is talk, and occasionally some action, about forcing a pedophile priest to be laicized, but it is very rare and is granted very reluctantly. Why? Once a priest, always a priest.

The primary Scriptural reference to insisting on permanence-at-all-cost priesthood is Hebrews 7:1–10, the section that describes Melchisedek as a type for Jesus, the High Priest—hence the phrase, "a priest forever according to the order of Melchisedek." But is that reference to Jesus literally applicable to all ordained priests everywhere under all circumstances? The doctrine of priestly permanence needs reevaluation by theologians more learned than I.

At the very least, the church could revert to the policy of the 1970s and make laicization an easier administrative procedure, which would, among other things, relieve the theological pressure of defending, and financially supporting, pedophile priests. That approach is not a fundamental revision of priesthood; it is an easy papal decision that has a modern precedent.

The pastor's questions deserve serious thought by many people. Pressured, last resort admissions of guilt, compliance, sorrow, sympathy for victims, and promises, even by the pope, are necessary but not sufficient. We must also rethink the fundamentals. Once a priest, always a priest?

CHAPTER 24

A Priest Forever?

June 2013

I was ordained a Catholic priest on May 7, 1966. I was laicized at the end of 1973. I always have to clarify that laicization is not a surgical procedure, but it does relieve me of priestly responsibilities and privileges.

Why I was ordained and why I left the priesthood are topics for other chats. Right now, I want to focus on whether I am still a priest or not. The answer has ramifications far beyond my personal story.

Unfortunately, canon law is what has passed for theology for the past thirty years, so canon law currently rules. Canon 290 states that "sacred ordination once validly received never becomes invalid." The catechism of the Catholic Church adds this clarification in paragraph 1582: "The sacrament of Holy Orders confers an *indelible spiritual character* and cannot be repeated or conferred temporarily" (italics in the catechism).

So, by that reading, I am still a priest but cannot function as a priest. I remain validly ordained with an *indelible spiritual character* even though I consciously and continually choose not to be a priest. Being laicized does not remove the *character*. To complicate matters more, laicization is a procedure that, for all practical purposes, was available only during the 1970s.

That *indelible spiritual character* keeps a person a priest even when he leaves the priesthood, even when he is officially laicized, even when he wants out and doesn't want back in. The church is consistent, however. Even when a bishop like Edward K. Braxton unjustly fires a priest like Fr. Bill Rowe for adding clarifying and inspiring words to the Eucharist, not even Edward K. Braxton or the Vatican can take away Fr. Bill's priesthood as he involuntarily loses all rights to function as a priest.

Once a priest, always a priest.

Suppose you are an oncologist, but at age forty-five, you can't deal with cancer anymore and you become an accountant. Are you still a doctor? Do you have an *indelible medical character*? Of course, your personal history includes your years as a cancer doctor, but once you lose your credentials, you are no longer a doctor. You are now an accountant.

Why is priesthood any different? Canon law doesn't answer that question, but it does add that the obligation of celibacy still persists unless the pope dispenses the priest from celibacy (Canon 291). Wow! A priest can lose all his rights but retains the obligation of celibacy. What kind of thinking leads to this bizarre conclusion?

It all goes back to that teaching about the *indelible spiritual character*. A similar character accompanies baptism and confirmation. To me, there is a stronger case for the spiritual character (whatever that really is, besides a metaphor) for baptism/confirmation as initiation into the Catholic community. But priesthood is a functional service to the community and it doesn't require a permanent "mark" to offer that service. A priest is as a priest does. Why does it have to be an irremovable state of being?

There are far-reaching consequences to this teaching. Here are a few:

- The local bishop feels an obligation to protect and defend the reputation of the church in his diocese. If a priest violates this reputation, even if it is criminal activity, such as pedophilia, the bishop feels his first responsibility is to protect the church from scandal. This line of thinking led to the cover-up policies that continue to plague us. Since the priest has an *indelible spiritual character* that ties him to the bishop, the bishop feels less inclined to turn the case over to civil authorities immediately. "We take care of our own" is the motto.

- The *indelible spiritual character* implies obligations not only to the bishop (or religious superior) but to God. Making this priestly designation permanent implies that God considers this ordination to be permanent also. It is hard to believe that God is so limited. If God accepts a priest who leaves the priesthood (for whatever reason), then the church's insistence on "permanency" is rooted in power, control, fear, and pride.

- The *indelible character* teaching eliminates a potential temporary priesthood; someone (male or female, married or celibate) becomes a priest for a number of years and then changes professions or retires.

- On the human level, this doctrine punishes priests who want to leave and does not punish those who deserve punishment.

Once a priest, always a priest is bad policy, rigid thinking with a shaky foundation, and complicates the real issue: priesthood open to all people, including married men and women.

CHAPTER 25

Women Priests

A Poem
August 2009

The Catholic Church, from its lofty perch, presumes to know God's will.
Though it's often said, with a little dread, that it doesn't fit the bill.
A case at hand, you understand, involves an ordained priest.
You must be male, in the current tale, to lead the Eucharistic feast.

The story's told, and it's very old, that Jesus wanted men
To lead us all to follow his call, just like it was back then.
A woman, you see, has biology that makes her second rate.
It's in her genes, and it surely means she must accept her fate.

With gifts galore, there's nothing more than bowing to a man.
She cannot change the ordered range to quash the female ban.
There's something wrong, but it's been so long, that nothing can be done.
The bishops say there is no way—except to be a nun.

The Scripture stars in the gender wars are much less absolute.
It's Jesus, they say, who leads the way and turns the ban to mute.
The women he knows are not his foes; they follow him everywhere.
The men, alas, run out of gas and leave him hanging there.

The early Church, when in a lurch, found women who could lead.
In love, in prayer, without compare, they handled every need.
Throughout the years, through many tears, the women served with grit.
Though often least, and never as priest, they found a loving fit.

The world at large had males in charge, and so the Church did too.
The men prevailed, as the Gospel failed, to teach this biased view.
The world today is moving away from total male control;
We slowly learn to make the turn and find our female soul.

We know the search within our Church for true equality
Will meet some strong and very wrong adverse reality.
The only voice to make the choice is older mitered men
Who choose to think without a blink that now must be like then.

The struggles ahead, it should be said, will not be quickly won.
But fight we must, to truly be just, before the battle's done.
Just wait and see, the time will be when women will preside
Because we know, as on we go, that God is on our side.

The time is now to make a vow to have some women priests.
The silly laws that make us pause obstruct the Holy Feast.
There must be ways in coming days that lead to women priests,
But of all the themes and all the schemes, may gender be the least.

CHAPTER 26

Contraception

March 2012

In an ongoing battle, the American bishops recently announced that their top priority is to fight the White House mandate that most religious employers must provide health-care coverage for employees, including contraceptive services presumably forbidden by Catholic teaching.

President Obama quickly changed the original mandate and said that insurance companies, not Catholic institutions, would assume the cost of the contraceptive coverage. Powerful cardinals and some bishops immediately counterpunched and categorically declared that the president's concession made absolutely no difference.

Really? Of course, it makes a difference. But Cardinal Dolan spoke publically and quickly and over two hundred bishops fell in line without comment or "Let's think about this a little and talk it over." In their desire to provide one, united voice on a complex issue, the bishops instantly supported the knee-jerk reaction of the newest cardinal and president of the United States Conference of Catholic Bishops.

That's how you spell "collegiality" these days.

Now, interestingly enough, the bishops expanded their concerns and registered a more general complaint about government intrusion on religious liberty. The bishops stretched the issue from contraception to this much broader concern about the church's freedom from government interference.

Wonder why they didn't stick to the contraceptive focus? Maybe because they already lost that fight forty years ago when Catholic women (and men) examined their collective conscience and concluded that using the birth control pill was morally acceptable despite the words of Pope Paul VI's encyclical, *Humanae Vitae*.

A quick review of that "birth control" encyclical is critical to any commentary on the current conflict. Birth control and optional celibacy for priests were two of the topics that were not allowed on the agenda of Vatican II. But shortly after the council closed in 1965, Pope Paul VI convened a multidimensional, high-level commission to review the church's birth control policy. After years of extensive research, study, and discussion, the commission concluded that artificial means of birth control should be permitted. There was a small minority report that disagreed with this conclusion based primarily on the historical argument that "no contraception" was always the teaching.

In his encyclical, the pope surprisingly followed the minority opinion. That is the modern basis for the current "no contraception" teaching. In the decades since *Humanae Vitae*, the vast majority of Catholics basically disregarded the teachings of the encyclical by using some "artificial" means to control birth.

In my opinion, the Holy Spirit was guiding the church to change its birth control policy through the deliberations and conclusions of the commission, and that same Spirit is now guiding the millions of Catholics who practice responsible, but so-called artificial, birth control. In other words, Pope Paul VI flat out got it wrong, and the Holy Spirit still respectfully disagrees with the pope.

Had the pope gotten it right in 1968, there would be no discussion today about providing contraceptive insurance for church employees. Of course it would be included. In fighting the insurance coverage today, the bishops are forced to defend the basic prohibition against artificial means of contraception all over again. It's an argument they haven't won in the past and cannot win in the present. And they know it. And it would be nice if at least a few of them would admit it.

It's no wonder they want to expand the issue to religious liberty. There always has been and there always will be conflicts between church and state on multiple grounds. And I agree that those boundaries need to be clarified often. Sometimes the state oversteps the lines, and sometimes the church goes too far and infringes on government responsibilities. It's a necessary tension, and it demands permanent diligence.

But don't cast this current debate as a religious liberty issue. The consequence of Pope Paul VI's error does not justify this opposition to a reasonable mandate to include contraceptive insurance coverage for employees of Catholic institutions, particularly since the church doesn't have to pay for the coverage.

The church loses even more credibility when it defends the indefensible, especially when the Holy Spirit lines up on the other side.

CHAPTER 27

Compliance

June 2010

The other night, I was wondering how bishops monitor parish compliance with liturgical norms, especially with the upcoming implementation of the New Roman Missal. All those parishes, all those celebrants! Must be a tough job. How do they do it?

I was still wondering when I went to bed, and I had a dream about it. As best as I can recall, here is my dream:

The scene: Batbishop and his caped, acolyte boyservant, Robert, are on a mission to ferret out, expose, and condemn illegal liturgical practices throughout the diocese.

Robert: Here we are at St. Wilomena's, Most Courageous Batbishop. Good thing we took the Bishmobile, so we can sneak in undetected and watch what goes on at this 9:00 Sunday morning Mass.

Batbishop: Yes, Robert, I have heard from usually, mostly, generally reliable sources that Fr. Liberal breaks clearly stated rubrics governing the celebration of the Holy Eucharist.

Robert: That is hard to believe, but I know about Fr. Liberal. My second cousin, once removed, on my mother's side, was in his previous parish, and she told me that sometimes he even laughs during the liturgy. She changed parishes.

Batbishop: A wise woman. But get ready. The Mass is beginning. Take notes, and I will tell you what to write.

Robert: Yes, Most Holy, Serene, Cardinal-in-waiting. I am ready.

Batbishop: The Opening Hymn. I'm not familiar with it—check later to make sure it is an approved hymn by a legitimate, church approved, liturgical publisher. It seems too cheery. Today is a solemn feast; we need somber music to set the proper tone for today's liturgy.

Robert: Yes, Most Wise, Intelligent, Chief Steward of the Mysteries of God.

Batbishop: Note that the lectors are sitting in the sanctuary, and one of them is a woman. Women can be lectors, Robert, but lectors do not belong in the sanctuary, especially women lectors.

Robert: An astute observation, Most Excellent Excellency.

Batbishop: Did you hear that? The people are not uniform in their response to "The Lord be with you." Some still say the old, inaccurate "And also with you" while some say the correct "And with your spirit." The confusion is Fr. Liberal's fault for not training his people properly.

Robert: I will underline my notes on that one, Most Superb Latin Linguist!

Batbishop: Here comes the homily. He is mixing some psychology in with his scripture references. Very dangerous tendency. There is a theological treatise by St. Thomas Aquinas that he should be using here. It fits nicely with the second reading. Fr. Liberal's content and tone is too superficial and not based directly on church teaching. It's more like that New Age spirituality nonsense. I will write him and tell him to teach church documents during his homilies. Better yet, I will send him a CD of my preaching so he will know what to say and how to say it.

Robert: Wow! Outstanding idea, Most Learned Theologian-Bishop!

Batbishop: I can't believe this! They are standing during the Eucharistic Prayer. It is clearly stated that in the United States, everyone must kneel during this most sacred part of the liturgy. It doesn't matter what they do in Europe or anywhere else; standing is a major violation of approved liturgical norms here. This is outrageous!

Robert: It's incredible, Most Just Shepherd! Holy Posture! Look over there! They don't even have kneelers in that part of the church!

Batbishop: That is no excuse, Robert. Fr. Liberal knew about these regulations a long time ago. No matter what, he should have installed kneelers. It's now a matter of obedience as well as liturgical practice.

Robert: Holy Insubordination! You should stop the Mass right now, condemn Fr. Liberal, and tell everyone they must kneel.

Batbishop: Yes, that would be justified, but I prefer to sneak out and write him a letter. We don't want any public confrontation. It might get into the newspapers or—Horrors!—television. They might try to turn me into the villain. You know how the media is, always trying to pin something on me.

Robert: Of course, Most Shrewd Leader! You can't trust Fr. Liberal or the media to obey you.

Batbishop: That's right, Robert. It is the joyful burden of the bishop to correct such outrageous behavior. My liturgical police do a fine job, but only I can handle these most serious violations.

Robert: Unquestionable, Most Mighty Inquisitor! God will reward you for your loyal dedication.

Batbishop: I have seen enough. Let's slip out now before his dreadful, secular announcements, and the liturgically improper recessional hymn. I have a letter to write.

Robert: Yes. Another successful foray into an enemy's parish. You'll win this war yet, Most Righteous Champion of Church Conformity.

I woke up in a sweat!

PART 3

You Gotta Be Kidding

This section highlights how the church persecutes progressives and defends the hierarchy at all costs. While the surprising arrival of Francis has changed the operation of the Vatican quickly and profoundly, it remains to be seen what the long-term impact of this refreshing papacy will be. Many of the distressing features of the hierarchy are deeply entrenched and difficult to eradicate. Besides, the vast majority of the bishops and cardinals were appointed by John Paul II or Benedict XVI.

There are a number of chats in this section that center on Fr. Bill Rowe. That extended focus is due to my long-term friendship with Bill and to the extreme with which the church is willing to go to punish a good man who steps out of line on minor liturgical matters. Bill is also a symbol for many other priests and laypersons who are treated terribly by church officials or policies.

CHAPTER 28

Revolution

October 2012

Recently Hans Kung, the noted Catholic theologian, has called for a revolution from below to force reform on the church.

"The only way for reform is from the bottom up," said Kung, who is a priest. "The priests and others in positions of responsibility need to stop being so subservient, to organize themselves and say that there are certain things that they simply will not put up with anymore."

Kung described the church as an "authoritarian system" with parallels to Germany's Nazi dictatorship. "The unconditional obedience demanded of bishops who swear their allegiance to the pope when they make their holy oath is almost as extreme as that of the German generals who were forced to swear an oath of allegiance to Hitler," he said.

Pretty strong stuff! Based on his positions for many decades, his public challenge is no surprise. Since his time as a young priest-expert at the Second Vatican Council fifty years ago, Kung has consistently championed the progressive themes embedded in the documents of that most authoritative teaching of, at least, the past 150 years.

What would a revolution from below look like?

1. Despite Fr. Kung's prestige and the fact that many in the church immediately agree with him, his call for revolution from below is highly improbable. Unlike other times in history when major reform took place, today's world is different. There are many options for people who are disaffected with the church hierarchy and teachings. It is easy to leave and attend another denomination or to join the majority of people in the United States who are unaffiliated with any religion. Why stay and fight for reform when there is no social or religious stigma for just quitting? So many people have already chosen this option that the likelihood of enough people joining the fight for reform is too small to create a revolution. The Vatican wins

by default. And they smile all the way to the high altar, with Cappa Magnas trailing royally behind.

2. On the other hand, if enough people stay in the Vatican Catholic Church who not only want reform but are willing to work for it, a few things, in my opinion, have to happen. Key to this reform will be the formation of, what I call, the Coalition of Progressive Catholics. (The acronym works: CPC.) Progressive priests, religious, and laity must come together, not necessarily on every issue, but on some key issues, so that a truly united, worldwide voice can emerge. A few leaders, representing millions of reformers, must speak publically and courageously to the pope and the Vatican.

» The CPC must include groups like Call to Action, the newly formed National Priest Association, Voice of the Faithful, Network, Leadership Conference of Women Religious, Corpus, sympathetic theologians and canon lawyers, a few bishops, liturgical reformers, Southern Illinois Association of Priests, Faithful of Southern Illinois, and other groups I don't know about who have similar progressive agendas. Any group willing to take the lead?

» Contact must be made with similar groups in other countries, like the priests' associations in Austria, Switzerland, and Australia, along with organized groups of laity throughout the world. A CPC organizing committee must reach out to identify and enlist participation from all of these groups and individuals who wish to participate.

» A few key issues must be identified and promoted. Some wording that includes greater collegiality in decision making must be one issue. The process for the selection of bishops is critical. A leadership committee can collect and assess other agenda items. Not too many. Just a few essential ones that millions of people will support.

» A plan must be developed which incorporates consequences for nonacceptance of the key issues. Perhaps something that withdraws financial support from specified church activities while preserving funding for charitable services. Perhaps widespread disregard for the New Missal, for example. The CPC will identify creative approaches to this need for specified consequences.

» Someone needs to articulate the vision of "loyal disobedience" in order to provide the theological underpinning for this revolution.

We need reform but not another Reformation. There are plenty of options already for being Christian in ways other than Catholic. Unless we create this revolution from below, Fr. Kung's challenge will remain rhetoric that we applaud but with no significant impact on the church.

And the Vatican will get their 1950 church back again while they continue to pick us off, one organization, one person at a time. Let's revolt before that happens.

Francis Follow-Up: This whole theme of revolt from below has been superseded by Francis, who is now leading a reformation from the top. But Kung's call remains as a necessary component of the leadership from Francis. Francis cannot do it alone because leaders must have participating followers— not just cheerleaders, but people who work to help implement the vision Francis, and Jesus, have. Besides, there needs to be some continuing pressure from below on some issues like women's ordination.

CHAPTER 29

What If …?

November 2010

What if a church leader, a pastor, bishop, nun, or layperson has narcissistic personality disorder? How would that look, and what would happen?

Narcissistic personality disorder (NPD) is more than looking in the mirror in the morning and wondering if you're going to have a bad hair day. NPD is a diagnosable, clinical disorder included in the *Diagnostic and Statistical Manual of Mental Disorders, Fourth Edition*, (*DSM-IV*), the official book of the American Psychiatric Association, which all psychiatrists, psychologists, and counselors use to diagnose clients.

Since mental illness is difficult to diagnose for even professional mental health providers, it would be foolish for me to attempt a diagnosis of any church leader—publically. But what if five of the nine characteristics of NPD found in the *DSM-IV* accurately describe a church leader? I say five out of nine because that is the criteria used in the *DSM-IV* to diagnosis NPD.

Here are the nine:

1. has a grandiose sense of self-importance (e.g. exaggerates achievements and talents, expects to be recognized as superior without commensurate achievements);

2. is preoccupied with fantasies of unlimited success, power, brilliance, beauty, or ideal love;

3. believes that he or she is "special" and unique and can only be understood by, or should associate with, other special or high-status people (or institutions);

4. requires excessive admiration;

5. has a sense of entitlement, i.e., unreasonable expectations of especially favorable treatment or automatic compliance with his or her expectations;

6. is interpersonally exploitative, i.e., takes advantage of others to achieve his or her own ends.

7. lacks empathy: is unwilling to recognize or identify with the feelings or needs of others;

8. is often envious of others or believes that others are envious of him or her;

9. shows arrogant, haughty behaviors or attitudes.

So, back to my first question: what if a church leader consistently exhibits at least five of these behaviors? What happens? Well, my best guess is: nothing! Here's why:

- Narcissists, classically, do not admit their disorder and therefore see no need to seek help.

- Since narcissism is a personality disorder and not a chemical imbalance, there is no medication that counteracts the illness.

- The church is extremely reluctant to admit it was a mistake to ordain a narcissist as a priest or make him a bishop. They are even more reluctant to remove him even if his narcissism becomes more evident. They would likely fire a layperson or a nun.

- A mental health intervention is also unlikely, but if it is attempted, it will have a greater chance of success if it is done by peers or superiors. A narcissist will not likely accept an intervention by someone he perceives as inferior to him.

The same basic question could be asked about Alzheimer's or other forms of mental illness. When a public figure, like a church leader, experiences these problems, treatment is more complicated but still possible if the person admits and accepts the diagnosis and commits to a plan for recovery. In fact, the mental illness can be incorporated into ministry very effectively when the person is open, honest, and manages the illness.

But if the church leader does not admit and accept the mental illness, the predictable disaster is devastating. The gospel shrinks to fit the illness. The ministry serves the illness first. Church teaching bows to the needs of the disorder. Christian community collapses into neurotic disarray, and worship devolves into perverted rituals for satisfying personal needs.

Schizophrenia, bipolar disorder, chronic depression, or Alzheimer's will manifest themselves in symptoms that will obviously impact the ministry of a church leader. A priest, bishop, or pope with one of these brain disorders may be relieved from ministry and provided some treatment. (Although who knows what happens if a pope has one of these illnesses?)

On the other hand, if the issue is NPD, there is no recourse. The narcissism thrives on the protection granted by the institution. If a bishop, in particular, has NPD, there is no one who will do anything about it. And it's the people of God who reap the poisoned harvest.

Francis Follow-Up: The *DSM-V* is now published and has changed its approach to these personality disorders. That change does not mean the behavior of a narcissist has improved. The behavior remains regardless of how the *DSM* describes or ignores it. The main point of this chat is still valid. Francis, of course, has not directly commented on this issue, but he is doing something different in terms of selecting bishops and any change in this area is welcome.

CHAPTER 30
An Episcopal Woodshed?

October 2011

Maybe I missed it. I hope so. But I see no response from other bishops, cardinals, the Apostolic Nuncio, the US Catholic Conference of Bishops, Vatican, or pope concerning the alleged criminal activity of Bishop Robert Finn of the Kansas City–St. Joseph diocese.

You probably know that Bishop Finn has been indicted by a grand jury on misdemeanor charges of failure to report child abuse in a case involving a priest accused of child pornography. Some people called for felony charges, but they went easy on him. In any case, the bishop is now the highest-ranking Catholic official in the country to face criminal prosecution in the decades-old child sexual abuse scandal.

This case is significant on multiple grounds, one of which is the indefensible position that the clergy, even bishops, are immune from civil and criminal law. Not anymore! The gates are open, and I can see the stampede heading our way.

But my question here centers on Bishop Finn's status within the church. What sanctions and penalties has he violated in canon law? What steps can the church take to discipline him regardless of the criminal process? And even more important, what will the church do with and to him?

These questions are above my pay grade and expertise. We need a canon lawyer to figure out the answers. I'm just chatting, but I do know something about canon law and I do have a *Code of Canon Law*, which I just looked up. Under the section on sanctions, I see lots of references to the ordinary (bishop) doing stuff about other people, but I can't find what the upper hierarchy does about errant bishops.

We know somebody can do something because Bishop Morris of Australia was publically criticized, sanctioned, forced to resign, whatever, but he was punished because he called for an open discussion about ordaining women. So, obviously, somebody can do something about some bishops on some issues.

So, who can and will do something about Bishop Finn? Who will take him to the episcopal woodshed and mete out appropriate disciplinary action?

The criminal case will run its own course, but, among other things, Finn obviously violated the bishops' "Charter for the Protection of Children and Young People."

Let me see, how does this work? The bishops hash out a charter, but individual bishops can exempt themselves from following their own rules, disregarding common sense and clear moral law. Do bishops claim a divine right to total immunity from any consequences of their actions? Each bishop is an independent sovereign, feudal lord of the diocese he temporarily leads? Is that how it works in practice? Once a bishop you get to run any and everything just the way you want to?

Somebody, show me it's different than that in practice. Please!

Other professions police themselves. Doctors, lawyers, plumbers, and electricians all have associations, which discipline people who do not follow standard, acceptable practice. My heavens, even Congress has an ethics committee, which periodically sanctions some of its own members!

The only ethics the bishops monitor is other people's behavior. Who monitors and sanctions them? And it is getting clearer and clearer every day that they need monitoring. Maybe someone who wears a red hat called Finn and politely told him he screwed up big-time. Or perhaps he got chewed out in capital letters privately. I hope so, but I doubt it.

The point is the reprimand and the punishment must be public, not just by the criminal court but by the church. Bishop Finn is a public figure leading the Catholic community in his diocese. Justice demands that he receives some public condemnation by the church.

You know what, now that I think about it, it's already too late. The bottom-line protectionism of the hierarchy has already been blatantly exposed. There should have been an immediate, public statement denouncing Finn's cover-up and charter violation by someone who has a bigger crosier than he does.

That episcopal woodshed needs to be built right next to the episcopal mansion with cameras linked to every HD, flat-screen TV in America. That would be a reality show worth watching.

Francis Follow-Up: Bishop Finn was convicted of a misdemeanor for failing to report suspected child abuse and sentenced to two years of court-supervised probation. Some called his sentence "too lenient." He remains bishop of Kansas City, with no woodshed in sight. Where are you, Francis?

At the end of September 2014, Francis showed up with an investigation of Bishop Finn. Thank heavens! No decision yet but at least there is now a Church investigation.

CHAPTER 31

Mellow

January 2011

Last week, we spent three days in Florida. The weather was sunny and in the seventies, a delightful contrast to the four inches of snow and freezing temperature in St. Louis, our home area, not to mention the blizzards in other parts of the country. My word for our brief vacation: mellow!

Nothing like mellow to take the edge off, let you see things from a different perspective! So many things in life depend on our own attitude that I sometimes wonder what is really "objective." Is my attitude, my perception of reality, the overriding factor in how I experience life? If I am mellow, is everything else also mellow?

Well, yes and no.

First the yes: certainly my personal disposition colors how I see everything. In fact, we often motivate people to see the bright side of things, to drink that half-full glass of water. We encourage people to bury negative attitudes and nourish a positive perspective. Good advice both psychologically and spiritually.

So, how does a positive-thinking person confront a truly negative piece of reality? Ignore it? Act like the negative isn't there? Excuse it? Figure it's someone else's problem? Focus on only the happy, positive pieces of reality? Make sure that your attitude stays positive, even as you glance at something negative?

That is one way out when confronted with evil. But that approach, while certainly valuable up to a point, is a cop-out in the final analysis. To withdraw from the negative side of life is to shrink our humanity and certainly our Christian faith down to me feeling good. Our challenge in life is to integrate the good and the bad with the intent of doing what we can to transform the bad into good, as is the message of the Resurrection.

A case in point: recently we watched the DVD of *Our Fathers*, the fact-based movie about the 2002 Boston clergy sex-abuse scandal. Some of you know the particulars of the case better than I do, but the movie seemed pretty accurate as I recall. If you haven't seen it, do so.

The film centers on the victims of Fr. John Geoghan and Cardinal Bernard

Law. It is now almost ten years after the core events went public, and it is time to summarize what we have learned from this tragedy:

1. Sex-abuse of young boys by Roman Catholic clergy is much more widespread than we assumed ten years ago. (Sex abuse of girls/women has not yet hit nationwide headlines.)

2. Understandably, the impact of this abuse on the victims is devastating, deep-seated, and long-lasting.

3. The official church minimized this impact to the point of denial.

4. The primary concern of the official church was to protect the abusing priest and the "reputation" of the church.

5. The hierarchy thought that a relatively short "treatment" cured the abusing priest.

6. Belated apologies and financial settlements do not atone for the original crimes.

7. The loss of trust in the hierarchy for the cover-up is widespread, deeply ingrained, and hard-nosed.

8. The church thinks it is above the law and is a law unto itself—no need for civil law.

9. False allegations expose the dangerous limitations of the current policy, deny rudimentary due process (innocent until proven guilty), ruin lives, and stigmatize the ministry of the accused.

10. The financial expense and the corresponding decline of donations bankrupt some dioceses and rob charitable services and ministries of much-needed funds.

11. The loss of confidence in church leadership explodes into all areas of church life.

12. The double standard embedded in the clerical culture highlights the elevated status of the clergy and the second-class status of the laity.

13. The promotions of Cardinal Law to the Vatican and other episcopal members of his staff to other dioceses destroy common-sense justice.

14. Let me know what else you have learned:

Whether I am mellow in Florida, crabby at home, or disinterested anywhere else, these facts and lessons of the sex abuse scandal remain destructively true. And we must face it in order to transform it.

CHAPTER 32
The Butler Didn't Do It

May 2012

Wow! It gets worse and worse every week. Now it's the pope's butler in the spotlight. He leaked some Vatican documents that incriminate Vatican power brokers in a variety of schemes involving banking policies, building contracts, and who knows what else. Next week will surely bring more revelations. Stay tuned, but I bet there are no laws in the Vatican that protect whistleblowers. And expect some hierarchical spin on this story that tries to make the butler the bad guy.

On the heels of the attack on the Girl Scouts, the women religious, the liturgy, the never-ending scandal of the sex abuse/cover-up disaster, and the attempt to manipulate the presidential election, this butler crisis adds another ton of fuel on the blazing fire we call the hierarchy. About all that's left to uncover are a few mistresses and some mysterious deaths—oh, that's right, we already have one of those: Pope John Paul I. That death, by the way, paved the path for the anti-Vatican II reigns of John Paul II and Benedict XVI.

Move over Borgias, the twenty-first century is taking over as one of the most corrupt periods in papal history. The hierarchy, at the Vatican, on the national level, and often at the diocesan and parish level, seems hell-bent on self-destruction. We progressives can protest till our voices go hoarse, our ink cartridges run dry, our demonstrations are unnoticed, and our press statements are not released. But, ironically, we may get some of the change we want because the excesses of the hierarchy may destroy its own current structure—evil feeding on evil and ultimately devouring itself. By insisting on more power and thought-control, they could lose what little credibility they still have. Soon, as Bob Dylan so eloquently sang, they'll be blowin' in the wind. You think?

So, in the midst of this inferno, what's a Catholic to do? Besides being angry in private and embarrassed in public, that is.

Here's my suggestion: compartmentalize, hold on, and wait it out!

I'm not a psychologist, but my guess is that, ordinarily, compartmentalizing may not be the best emotional tactic to promote. To isolate one part of our experience and file it away somewhere in our psyche sounds risky even to an amateur like me. On the other hand, it is one way to keep this terrible negative stuff away from undermining our spiritual journey with and toward God.

The key is to compartmentalize consciously. Acknowledge the bad stuff, name it as accurately as you can, protest it, and try to change it. But at some point, let it go, lock it up in the negative church file in your psyche, forget it, and go connect with God, find your peace, and live your life in love. Later, come back to the negative stuff. Can you do both of these seemingly diametrically opposed functions? Yes, you can. If you compartmentalize consciously.

I suspect that this technique is used successfully somewhat frequently. We see it in our support group for people who lost a loved one to suicide. The shock, loss, and pain that accompanies the suicide often leaves grievers so immobilized emotionally that they have to compartmentalize their grief periodically in order to function at all. We go back to the grief consciously in our group but at some other times, the grief has to be ignored deliberately for the sake of basic sanity.

There are other examples: other types of death, natural disasters, war, intense cruelty, situations over which we have no control, breakups in relationships. Do not ignore or bury these experiences. But sometimes we can set them aside and refresh ourselves with other aspects of our life before we come back to the pain. Deliberate compartmentalization provides an alternative to complete withdrawal, perpetual anger, or simply giving in for the sake of pseudo peace. With the negative church stuff, compartmentalizing is an alternative I suggest and use myself.

Some of us have to keep pounding away at the destructive elements of the church (and ourselves) in order to ferret out some of the cancers and warts that inevitably travel with the people of God as we move into the future. And when our ferreting isn't successful, we have to simply say it because it needs to be said. So be it.

In any case, during this current intrigue and the many intrigues to come, just remember that the butler didn't do it. He's the hero. In my book, he is closer to sainthood than anyone else who stalked the halls of the Vatican since Pope John XXIII.

Viva that Papa! And this butler!

Francis Follow-Up: I suspect that the revelations from the butler are now part of the changes Francis is making within the curia and the Vatican Bank. Apparently, Francis had a mandate from the cardinals who elected him to reform the curia and to clean up the financial mess at the Vatican Bank. He is aggressively pursuing that goal: people have been fired, others replaced, and outside auditors are making recommendations to bring the bank into conformity with international standards. Who knows what is next? In any case, I still root for the butler.

CHAPTER 33

Maciel

May 2010

I started reading the *National Catholic Reporter's* lead story in the April 16, 2010, edition titled "New Maciel Revelations," but I didn't get very far. I simply stopped reading. Disgusted. Sad. Angry. Weary. Embarrassed. No surprise though, more like "I told you so."

Fr. Marcial Maciel Degollado, the founder of the Legionnaires of Christ, ultraconservative, friend of Pope John Paul II, influence peddler to the Vatican curia, pedophile, father of several children with different women, superior fundraiser, effective recruiter for his community. The Bernie Madoff of institutional Catholicism. The Tiger Woods of the church.

It isn't that he is the first and only deceitful, self-serving, arrogant major religious figure. A little knowledge of church history reveals many of these sordid stories, and Catholics aren't alone. Religion can bring out the best and the worst in us.

It's more than a question of how could Maciel be so successful and yet so deceitful, or why would he do these things while promoting his religious mission. Those are not my questions, though I am happy others are answering them. My question is more personal: what do I do with Maciel?

There are options. I could simply write him off as another example of a talented, power-hungry, pleasure-seeking cleric who used the church as an easy playground for his grandiose, indulgent desires. I would then nod my head knowingly, utter a dismissive "That's human nature," and forget about him.

I could also take some level of satisfaction at his downfall because I am a progressive Catholic and he was a conservative who promoted and built a model of the church that I detest. His convenient theological convictions worked well for his silent, destructive motives, and it would be easy to equate his theology with his perversion. He could become my poster priest for all that is wrong and dangerous with his brand of conservatism.

Another option would be to discredit him but support his community and its works. Though I disagree with their theological presumptions, operational procedures, and core spirituality, I could admit that many of his followers are likely dedicated, holy people who contribute a lot of time, talent, and treasure to the mission of the Legionnaires of Christ. While the order obviously needs reform, this option would conclude that the primary purpose of the community is valid and deserves some level of acceptance.

A fourth possibility would be to fight him, his memory, and his community as much as I can in the hope that his order would disintegrate, his priests disburse, his fortune be distributed to the poor, his institutions be destroyed (or administered by non-Legionnaires), and his disgraced legacy survive many generations as a warning to possible similar demagogues. His case could enter the moral theology textbooks as an example of what can happen when proper safeguards are not in place in the formation of new religious communities.

There is also the option that I presume some of the Legionnaires chose. Fr. Maciel was a flawed but brilliant, Holy Spirit–inspired religious leader, who deserves some respect despite his sinfulness. "Let anyone who is without sin cast the first stone." His good works outweigh his sins and, while immediate canonization is now impossible, at least acknowledge the good he has done. The Holy Spirit works in unpredictable ways and sometimes chooses very frail vessels to continue the mission of Jesus.

Yet another possibility: this is the last straw. I'm outta' here. Consider me a "fallen away" Catholic. But, who's fallen from whom? (This is not a personal option, but I wonder if some other people might have this reaction.)

Do you have a clear option on how you will react to the unfolding scandal of Fr. Marcial Maciel Degollado? This story will occupy the media for some time, along with the other sex abuse and cover-up themes that seem to be the current face of worldwide Catholicism. Frankly, I would prefer to chat about more positive topics, inspiring people, and hopeful events, but when I sit at my computer to write another Church Chat, I can't ignore these major, though negative, realities. Maybe next month, I can tap my basically optimistic nature and go with my more positive flow.

In the meantime, I still have to decide which option I will choose for my reaction to Maciel.

Francis Follow-Up: Maciel remains in this *Church Chat* book, even though the story may now be dated, as a reminder of how flawed the church can be. I suspect that there are variations on the Maciel story in the church right now. We need to be vigilant in identifying these destructive individuals, organizations, and communities. Maciel is a constant example of what and who should be condemned. As far as I know, Francis has not commented on Maciel, but I can't imagine this pope welcoming Maciel at the Vatican as did John Paul II.

CHAPTER 34

There's Gotta Be More

September 2011

I don't do thorough research on all the issues surrounding my chat topics. Frankly, my life is too busy to keep up with everything. Besides, I'm only chatting, and when we chat, we say things that we think we know or we know something about, but we express our opinion anyway. We chat.

Nevertheless, the topic of this column still has me scratching my head, even after I did do some research. What am I missing? I'm talking about Bishop William Morris from Australia and Fr. Roy Bourgeois, the Maryknoll priest. Both of these men have publically stated that the church should, at least, discuss the possibility of ordaining women to the priesthood. Their stories are not the same in the details, but, in one way or another, they are both getting kicked out because they support the ordination of women.

Kicking them out? Where is that coming from? And, here's my next question: why aren't we all getting kicked out? Or at least, all of us who support the ordination of women? That, by the way, is millions of Catholics, most likely hundreds of millions.

Okay, these two guys are clerics and therefore more eligible for being fired from something. They have an official public position that, it appears, can arbitrarily and one-sidedly be taken away. I support the ordination of women (have for forty years), but I don't think they can fire me from the tenth pew on the left side of the center aisle of my parish church at the 8:00 a.m. Sunday liturgy. Or can they?

Anyway, why are the Vaticanistas picking on Bishop Morris and Fr. Bourgeois?

Maybe these two are chosen examples for the rest of us. Don't tread on this issue! If any of you do, we will punish you severely. No liturgical waterboarding here, we will move directly to condemnation, conviction, and execution. After all, the pope fallibly declared that it is an infallible doctrine of the church that only men can be ordained validly. So, I guess the plan is to select two relatively unknown church leaders in different parts of the world and kick them out of their public position in order to warn the rest of us to get back into the proper thought-control line.

Doesn't seem to be working out that way, does it? These two clerics are now more well-known than they ever would have been and have become martyrs to the cause, galvanizing women ordination supporters and exposing the terrified desperation of the Vaticanistas.

There's gotta be more to the story than that!

Perhaps these two men are being punished for other things, along with their advocacy for women's ordination. I don't know what the "other things" would be for Bishop Morris, but I do know that Fr. Bourgeois is also a courageous peace activist. Are these unnamed offenses the real reason they are being kicked out? If that's the case, I have a three-year-old grandson who knows how unfair that is.

And talk about cowards! To fire someone for unspecified "other reasons" while claiming it is because of women's ordination is Machiavellian malfeasance, to say the least. Makes me wonder if the dresses they wear interfere with their thinking.

Then, the context in which this prosecutorial fiasco takes place is infuriating. Known pedophiles and serial sexual predators get protection in order to prevent scandal, and bishops are granted automatic and perpetual immunity from any consequences of any of their actions. I'm talking total immunity from everything! No accountability for sexual cover-ups; financial disasters (can you hear me, Cardinal Maida?); arbitrary, self-serving policy decisions; etc.—except, of course, Bishop Morris.

They will have to kick me out of this thoroughly dysfunctional system (I remain for other reasons), but this vendetta against Morris and Bourgeois exposes the worst of the worst. That's why there's gotta be more to this story, something I'm missing. Or can they really be *that* vindictive, desperate, stupid, defensive, fearful, and, as my mother used to say, bullheaded?

At this point, it looks like my mother is right once again.

CHAPTER 35

Schism?

April 2012

The 1970 book *Future Shock* by Alvin Toffler taught us that it was always better to anticipate and plan for the future than to let it happen to us—at least, as much as we can.

The latest vicious attack on the Leadership Conference of Women Religious (LCWR) by the Vatican disrupts any plans for the future of the church in the United States. In case you are not aware of the basic story, here's one link: http://ncronline.org/blogs/grace-margins/lcwr-radical-obedience-voice-god-our-time.

Is this the last straw in a steady stream of moldy hay strewn across the world by the Vatican? Is this the challenge that eventually ends up in a formal schism? How will over forty-five thousand sisters respond to this test? And how will the rest of us respond?

This assault is not like the condemnation of Fr. Tony Flannery or Fr. Roy Bourgeois or countless others. This public confrontation is with a large group of dedicated religious women, honored by most Catholics of diverse opinions. Bullies who pick on individuals often get away with it. These same thugs who pick on an organized group of intelligent, service-minded, holy, courageous sisters have a different and more dangerous fight on their hands.

My advice to the Vatican bullies: duck!

One of my reactions to this foolhardy attempt to control the thoughts of all these nuns is to revisit the wisdom of Toffler. So, here are three scenarios for the Catholic Church of the future:

1. After some give-and-take (give by the LCWR and take by the Vatican), the LCWR agrees to "modify" its official positions enough (even if the positions are not currently official) to call off the Vatican bloodhounds. Individual sisters continue to express their personal opinions on the doctrinal issues in dispute (mostly sex-related topics, as usual). Some religious communities withdraw from LCWR, and some sisters leave

the church. But the Vatican achieves its main goal of controlling and weakening the organization. After some vocal protests by progressives in the church, things settle down and the conservative stranglehold on the church gets tighter. More people are scandalized by the attack and connect with other denominations or bitterly, forget the whole church thing completely.

2. The LCWR fights back aggressively, refuses to accept the condemnation, and forces the Vatican to take more punitive steps. The semipolite meetings with Archbishop Peter Sartain end in a stalemate. The Vatican threatens to excommunicate all the nuns, but with the public support of millions of lay Catholics, thousands of priests, and even a few bishops, the threat goes no further. By this time, a new pope tries to bury the conflict, and eventually, there is a permanent standoff, with suspicion and distrust on both sides—like it is now, but with the heat turned up very high.

3. After initial forays, threats, and veil twisting (but there are no veils anymore!), after volumes of outrage from around the world, after pledges of support in private and in public, after all options are thoroughly discussed, the LCWR aligns with other progressive organizations around the world and formally leaves the institutional church. This combined community declares themselves the Reformed Catholic Church and uses Vatican II as its guiding principles. Schism. This RCC begins with some bishops, thousands of priests, multiple thousands of nuns, and millions of laypeople. The current Catholic Church becomes even more conservative and gets their wish of being "leaner and meaner."

While I am at it, here's another prediction: the Vatican response to the "visitation" they forced on the nuns last year will be equally condemnatory. They want the "good sisters" back in their convents, back in their veils, and smiling demurely under their obese, episcopal thumbs.

Ain't gonna happen!

The value of this projecting process is not to say, "See, I told you so," five years from now or to admit that you missed the prediction. The value is to articulate more clearly what is now semiconscious, to separate wishes from realistic expectations, and to plan accordingly.

Futurizing is clearly not an exact science. What will the church be like five years from now? Do any of the three scenarios above get close to what you see?

If not, try to do one yourself. Not so much what you wish would happen, but what do you honestly think will happen?

Pent-up resentment to centuries of chauvinistic arrogance and institutional domination will not go unchallenged.

Schism?

Francis Follow-Up: It seems at this point in mid-2014 that Francis has basically ignored the investigation or at least moved it to his back burner. Cardinal Gerhard Mueller, head of the Congregation for Doctrine of the Faith, has continued the attack on the LCWR, but my guess is that Francis will call off this direct attack and let things simmer down and ultimately fizzle out. Condemning American nuns runs so contrary to everything else Francis is doing that I can't see him joining the attack. If there is a schism, my guess is that it will come from the far right, perhaps led by Cardinal Mueller. But I'm just chatting.

CHAPTER 36

Loyalty to ...?

February 2012

I have known him since high school, and his name is integrity. Unassuming, humble, intelligent, compassionate, courageous, servant, pastor, dedicated—some of the adjectives that fit Fr. Bill Rowe. What doesn't fit is retired.

And yet, this summer, retired is what he will be. Unwillingly. Unnecessarily.

Bill was "forced" into retirement not by any moral issue (sexual abuse, stealing, degrading parishioners, laziness, etc.) or by any heresy (denying the existence of God, divinity/humanity of Jesus, rejecting sacraments, etc.) or even over social justice protests (civil rights, war, women's ordination, etc.).

He was backed into a tiny liturgical corner over celebrating the Eucharist and changing some of the bizarre Latinized English words and phrases in the missal. He kept the basic meaning of the text in his ad-lib prayers but used words that were more understandable and meaningful to his parishioners.

And you all know what I mean by "bizarre Latinized English words" in the prayers at Mass because you have heard them for years, especially since last November and the introduction of the ridiculous "New Missal."

Bill's bishop, His Excellency, the Most Reverend Edward K. Braxton, PhD, STD, insisted that he say the prayers as literally written in the book. Bill said he couldn't do that and that he would resign before he would comply because that would be more pastoral than a prolonged public fight over his noncompliance. His Excellency, the Most Reverend Edward K. Braxton, PhD, STD, said, in effect, "I accept your resignation."

Other columnists, commentators, and letter writers have come to Bill's defense on a number of fronts. My comments deal with two underlying issues: loyalty and proportionality.

How does a Vatican II priest remain loyal to the current version of the institutional Catholic Church that rejects the main themes of Vatican II? That is not just an academic question; it is one that haunts thousands of priests (religious and laypeople also) every day, personally and pastorally. Many of these priests suck it up, talk about it only among trusted friends, do their pastoral work as best they can, try to ignore the broader institutional church, love God and their parishioners, and hope for the best.

They remain loyal enough in their external behavior and words to avoid a confrontation with their bishop because they either don't have the stomach for that fight, fear punishment, or because they figure it is better for the people if they maintain enough loyalty to avoid public confrontation.

They are in a very difficult situation. They have Vatican II (the most authoritative teaching of the church in centuries) to back them up, but the current hierarchy is clearly not following the teachings and initiatives of Vatican II. Besides, there is the example of Jesus—it is obvious what Jesus did and would do in similar situations. Bill Rowe is in good company when personalizing rituals (see Mark 7, for just one example).

Loyalty is slippery. In the church, there are multiple loyalties: loyalty to a bishop, fidelity to church teachings like Vatican II, allegiance to the gospel, faithfulness to current administrative policies, and personal integrity. Sometimes, for some people, these varied loyalties conflict.

So, to whom or what are these priests loyal? Bill Rowe drew the line at the words of the Eucharist.

Well, some say, what's the big deal? Just follow the book, do what the boss says, recite the stupid words, and keep doing good in the parish. I suspect that many priests simply don't care that much about the words they read from the missal anyway. For Bill, that approach would violate his personal integrity so he chose insubordination and resignation. That's how much he *does* care about those words. He is more concerned about providing a meaningful, understandable worship experience for his parish community in rural, eastern Illinois than about the church's institutional mandate to use only prescribed words in a book.

For this, he is forced to resign? He is when you throw a bully bishop like His Excellency, the Most Reverend Edward K. Braxton, PhD, STD, into the mix. Frankly, I can't recall any priest anywhere who was forced to resign because of liturgical irregularities. There are many moral and some theological reasons why some priests should be forced to resign or be just plain fired, but not for clarifying archaic liturgical prayers. The consequence is monumentally out of proportion to the "crime."

I told you Fr. Bill Rowe is a man of integrity, courage, and compassion.

CHAPTER 37

Church, Inc.

February 2012

The ongoing conflict between Fr. Bill Rowe and His Excellency, the Most Reverend Edward K. Braxton, PhD, STD, raises many questions.

For those of you who don't know the basic story, here's a very brief summary: Fr. Rowe ad-libs some of the prayers for the Eucharist and adds some commentary during the Mass. He does so because he believes these creative embellishments make the Eucharist more meaningful for the people and more honest to his own prayer. His Excellency, the Most Reverend Edward K. Braxton, PhD, STD, warned him not to deviate at all from the prescribed text and then forced him to resign this coming June when he refused.

There are more nuances to the story, which is being reported widely and changes periodically as it unfolds, but those are the basics. In the Diocese of Belleville, Illinois, where this conflict is taking place, there are many letters to the editor, personal conversations, and wide-ranging discussions about this clash between a generally popular pastor and a generally unpopular bishop. One theme that often emerges is what I call the "Church, Inc." perception, which is usually advanced by those who support the bishop in this matter.

The argument goes something like this: a manager in a company or agency is expected to follow policies and guidelines as determined by upper management, owners, or the board of directors. Not following those policies runs the risk of unwanted inefficiency, loss of brand identification, and the disruption of product or service reliability. A bishop can reasonably expect the same compliance from his pastors, especially when the policy originates from the Vatican. Disciplinary action is necessary in all of these situations, including the church, in order to maintain clarity of mission and quality of the product or service provided.

Since almost everyone works in an environment that operates under this core governing system, most people are familiar with and basically accept this sensible approach to managing large and complex organizations.

Why would the church be any different? Why shouldn't Bishop Braxton force the retirement of Fr. Rowe for not complying with the prescribed, liturgical texts? Because the church is not a corporation, and the punishment is not proportioned to the deviation.

Chapter 1 of The Dogmatic Constitution on the Church from the Second Vatican Council is titled "The Mystery of the Church." The title itself gives us a clue that the church is more than a corporation, even if it has a hierarchical structure. The church is about God-among-us. A company is about making money. An agency is about a specific service. While there may be some common qualities in all three, the church is qualitatively and essentially different.

Well, you may say, if Fr. Rowe does his own thing at Eucharist, then anyone else can do their own thing and we end up splintered and in a mess. We have to draw a line somewhere, or the commonality of the liturgy is lost completely. Uniformity prevents chaos. I agree up to a point. And we could discuss where the line could be drawn. My point is: it should not be drawn at Fr. Bill Rowe.

Here's why: he does not violate the structure or intent of the Eucharist. It is a valid, intact liturgy. He adapts the three assigned prayers (opening prayer, offertory prayer, and closing prayer) to his homily and the hymns. Quoting Fr. Rowe: "In the Eucharistic prayer I sometimes insert a phrase to continue the theme, e.g. for Ash Wednesday, I inserted the idea of changing our hearts and return to the Gospel and also, from the ashes of our failures God promises to give us a new life and Spirit."

That's what he does. He enhances the liturgy. He not only prepares a homily; he prepares for the whole Eucharistic experience and integrates the additional elements into the prescribed ritual. He doesn't take away; he augments, clarifies, and makes the rich themes of the liturgy more accessible to the community.

Sounds like a creative, devoted, intelligent, prayerful presider to me. Would that everyone in every parish be so fortunate! To punish him when other priests mumble through the ritual or cannot be understood or preach insulting, irrelevant drivel or simply paraphrase the gospel and call it preaching is picking out one of the best and calling him the worst. Absurd!

Not only does the punishment not fit the crime, but, as St. Matthew reminds us, "Remove the plank from your own eye first; then you will see clearly to take the speck from your brother's eye" (7:5).

CHAPTER 38

"I Do That"

July 2012

I was going to write this column two weeks ago when I first heard about it. But I didn't believe it and wanted to verify what I had heard. So I did verify, and found out it is worse than I thought.

I figured His Excellency, the Most Reverend Edward K. Braxton, PhD, STD, bishop of Belleville, Illinois, my home diocese, would remove Fr. Bill Rowe from his assignment as pastor of St. Mary's Church in Mt. Carmel, Illinois. But I didn't think His Excellency, the Most Reverend Edward K. Braxton, PhD, STD, would strip Bill of all his priestly faculties, which means he cannot function as a priest in any capacity anywhere.

That's blatant overkill. And what did Fr. Rowe do to warrant this extreme punishment? As you may recall from some previous chats, he adapted some of the prayers of the Eucharist, never changing the words of institution, but adding comments that clarified the obscure language and emphasized a consistent theme throughout the liturgy.

I have known Bill since high school and his middle name is integrity. He would not violate his conscience and preside over a liturgy that he knew was at least partially incoherent to his congregation. Sounds more like St. Thomas More, the Man for All Seasons, than a stubborn, do-it-my-way-only rebel.

Here is just one part of this outrageous punishment: many other priests do the same thing with complete immunity. I have participated in Eucharists where the celebrant added comments during the ritual, explained what was going on, clarified, or adapted the liturgy to a particular event or theme. It happens, and I bet all of you have been part of it yourself. It happens a lot.

So, in order to be consistent, all of these priests should also be banned. Disregard everything else they do in their ministry. Ignore their compassion, dedication, talents, commitment, and personal holiness. Kick them out because they add or change some of the words of an archaic liturgy. Form a group of litur-nazis to ferret them out, report them to the local bishop, and fire them all.

How many would there be? My guess is: a lot. And many of them would be among the most respected and effective priests in the country.

I have a preemptive counterplan. How about a national website where priests could sign on and admit "I Do That!"? It would be the "I Do That" movement. A companion website or another section of the same website could be for laypeople who would sign a statement that they support the priests who sign the "I Do That" admission. It is time the people of God take back our church.

It sounds scary for the celebrants, doesn't it? What if His Excellency, the Most Reverend Edward K. Braxton, PhD, STD, and other bishops like him, take the same action against other priests like he did with Fr. Rowe?

Well, it is scary and would take bravery and conviction to sign. But the vulnerability would be lessened if the promotion for the movement would include a provision that no one would sign until the word got out to the whole country and everyone would be asked to sign at the same time on a designated day. If thousands sign on that one day, there would be protection in numbers. And the lay website would be activated at the same time. There would be immediate, nationwide, public protest if any bishop took any action against any signee. Do it publicly and in great numbers. It would be a loud, dramatic, social network protest. It would be our Tahrir Square, Tiananmen Square, Selma march.

Unless something like this takes place soon, this kind of excessive punishment will continue. Bill Rowe may be the first, but he will not be the last. Once His Excellency, the Most Reverend Edward K. Braxton, PhD, STD, gets away with ousting Bill, the path is clear for him and other bishops to do the same to other priests for liturgical and other supposed major offenses. Stop this trend now, or they will pick off one priest at a time. Don't wait until it happens to a priest you know and love.

The "I Do That!" movement gives us one chance to balance things out a little. There may be other approaches, but going through official channels of appeals and protest will not work. Over the last three decades, the upper hierarchy has clamped down, buttoned up, and squeezed out everyone but themselves from any influence on anything. Fear and compliance stalk the formerly hallowed halls of chancery offices throughout the country.

So, what do you think? Is the "I Do That!" movement feasible? Will you participate? Should I proceed with more organization and planning? Let me know, and remember Fr. Bill Rowe!

CHAPTER 39

www.iamfrrowe.org

August 2012

Yep, that's right. The title of this chat is a website. And, of course, I want you to go to it, read it, add your name to the petition page, and forward it to a million of your closest friends.

You may recall that over the past few months I have chatted about Fr. Bill Rowe, the pastor who was fired from the priesthood by his bishop for enhancing the Eucharistic liturgy by adding some clarifying words to some of the official texts of the ritual. Fr. Bill is also a personal friend of mine since seminary high school, which amounts to more decades than I want to remember.

I have said it before, and I will say it again: Bill is one of the most compassionate, priestly servants anyone can imagine. His humble integrity, his personal dedication, his concern for others, and his inspiring pastoral leadership is outstanding. For Bishop Braxton to attack him for liturgical improprieties is like condemning Mother Teresa for leaving her convent to comfort the poor of Calcutta or like firing Olympic gold medalist swimmer Mark Phelps for spending too much time in the water.

When Fr. Bill was removed not only from his parish but also from the priesthood by taking away all of his authority to function as a priest, some of his friends created this website to express their support for him and their outrage at the disproportionate harshness of the punishment. This overkill is even more preposterous in light of the way the church has handled pedophile priests, church thieves, lazy pastors, and downright mean ministers. This site invites you—no, urges you—to join them in this support and outrage.

To indicate the kind of person Bill is: he is now volunteering as a lay minister in another city in Southern Illinois.

Here are some features of the site:

- It is a "robust" site in that, along with the specifics of Fr. Rowe's experience, there are summaries of events and church teachings that influenced him in his ministry: Vatican II, the 1998 Missal, church history, what Catholics believe, etc.

- Under the "News" tab, watch the short video of an interview with Fr. Bill to get a feel for his personality, style, and courage. Check some of the other news stories to see how his situation is being reported.

- Don't miss the items in the "What Happened" section: "Fr. Rowe's Recollections and Charges & Responses." These two entries are a log of what happened. The charges are literally unbelievable: unsubstantiated, erroneous accusations totally unrelated to liturgical practice used as an obvious attempt to pile on canonical justification for the removal of a pastor. If Bill had not appealed the decision, these charges would have gone to the Vatican unchallenged.

- You will note in this continuing log of events that some priests from the Belleville diocese "signed on" to his removal. This testimony is part of the removal process. What you may not know is the overpowering and intimidating presence of Bishop Braxton. These priests, whom I also know and some of whom are also friends of Bill, will have to deal with their conscience as they reflect on their part in this injustice.

- The petition page makes clear that no one denies that Fr. Bill breaks the liturgical norm of not changing the explicit words in the ritual. He enhances and clarifies some obscure wordings to help his people (and himself) pray better. Many other priests do the same thing. To be consistent, shouldn't they all be fired? The petition says: you can't fire all of them!

- If you want to add a testimonial or comment, there is a forum tab for that. See what others are saying.

- Please note that there is a very active Facebook page as well. Comment there also.

Some final, and fair, questions: What is the ultimate point of this site? What can be done with the signatures collected? Will it reinstate Fr. Bill as a priest? Will it galvanize so much support that bishops will hesitate to punish other priests? Will it, along with other current events, help crystallize the obvious chasm between the institutional church and the church as community? Will it provide, as the tagline says, solidarity, courage, and priorities?

I hope so. Sign on, and let's find out. www.iamfrrowe.org.

Francis Follow-Up: The site is still active so you can continue to add your comments. The Facebook page has many supportive comments. The pastor who took Bill's place announced that he was leaving the priesthood. His motives for leaving are not publically related to Bill's situation, but he clearly had a tough assignment due to Bill's continuing popularity in the parish and the overwhelming conviction that he was treated so unjustly. Even more recently, the deacon who was appointed administrator of the parish after the pastor who left has now resigned that position and has taken a leave of absence from the deaconate. All because Bill enhanced the liturgy? No. All because Bishop Braxton decided to defrock him. By their fruits, you shall know them. In July 2014, a new pastor will take over the parish, a pastor with the reputation of being one the most conservative priests in the diocese. One result of this whole sordid disaster: there are many fewer people attending Mass at the parish. What would Francis do?

CHAPTER 40

Vatican Schism

September 2012

There are certainly other issues in the church that I can write about. Lots of low-hanging fruit. And they all deserve picking. And when I get through with most of this spoiled fruit, there are thousands of good, inspiring, holy things to chat about.

But I have to stay with the Fr. Bill Rowe persecution at least one more time. That's because this case includes many dimensions that transcend the specifics of his story and illustrate some of the rotten fruit that continues to grow on the tree of the church.

As a reminder, the website is www.iamfrrowe.org. If you haven't done so already, please sign the petition page after you read the details of this incredible punishment. Forward the site to others and come back to it periodically to see the comments on the signature page or on Facebook.

For this chat, I want to quote one of the comments from the signature page. In case you missed it, here's how it reads:

> The web site fails to note that the new English Missal translations are not only unprayable; they are illicit because the highest authority of the Church, the Second Vatican Council, by a 99.9% vote, gave full and final responsibility for translations to language bishops' conferences and made accessibility to all, not "more sacred language," the primary norm. Rome hijacked a fine 1998 proper translation, excluded all who had a hand in it from its translation process, and created new norms, which one liturgy expert calls the dumbest thing ever to come out of Rome on liturgy. The Vatican is in schism in repealing Vatican II and the Church is now headed by a long-time coddler of pedophiles who should be driven from office (and never elected pope). His predecessor was another, being hurriedly canonized before the people wake up to his record. Dr. William Slavick, ME Signature #393

I don't know Dr. Slavick, but his observation about "The Vatican is in schism ..." intrigues me.

One dictionary definition of *schism* is: a formal division within, or separation from, a church or religious body over some doctrinal difference; the state of a sect or body formed by such division; the offense of causing or seeking to cause such a division.

Sounds right to me. Dr. Slavick is correct: the current Vatican is a small, schismatic sect, separated from the church of the Second Vatican Council.

So, why do they still call the shots for the whole church? And get away with it? And what can we do about it?

Quick answers:

1. They call the shots because a few power-hungry, self-righteous Red Hats bulldozed their way up hierarchical ladders under the protective and encouraging patronage of John Paul II and are now sitting on entrenched thrones sneering at the rest of us and controlling their fiefdoms through doctrinal guillotines, unaccountably harsh punishments (e.g., Fr. Rowe), blatant sexism, a medieval governance system, etc., etc., etc.

2. They get away with it because over the last forty years they have deliberately appointed thousands of bishops whose core personalities demand absolute loyalty, fear of authority figures, doctrinal slavery, and personal ambition. These bishops are incapable of the courage it takes to demand collegiality or to speak out against the dictates of the intimidating higher clergy. Those bishops who are best at these qualities climb the ladder. One example: they don't even dare to speak about discussing the possibility of ordaining women or even optional celibacy. That level of thought control is not even present within the Pentagon.

3. What can we do about it? Not much. Some more reasonable bishops have to get together and say: Enough! Priests need to organize and say: Enough! Some outright, selective public disobedience by priests would be a start. How about an organized, publicized, designated Sunday for thousands of priests to use last year's missal? The hierarchical stranglehold will not be broken from the top down. It must be bottom up. There will be martyrs, like Fr. Bill Rowe. But his approach of humility and service, coupled with unwavering conviction and courage, must be the model. It is the equivalent of Gandhi's and

Martin Luther King Jr.'s nonviolent protests, which is also the way of Jesus. We lay folks must join in by speaking up even while we walk our spiritual journey.

Dr. Slavick made the correct call. Instant replay confirms it. The Vatican is in schism with the church of Vatican II. And the evidence is everywhere, including Mt. Carmel, Illinois, where Fr. Bill Rowe, the pastor of St. Mary's parish, is stripped of the power to exercise his priesthood.

Remember: bottom up!

Francis Follow-Up: The arrival of Pope Francis has dramatically changed the dynamic inherent in this chat. But I kept it in this book because it represents the feelings of many progressives up to the time Francis was selected. How much impact and what will be the specifics of a Francis reform remains to be seen. The most hopeful thing so far is not a specific policy change but an obvious and clear change in the atmosphere around the papacy. I doubt, for example, if Bishop Braxton could get any approval from anyone in the Vatican to defrock Fr. Bill Rowe today.

CHAPTER 41

Fear

April 2012

To be honest, I didn't know who Father Tony Flannery was until last week. I know now that he is a sixty-five-year-old Redemptorist who writes a column for his order's monthly magazine *Reality*. Or, at least, he used to write one.

The Vatican silenced him and apparently sent him to six weeks of prayer and meditation at a monastery. I guess he has to get his mind right, which means he needs Vaticanization. He keeps oozing out of the cookie-cutter.

He was shut down because he supports a married priesthood, women's ordination, and other progressive Catholic issues, including criticizing the Irish hierarchy for their handling of the sex abuse scandal. To get more information on this story go to http://www.thedailybeast.com/articles/2012/04/11/vatican-silences-father-flannery.html.

Just when you think the Inquisition is an embarrassing tragedy of the Middle Ages, it shows up again in our post-modern twenty-first century. Surely, they won't dust off those old racks they used to force suspected "heretics" to recant their wayward ideas, will they? Surely, they can't go that far! On the other hand, what monastery was he sent to?

I suspect that this story will have some legs. For now, I have two general comments:

1. Fr. Flannery received immediate and strong support from at least two priests' organizations: the eight-hundred-member Association of Catholic Priests in Ireland and Austria's We Are the Church group, which counts thousands of priests throughout Europe as members. Where is a similar response and support from the United States?

   There is no response from the United States because there is no comparable priest organization here. With the obvious attack on Vatican II over the past three decades and the increasingly bold, direct assault on priests like Fr. Flannery, why haven't a sizeable number of priests nationwide banded together to be able to respond to issues like this?

It is frustratingly clear that the United States' hierarchy, as a body, bishops, and priests, simply don't have the courage to defend Vatican II and to champion issues like optional celibacy and women's ordination. Presumably, some bishops privately are at least willing to discuss these issues, and there are certainly some priests who not only believe in the liberal agenda, but who speak about it publicly. But there is no courage or willingness to get organized so there could be a clear, forceful, multitoned voice representing a progressive wing of the hierarchy, including priests.

The bishops are afraid of the Vatican, and the priests are afraid of the bishops. Fear is not a worthy emotion for leaders of our church. Will all those who are not afraid please stand up?

It looks like priests in Ireland and Austria are standing up. There were some priests in Milwaukee some years ago, some others in Boston, and a handful in Southern Illinois who have taken some courageous stands, but there still isn't a nationwide, coordinated voice representing priests who articulate a progressive Catholic agenda based on the gospel and utilizing the teachings of Vatican II and liberal theology of the past fifty years.

Come on, guys, get it together. I know you're out there. We all need you, as individuals and as a body. They can't send all of you to Fr. Flannery's monastery.

2. On the lay side of the church coin, there are some organizations that push this envelope. Call to Action, Voice of the Faithful, and the Faithful of Southern Illinois are a few that come to mind. These groups and others I don't know about need more members and supporters. Not everyone has to picket cathedrals and chancery offices, but there should be many more people publicly declaring what they are against and what they are for. The conservatives are highjacking our church, and it's time we balance things out.

It's not a hard case to make: just quote the gospel. Service to the poor, justice to the victims, and love for all trumps power to the hierarchy, ritual exactness, and priorities established by (presumed) celibates regarding sexual issues.

More laity needs to speak up. We have less to lose than our priest friends. The Vatican can't send us to Fr. Flannery's monastery. Join a group, send letters to the editors, invite progressive speakers to your area, create and/or sign petitions, speak up to your friends and neighbors, get beyond your parish, take an interest in your diocese and the universal church.

And most of all reject fear.

Francis Follow-Up: There now is an Association of United States Catholic Priests—http://www.usCatholicpriests.org/—who are attempting to unite many priests around some of the issues facing the church. It will take a few more years to see how this organization matures, what positions they take, and what their impact will be. At this point, it looks promising, and their recent conference in St. Louis in June of 2014 was well attended. They are becoming a necessary voice in the American church. More time is needed, but with the other priests' associations around the world and by eventually connecting with lay groups, a major force could emerge that could enliven the gospel and give flesh to Vatican II.

CHAPTER 42

If I Only Knew Then ...

February 2013

If I only knew then what I know now, I would have_____ (fill in the blank). We say it often enough, and it often enough is an accurate assessment. After more experience, we have a different perspective than we had originally. We would act differently, more wisely, handle the situation better. It implies that we are not responsible for what we didn't know then, even if we admit we were naive. It's just the way life is. Experience teaches, and we hope we learn.

I hear the phrase and use it myself as a grandparent reflecting on the experience of parenting. Another quick example: after years of experience on a job, we may hear it when the conversation turns to what it was like when we started the job.

Common enough observation. And universally accepted as true.

Most of the time.

Sometimes, this commonly accepted axiom is used as an excuse, a cover-up for what should have been known in the first place but was ignored. A case in point is the recent coverage of Los Angeles Cardinal Roger Mahoney's scandalous and criminal handling of child sex-abuse cases. Between the lines of the reporting is the premise that "If I only knew then what I know now about child sex abuse, I would have acted differently."

Resorting to this revered truism in this case is not only misleading; it is a calculated lie. To Cardinal Mahoney and all others like him, I say: "You knew then that the sexual abuse of children is a heinous, criminal, damaging act. You chose to minimize it because of your sinfully distorted view of the church and your role in it."

There are some things that are so clearly wrong that years of experience are not needed to see that they are wrong. Child sex abuse is one of them.

But there are other examples as well. Mandatory celibacy for priests is another one. We have known for centuries that requiring celibacy for priesthood is ridiculous and damaging. Laypeople may have known it as a fact long before some priests and bishops knew it, but for at least the last century, priests knew it too. Even many brainwashed seminarians knew it but didn't say anything because if they did, well, they wouldn't be seminarians anymore.

Ordination of women to the priesthood is another case in point. We have known for at least fifty years that the arguments against women's ordination are unfounded. When we get through all the theological jargon, misquoting of scripture, appeals to an unenlightened tradition, misguided acceptance of the cultural imposition of second-class status on women, all that is left is anatomy. And it is self-evidently preposterous to think that God, and therefore Jesus, limits priestly service because of anatomy.

We have known for a long time, but it gets increasingly clearer, that the hierarchical structure of our current church is not only dysfunctional and destructive; it is flat-out wrong. It looks Orwellian to me, with a heavy emphasis on thought control. It certainly isn't collegial, as Vatican II envisioned. Is it a monarchy, a dictatorship, an oligarchy, a gang, a mob? It is not a democracy or a republic. Whatever it is in practice, we have known it for a long time. And we know its destructive power. It looks like a structure mired in the Middle Ages, fundamentally incapable of communicating effectively with the twenty-first century no matter how many Tweets the pope supposedly generates, and an organizational museum piece hanging in the backroom of history. We know it, and we know it is wrong.

Is there hope? Of course, there is. God is bigger than our structures and policies and certainly much more loving, accepting, and forgiving, if forgiveness is really needed. Can we find God in the midst of the currently constituted Catholic Church? Of course, we can. Fortunately, the Holy Spirit knows how to breathe underwater. The Spirit will find us, even when we are not looking. We don't have to leave the church to find the Spirit. Just poke around in different parts of the church, and the Spirit will find you.

Why even chat about the bad stuff? Because some of us have to, just to point out alternatives and not let the bad guys (and they are mostly guys!) claim they speak and act for all of us.

So, don't let the axiom of "If I only knew then what I know now" fool you. They knew. They knew.

Francis Follow-Up: Once again, Francis demonstrates a more enlightened approach to these issues, but it was only a few years ago that the picture painted in this chat about culpable blindness to obvious sinful behavior permeated our Catholic religious culture. With Francis, we get honesty, transparency, simplicity, compassion, and love. Did our two previous popes have these same qualities? If they did, it was not as apparent.

PART 4

Culture Versus Catholic

Faith and culture mingle. Believers live in a specific place at a precise time within a particular society. The surrounding culture, the beliefs, customs, attitudes, priorities, expectations of the society at large, influences how believers express their faith. Sometimes culture and Catholicism clash, and sometimes they mesh. This section of *Church Chat* explores some of these points of intersection.

CHAPTER 43

Cafeteria Catholics

September 2011

Of course I am a cafeteria Catholic. Aren't we all?

First of all, I love the food image. Making difficult choices among delectable edibles is my idea of a good time. At a buffet I visit too often, I have a wide array of salads, meats, vegetables, and desserts to choose from, but I almost always pick the same three or four items. I wonder why!

Secondly, cafeteria Catholic is a pretty good analogy for all Catholics—progressive, conservative, and middle-of-the-roaders (MORs). There are multiple church teachings, not unlike a long buffet, and all Catholics are picking and choosing their way through the line.

Most often, *cafeteria Catholic* is a negative term used by conservatives to criticize progressive or middle-of-the-road Catholics. The implication is that the progressives and MORs are weak, disloyal, and inadequate Catholics who need to either follow all the teachings (eat all that food?) or leave. What these conservative critics don't accept is that they too pick and choose among church teachings and gorge on some teachings while skipping others, like that tasty vegetable called primacy of conscience.

Their main course is papal infallibility and its condiment, the magisterium. It's like they eat too much red meat and leave out the fish and chicken. It's a platter full of rare sirloin. This diet causes "creeping infallibilism," which means that they treat those teachings that are not infallible as if they are infallible. Actually, infallible is an either/or. The teaching either is or it is not infallible. Period. Everything else can and should be questioned and discussed, without damage to personal or magisterial faith.

Actually, even the infallible, creedal statements are open for restatement. As Pope John XXIII said, the core faith can be expressed in a variety of ways, just like chicken can be prepared in a variety of ways and still remain chicken. The fact that a doctrine has been "defined" in a particular, usually Aristotelian, philosophical language doesn't mean that the underlying mystery cannot also be expressed in different, non-Aristotelian language. All faith language is a limited attempt to describe the mystery of God. No language, not even the words of defined statements, completely captures the faith we profess. Defined statements are one reliable way of expressing our faith, but not the only, exclusive way to talk about the mystery. The veal marsala may be a reliable way to prepare veal, but it isn't the only way.

By the way, you will find Aristotle in the philosophical cafeteria down the street, not in the Catholic faith buffet.

How do Catholics choose their food while they slowly stroll down the cafeteria line? My guess is that we believe what our personality allows us to believe. If we like to help others, we will pick those teachings that emphasize service. If we like to control things, we will pile our plates with those teachings that reinforce our desire to control. If we like to think abstractly, we will favor those teachings that feed our desire to reflect. In other words, a determining factor in choosing which teachings we emphasize starts with our own personality.

We bring our specific appetite with us when we enter the Catholic teaching cafeteria. The appetite of conservative Catholics is no better than the appetites of progressives or MORs. So, excuse me, but I want a piece of that pecan pie.

CHAPTER 44

Those People

May 2011

First of all, if you haven't already done so, read this article in the *National Catholic Reporter*, April 15 issue: http://ncronline.org/news/hidden-exodus-Catholics-becoming-protestants. This report by Fr. Thomas Reese highlights the US Religious Landscape Survey by the Pew Research Center's Forum on Religion and Public Life.

For those of you who didn't just read the article, it's about Catholics who become Protestants. Now, read the article!

There's a lot to quote, but here's my current focus: "Any other institution that lost one-third of its members would want to know why. But the U.S. bishops have never devoted any time at their national meetings to discussing the exodus. Nor have they spent a dime trying to find out why it is happening."

Now why don't they address this exodus, do you imagine? Since they haven't answered this question, we are left to imagining. So imagine, I will.

I have always resisted lumping a large group of people together under a "they." Usually, "they" are not a "they"; there are generally significant differences among any group. But if the bishops were candy, they would all be M&Ms with a variety of colors. There are no Snickers, Butterfingers, Milky Ways, and certainly no Hershey Kisses. And where are my favorites, Almond Joys? Only M&Ms. So, in this case, I will say "they."

Here are some reasons why they don't want to know why people leave the Catholic Church:

1. They already know why those people leave. Who needs surveys? Those people have little faith to begin with, and so they just leave because their commitment is minimal. Let them go. Who needs them? A leaner, smaller, more loyal membership works better anyway. Dump the dead weight. Good riddance.

2. Those people can't accept the teachings of the church because those people are too heavily influenced by the secular culture of the United States. Their faith has been corrupted by the consumerism, commercialism, superficiality, and relativism of the general population. Those people can't see beyond sitcoms, latest movies, fashion, sports, and digest news. They are incapable of seeing the truth as proclaimed by church teaching. So, they gradually just leave for an easier faith or no faith at all. All we can do is teach harder, longer, and stronger, but when they have deaf ears, there is nothing else we can do. They will suffer the consequences.

3. Most of those people are too smart for their own good. They think they can figure out things about God, faith, morality without the bishops' guidance. Those people are too proud to accept the teachings of the magisterium as articulated by the bishops. Their pride drives them away, and unless we are able to break their pride, they will continue to leave.

4. The fear factor is gone. Since those people are no longer afraid of mortal sin or hell, they feel free to leave. This lack of fear is especially evident among younger people.

5. We have higher priorities, like bringing back more Latinized language to the liturgy and reasserting our positions against abortion, same-sex marriage, optional clerical celibacy and the ordination of women. Losing membership isn't nearly as important as these issues, and if we add this exodus issue, we will dilute our essential message about our core concerns.

6. Other?

Anyway, those are some of the reasons I imagine are operating as the bishops take no notice of the millions of people who are slipping out the back door of the church. It seems the Vatican isn't too concerned either, perhaps because, as John Allen says, the Vatican's hope for growth of the church is focused on what he calls the "global south," countries south of the equator.

If you know any of "those people," perhaps you can tell them why the bishops are not conducting exit interviews. On second thought, it's probably better just to be nice to "those people."

CHAPTER 45

All Are Welcome

September 2011

It's a good hymn. Catchy tune. Fine lyrics. It's usually used as a processional hymn, to begin the liturgy. Generally, it's sung by the congregation with some gusto, at least in my parish. It's also a lie.

The lie is in the words: "All are welcome; all are welcome, in this place." I wish it were true, but it obviously isn't. We can sing as loud as we want, even sing on key; we can add harmony, a choir, and an orchestra—but it still remains a lie.

Clearly, not everyone is welcome. If you are divorced, remarried without an annulment, you're not welcome. If you are gay, in a committed relationship, you really should stay home. If you are a former priest, without laicization papers, please worship elsewhere. If you are not a baptized Catholic, there are other churches for you. If you haven't been to church in ten years, don't bother to come this Sunday either.

Oh, yes, that's right; I almost forgot: you can come in the doors and sit with us. You can even sing along, maybe you will get to sing "All Are Welcome." We will even allow you to listen to the readings and the homily. But, above all, you may *not* go to Communion. You are not welcome to go to Communion. Is that clear?

You see, you must be worthy to receive the sacrament of the Lord. Who's worthy, and who's not? Well, that gets tricky when you consider secret, sinning Catholics. Then again, we know that all the people in the above categories, and more, are not worthy.

So, let's review: secret sinners sneak into the Communion line, inherently accepting the dire consequences of their fraudulent participation, but the above-mentioned folks are excluded outright. Does somebody have a scorecard so I can keep it straight? After all, we do have an obligation to protect the worthiness of the sacrament and the sanctity of the Lord. I want to make sure I don't slip onto that unworthy list and unwittingly wind up with some of those dire consequences.

I wonder what the Last Supper would have been like with our current worthiness standards. I think we would have had to ask Peter to leave—the denials he came up with a few hours later really should disqualify him from the first Eucharist and certainly the priesthood. Then, there's that tax-collecting Mathew. Do you really feel he's acceptable? Of course, there's Judas too. He left before the Eucharist, right? So, he wasn't there for the first consecration. Or was he? The one I wonder about is Simon of the Zealot party. I mean, what do we actually know about him? Zealots are not very reliable, you know. Is he worthy? And, by the way, what do we know about the marriage status of all of these guys? Makes you wonder.

If all twelve of these apostles got into the Communion line in your parish, would they meet all of the worthiness standards we now have for receiving the Eucharist faithfully? It's just a question.

Why don't we just simply open the Body and the Blood of Jesus to everyone? He did. All the time. As a lifestyle. The only ones he turned away were the ones who made rules about worthiness. Why do we feel we must protect Him from so-called sinners and nonbelievers? Seems like we turned His acceptance and total availability into a self-serving, protective society of insiders. I doubt if He likes that. We don't have to protect Him from the unworthy of the world. He can handle it without our interference.

So, the least we can do is not sing the "All Are Welcome" hymn or change the words to "Some Are Welcome." We could put an asterisk by "some" and list at the bottom of the page those who aren't welcome. Better yet, for the sake of space, let's list those who are welcome. It's a shorter list.

CHAPTER 46

The Us Pause Movement

December 2012

"… for us men and for our salvation …"

Now, really, couldn't we simply drop the word *men* in this line from the creed we pray at Mass? What would that hurt? In fact, wouldn't it clarify the obvious meaning of the text? Surely, we don't want to exclude women from the "us" and "our salvation." That would be heresy and just plain stupid.

It really is a simple, little request. It would take some time for all of us to stop adding "men" to the creed just because we've been saying it this way all of our lives. But in time, we could do it easily enough.

Here are just two benefits of dropping "men" from this part of the creed:

1. It would be more faithful to the Latin text: *Qui propter nos homines et propter nostram salute.* "Homines" in Latin refers to "human beings." If they wanted to make it male only, they would use the Latin word "vir," which refers to male, masculine, as opposed to feminine. English, of course, doesn't have two words for "man" so saying "for us men" is inherently misleading. By deleting the word "men," we would simply pray "… for us and for our salvation …," which is the meaning and intention of the Latin word *homines* anyway. This phrasing would, in fact, be more faithful to the meaning of the Latin text.

2. It would be a token concession to the overwhelming sexist language of the scriptures, Church documents, prayer, and liturgy. God, of course, is neither male nor female, but beyond both. (On the other hand, my wife says that maybe only men need salvation. I hadn't thought about that, and I'm not going there!)

Simple, right? So, what's the problem? Surely, no one would mind if we drop the reference to men.

Well, maybe some people would mind. Perhaps the Congregation for the

Doctrine of the Faith in Rome and the Sacred Congregation for the Sacraments and Divine Worship would mind. Maybe the people who think that the literal fourth-century wording of the creed is required for all people, in all times, in all cultures would mind. After all, it would be tampering with the text, even to make the text clearer. All those fine folks would mind. Most of us wouldn't, but they would and they decide.

I am realistic enough to know that this tiny, insignificant, inconsequential change will not happen officially in my lifetime or maybe my grandson's lifetime. But I do have an alternative suggestion.

Just stop saying it. Just pray "… for us (pause) and for our salvation …" I've been doing that for years, and I admit that, while it is personally satisfying, it has no impact on the community. To make it clear to everyone, a group of people have to skip the word, "men." Just think, if one small group would do it and then another and another, it's possible that at one Mass in one parish, a whole community (probably except the celebrant and a few people who forget) would omit "men" from this one part of the creed. Wouldn't that be something? It would probably make the news, and other people would catch on. It would become the "us Pause" movement, then a trend, and finally, perhaps in my grandson's lifetime, a common practice.

Then the bishops and other somber congregations, after some predictable, pompous, and threatening proclamations, would say, "Oh well, what's the difference?" And at that point, the offending "men" would officially drop from the creed.

It could happen. Let's try and see.

CHAPTER 47

Global South

October 2011

I did it again. I went to another John Allen talk, the CNN Vatican correspondent, regular contributor to the *National Catholic Reporter*, author, and lecturer. About two years ago, I attended my first Allen presentation and wrote a chat about Catholic identity, one of the ten trends he sees in the church today. My question was: why is Catholic identity so important? That remains unanswered.

Why did I recently go to another Allen presentation, even though he had a similar message? Probably because I thought there was another chat in there somewhere. And so there is!

Folded into his remarks then and now was a description of the global south and its impact on Vatican policy.

He maintains that the religious agenda is very different in a United States / Western European setting than it is in the global south—South America, Africa, and parts of Asia. In the global north, the questions are usually framed in "liberal versus conservative" issues (birth control, liturgical norms, church authority, optional clerical celibacy, ordination of women, homosexuality, etc.) In the global south, the issues are more related to justice, poverty, and Catholicism as being recognizably different from common cultural values and other religions.

Allen provides a helpful analysis of worldwide Catholicism. But the issues of the global south and their millions of very young Catholics do not determine the issues of the United States. Like Jesus lived and St. Paul taught, Christianity is incarnational, embedded in the culture and society of multiple arenas. If I understand Allen's comments correctly, some powerful church leaders shape policy and promote teachings that try to neutralize this diversity in favor of an identifiable, worldwide uniformity. They want clear, universal answers to Catholic questions.

Progressive Catholics in the United States and Western Europe seem marginalized in this global strategy. We are simply outnumbered, and our issues are considered trivial, unworthy of attention. We are written off as bitter, whining, generally aging, frustrated malcontents unable to adjust to a new agenda. We do not have a place at the table (although this is what Allen calls for) if the issues are celibacy, women's ordination, homosexuality, birth control, appointment of bishops, liturgical norms, etc. Our positions on these issues are not considered, and we are condemned for holding them. We are dismissed in favor of the issues facing the global south.

Hold on just a minute! Why is this an either/or? Why are the issues of the youthful global south pitted against the issues of the aging north? Makes no sense. Aging Vatican II progressives have been champions of social justice for forty years. The universal church could choose to deal with all these issues; there is no need to side with the issues of one part of the world as opposed to another part of the world. No need at all.

It seems to me that Popes John Paul II and Benedict XVI and most of the bishops they have selected over the last thirty years have deliberately chosen to starve the global north issues. I don't say this in anger; it just appears to be objective reality. They obviously starved infant, core Vatican II themes like collegiality, subsidiarity, and gender equality while they clearly nourished a Vatican I church with its sexism, clericalism, and devotionalism that spawned and coddled Evangelical Catholicism.

I don't want a fight with John Allen because I respect him so much and because I would lose! But the picture I got from his presentation both times is that the Vatican is a passive observer of the ten trends he identifies. The Vatican looks around the world, sees what is happening, and responds to what it sees.

My view is that the Vatican is an active player in shaping many of those trends, particularly the ones that are internal to the church. The Vatican wields enormous power in determining which "trends" grow and which ones wither. The Vatican has an agenda, and they implement it subtly and not so subtly.

Allan rightly maintains that there are "tribes" in the church and in society and the tribes don't dialogue with each other. So true. But to dialogue fruitfully and as friends, we must start with calling a miter, a miter.

Francis Follow-Up: The Francis impact verifies my main point in this chat. The pope and the Vatican are major players in creating and shaping some of the trends in the church rather than observing and reacting to them. With over a billion Catholics in the world, the priorities of the Catholic Church not only influence Catholics but also society in general. Francis is clearly changing some of those priorities, which makes him and the church a change-maker in the world as well as internally.

CHAPTER 48

Religious Liberty

September 2012

I must be missing something. I've been thinking about this for a number of months, did some reading about it, tried to sort it out, and wanted to be supportive, but it just never came together.

Religious liberty. Not religious liberty in general, or theoretically, but the specific religious liberty that's caused all the commotion the past few months, the issue attached to the US Department of Health and Human Services (HHS) ruling that requires most health-care plans to cover contraception and sterilization procedures. The most critical questions arise when Catholic institutions like hospitals and universities are included. There are obviously many details and implications in this ruling, but I can't get past the big picture.

Is it really a violation of religious liberty when these Catholic institutions, which take millions of government, taxpayer dollars, refuse to follow government policies? Is the government denying these institutions their religious liberty by requiring them to treat all citizens, including their employees, equally? Or are these institutions denying their employees their civil rights?

There are centuries of law embedded in these questions, and I am certainly not qualified to dissect these issues and make profound pronouncements about what's right or wrong here.

But I am a practicing Catholic and I do have the right to question what our episcopal leadership is claiming. My questions remain, and my confusion is real.

Here are some reasons why I am confused:

- If religious institutions take no money from government sources, then these institutions can, in my mind, limit their benefits package for employees however they want when they employ members of their faith.

- If they do take money from the government, then they are required to follow the stipulations that accompany that money. The government must represent and respect the rights of all citizens and follow the rulings of our judicial system. If some of those rulings are considered unjust or immoral, appeals are available through our judicial system. Or pass a new law.

- This may come as a surprise to some people, but the United States is not, and never was, a Christian nation. The purpose, mission, and parameters of a country are contained in its constitution, and our constitution does not establish a Christian nation. In fact, the First Amendment distinctly and deliberately insists that "Congress shall make no law respecting an establishment of religion ..." My guess is that our founding fathers had had enough of European "Christendom," the marriage of church and state. They wanted nothing to do with it. Some Muslim nations are trying it again today with predictable negative results.

- In terms of contraceptive measures, there is no civil law against their use, and according to all polls, most people in the country use, have used, or will use some form of artificial contraceptive. The church can condemn that usage, exhort its members not to use them, even reject users as members, but they can't force or expect the government to enforce their beliefs. The government must follow the constitution and the laws of the land. If we don't like a law, then we can try to persuade people to change it. But we cannot expect the government *not* to apply the law or condemn them when they do enforce it.

- Specifically, the bishops have lost the battle against contraceptive use and abortion. They can continue appealing to individual consciences, but the government must follow the constitution and law of the land.

- So, here's one thing I don't get: how is it a violation of religious liberty when the government requires an institution that hires from the general population, serves the general public, and uses public funds to follow the laws of the country and apply benefits equally to all its employees?

That's part of my confusion about this issue. Then the bishops launched their "Fortnight for Freedom" campaign a few months ago. (By the way, when was the last time you used "fortnight" in a sentence? It's not your typical effective campaign language.) Not surprisingly, the campaign didn't accomplish much.

I admit that I didn't get involved with it. It's all too confusing. I am all for religious liberty and still applaud Vatican II's Declaration on Religious Freedom. But I just can't connect the dots from that document to this campaign.

Where have all the dots gone?

CHAPTER 49

Democracy

October 2012

Duck! Here comes another negative political ad! Tis the season for mudslinging, distorted truth, permissible slander, perception management, and sculptured sound bites. Isn't democracy fun?

If the attack ads are so effective, why don't we see more of them all year long? You know, the GEICO gecko karate-kicking the Progressive Insurance lady in the head, a Buick morphing into a transformer and smashing a Toyota, Miller Lite accusing Bud Lite that their secret ingredient is arsenic. More and more fun!

It's the price we pay for democracy. In politics, candidates raise millions of dollars, which they eagerly hand off to marketing firms so that the firms can create the message the politicians (and super-PACs) want. The firms then eagerly hand off the remaining funds to media outlets who always are the winners because they ultimately get most of the money, regardless of who wins the elections. Nice system, especially if you work as a media outlet.

In the midst of this delicious, democratic frivolity and waste stand a number of companies and institutions that function undemocratically. The military and the Catholic Church come to mind immediately. The military needs a strong hierarchical structure because their mission is to defend the country, a task that demands organization, chain of command, and disciplined participants.

But why does the Catholic Church need a military-style structure to accomplish its mission of being Christ in our world? Especially in a society so imbued with democracy that it even tolerates the excesses of a political season? Especially when Jesus vehemently condemned this kind of authoritarian system?

Jesus was certainly no politician, and He lived in a decidedly undemocratic society. So, can His teaching and His experience be transported into our messy democratic society?

I sure hope so. If not, the gospel is reduced to a guidebook for individuals on their personal spiritual journeys. Our faith in Jesus demands some focus on community, which includes our society and how we govern ourselves.

Can democratic principles coexist with the hierarchical structure of the Catholic Church? Not easily. But there are at least two helpful, democratic principles included in official church teaching: collegiality and subsidiarity.

Collegiality includes some aspects of shared decision making (Vatican II, Constitution on the Church, Chapter 3, Paragraph 22, etc.).

Subsidiarity teaches that a "community of a higher order should not interfere in the internal life of a community of a lower order ..." (Catechism of the Catholic Church, Paragraph 1883).

Admittedly, these teachings are surrounded, almost engulfed, by elaborate and repeated teachings about the primacy of the pope and the steadfast hierarchical structure of the church. But these official teachings on collegiality and subsidiarity do exist.

So, the main problem is not the teaching itself; the problem is choice. There is a choice on how these teachings will be implemented or ignored. Choice means it is a free will decision by church leaders, including the pope.

Here are two recent examples of how collegiality and subsidiarity are deliberately being ignored:

- Collegiality: the outright hijacking of the English translation of the Missal by Vaticanistas disavowed the English-speaking bishops of their right to make these decisions. On the other hand, these bishops did not insist strenuously enough on their rights.

- Subsidiarity: the Vatican process for the selection of bishops ignores and rejects any input from the clergy and people of the diocese in need of a bishop.

Without changing any of our official teaching, we could have a significantly different, current Catholic Church experience. By taking collegiality and subsidiarity seriously and creating ways to apply these principles wisely, we could have vibrant parish communities all over the world; dioceses that identify, nurture, and celebrate the varied gifts of all the people of God; national conferences that honestly deal with major issues; and a Vatican that inspires, leads, and orchestrates these gifts of the Spirit.

It could be a bottom-up, hierarchical church rather than a top-down church as it is now. With collegiality and subsidiarity as the guiding principles, we could turn everything around and still retain our current teaching.

But our church leaders choose to enforce the top-down approach. It is a choice, not a teaching. In response, Hans Kung is calling for a bottom-up revolution (http://ncronline.org/blogs/hans-kung-calls-open-church-revolt).

When that time comes, can attack ads be far behind? Any sympathetic marketing firms and super-PACs out there?

Francis Update: Francis certainly didn't read this chat, but he is acting like he did. More accurately, he and I must think somewhat alike in this area. In any case, he's doing what I called for here. In my mind, his initial efforts at collegiality and subsidiarity may wind up the most significant changes he will make. I hope so.

CHAPTER 50

Church and Politics

October 2013

I am clearly headed for uncharted waters. Many of my previous chats have centered on internal church issues, and I have avoided dipping into the treacherous pool of politics. But I can't avoid it any longer.

I check my emails every day, and, along with the funny ones, junk ones, motivational ones, and the personal ones, I get links to the latest news from the Vatican (usually what Francis did yesterday) followed by links to the government shutdown, debt ceiling, the Affordable Care Act, and who is calling whom what. You too?

These two streams—church stuff and politics—each have a vibrant life of their own. My question is: how do they intersect? Just to narrow it down, let's limit the question here to Catholics and politics.

Some say that faith belongs in the private, personal world while politics handles the social, public sphere. Believers who mingle in politics are misguided violators of the separation of church and state principle.

I disagree. Genuine faith is social by nature, demanding interaction with other people and society in general. Church and state must overlap. Our First Amendment is wise when it says that "Congress shall make no law respecting an establishment of religion ..." but that does not mean that religion is trapped in the prison of private faith.

So, back to the core question: how do Catholics and politics intersect?

There are genuine Catholics who are Republicans and genuine Catholics who are Democrats. There are, of course, wide variations within both groups in terms of how much their faith influences their politics. Navigating between church and politics, whether you're Democrat, Republican, Libertarian, or Independent, is tricky business.

Where to start? Well, I brought it up with our small faith group, and we had a ... lively discussion! Then I reread the *Church in the Modern World*, Vatican II's landmark teaching on the subject. I do not have simple answers to the complex issue of church and politics, but here are some current comments:

- The goal for both Republican Catholics and Democratic Catholics is to love their neighbors. They will differ on the means to express that love, but it must remain the goal. It is the clear and insistent command of the gospel that does not change when a person chooses politics as a profession.

  » Love means to think well of others, wish them the best, and to do what you can to help them.

  » Catholic voters must cast their vote for the candidate they believe will express this love the best.

  » Any other motive for running for office or voting diminishes the candidate or the voter, and the Catholic faith.

- Politicians who consciously attempt to benefit only one segment of the population violate their faith as well as their political duty.

- Catholic politicians of either party who campaign or legislate on just one issue minimize the gospel, betray their faith, and cheat their constituents.

- Politics is the art of the possible. Faith acknowledges dependence on a higher power. Together, they humbly get things done for the common good.

Am I aiming too high? Futile words flung on a slippery wall? Pie-in-the-sky religious mumble-jumble? Naïve wish list floating serenely above the hurricanes of today's politics?

In a political world of gerrymandered districts, in-your-face confrontations where compromise is a dirty word, multimillion-dollar, bought campaigns, candidates outextreming each other, is there any hope that any genuine faith can impact any politician with any real leverage?

In an era when politics is morphing into *The Jerry Springer Show*, is there room for a Catholic reading of the gospel? *The Church in the Modern World*? At a time when self-promoting pundits pound the airwaves with their profitable, endless, truth-defying tirades, is there a slim chance that ordinary citizens can discover policies that are consistent with the gospel? Is it doom and gloom? Do we have couch potato seats to the thundering end of a great political experiment?

Not yet. But the rescue is not in the hands of the politicians, Catholic or not. The hope is in the American people, in this case, American Catholics because the blame, ultimately, is on the American people.

How to fix it? First read and pray the gospel from a political perspective. Then disregard the sexist language (it was written in the midsixties after all) and read the still modern *Church in the Modern World*. You take it from there.

CHAPTER 51

Lunch

November 2012

Two friends, both active Catholics, meet at Applebee's for lunch. Vince and Paul have been friends since high school, having many common interests, mutual friends, and decades of shared experiences. They disagree in two major areas, religion and politics, so they don't talk about those topics very much since they value their friendship and enjoy lunch together about once a month.

After the hostess seats them in a booth, Vince says: "Well, I guess our votes cancelled each other out, but I'm glad it's over. All those negative ads just got me mad."

"On that, we agree," Paul replies with a smile and adds, "Many of the polls were flat-out wrong; it wasn't nearly as close as they predicted. Makes me wonder if they were rigged."

The waiter comes, introduces himself as Andy, hands them their menus, and asks for their drink orders. They both say tea.

Vince picks up the conversation: "I noticed that the bishops didn't do well either. Obama wins, and I think it is three states, including Maryland, that approved gay marriage. I never thought I would see the day."

Both men are quiet for a while as they realize they are now talking about the two topics they usually skirt. Simultaneously. While they study their menus, the friends struggle with how they can continue the conversation without damaging their relationship.

Paul, somewhat distractedly, admits: "I'm really not that surprised those states voted in favor of gay marriage. It's been headed that way for a number of years, and, eventually, with the younger generations, it will be pretty much accepted in most places."

Vince looks up from his menu and cautiously replies: "I hate to see that day. Our society is heading in the wrong moral direction to begin with, and gay marriage is a terrible step in that wrong direction."

The two friends notice that Andy has returned for their orders. Vince chooses the roast beef, bacon, and mushroom melt, and Paul decides on the three-cheese chicken penne.

Paul delicately goes back to the conversation. "I don't know, Vince. I never felt that strongly about gay marriage, but, frankly, I never thought about it too much at all. I always figured it was wrong, but over the last few years, I've been following it more closely and I am looking at it a little differently now."

"Wait a minute," responds Vince a little more agitated than he wants to be. "You're not in favor of gay marriage, are you? Church teaching has been and is very clear about this: marriage is for one man and one woman. Period. End of discussion. The bishops say that homosexuality is intrinsically disordered. You can't get around that."

After some uncomfortable silence and a few comments about sports, Andy brings their food. Paul decides to clarify his position a little. "I'm not sure the gay marriage thing is as black and white as you say. The core of marriage is about relationship, commitment, forgiveness, growth, respect, understanding, love. It is not primarily biological or, to be blunt, genital. And we don't have to worry about procreating; as a race, we've done that very well. So, I'm beginning to think that, if marriage is really about a unique relationship, it could also include two men or two women."

"But," Vince objects, "official gay marriages will ruin the sanctity of marriage."

Paul answers more quickly and more sarcastically than he wants: "More than half of heterosexual marriages end in divorce now. Straight couples have already ruined the sanctity of marriage. Living together without marriage is rampant. The impact of gay marriages is minor compared with the damage already done."

More silence. More sports. But Vince was not finished with the gay marriage topic. "I don't buy it, Paul. In my mind, gays will have to abstain from sexual activity and do the best they can. I can't imagine God seeing it any other way. I will try not to judge homosexuals, but I believe God will judge them negatively."

"That's okay, Vince. I'm not trying to convince you." And he added with a smile that only old friends recognize, "I know I can't do that anyway! I'm just telling you what I'm thinking these days."

By this time, Andy has cleared the table and brought their checks. The friends set the next date and place for lunch and leave. Vince is a few steps ahead of Paul, and as they are walking to the door, Andy stops Paul and says, his voice quivering, "I overheard part of your conversation. Thank you for defending me and my partner."

CHAPTER 52

Homosexuality

February 2011

Here's the church's teaching on homosexuality: "... basing itself on Sacred Scripture, which presents homosexual acts as acts of grave depravity, tradition has always declared that 'homosexual acts are intrinsically disordered.' They are contrary to the natural law. They close the sexual act to the gift of life. They do not proceed from a genuine affective and sexual complementarity. Under no circumstances can they be approved" (Catechism of the Catholic Church, Paragraph 2357).

Here is one of my twenty-seven questions: how do laypeople, especially laypeople who have friends or relatives who are gay or lesbian, deal with this teaching? How are they supposed to implement it?

A number of possibilities come to mind:

1. Enforce the teaching: with "respect, compassion, and sensitivity" (Catechism, Paragraph 2358), you could talk to your gay or lesbian relatives or friends, using the language of paragraph 2357 to make sure you get it right. But I have no suggestions on how you deliver that message with "respect, compassion and sensitivity." Sorry, you are on your own for that. By the way, if you choose this option, you might need to prepare yourself for the end of the relationship.

2. Hint at the teaching: don't be as direct as #1, but when you get the chance, make some general comment like "The Church teaches that homosexual acts are wrong" or "The Bible condemns homosexuality" or "It is God's will that we all be heterosexual" or "All gays must be celibate." Don't apply these statements directly to your loved ones, but make sure they hear you say it. Don't be too surprised, however, if you don't hear from your gay or lesbian friends or relatives for a long time.

3. Make distinctions: you may try to preserve your relationship with your loved one by making the classic distinction reflected in the adage: "God loves the sinner but hates the sin." But drawing that

line between sin and sinner is always tricky, and the premise of the adage is that they are sinners to begin with. You could also make the distinction between "objective sin" and "subjective sin"—homosexual acts are sinful in the abstract, as an intellectual moral reflection, but not necessarily a sin as applied to an individual person who may have a psychological condition that prevents him/her from recognizing the objectively sinful nature of the acts. Huh?

4. Ignore the teaching: when relating to your gay or lesbian friends or relatives, you can simply ignore the teaching, much like many people seem to ignore the teaching on birth control. But does that disregard leave a residue of resentment either toward the church teaching or toward your friends or relatives or both? If so, what do you do with your resentment?

5. Disagree with the teaching: you can directly contradict the teaching and tell your gay or lesbian friends or relatives that you disagree. You may go so far as to say that sexual acts between people who love each other of either sex are legitimate expressions of that love. You may even mention that sexual acts between consenting adults are not that important morally and that respect, caring, understanding, and forgiving are much more significant to love than sexual acts. You might suggest that God's command to the human race to "increase and multiply" has been fulfilled quite successfully. But if you do choose this option, with these kinds of opinions, you need to accept that you are not following the teachings of the church and you are in opposition to those tenets. Can you live with that "disloyalty" to the church and still remain with the church?

6. Educate yourself about this teaching: you can do some more research on homosexuality and church teaching. For example, what is the biblical teaching on homosexuality, according to current scripture scholarship? What is the role of conscience in relationship to church teaching? Is homosexuality an "abnormality" of human nature or a natural part of who we are as a race? How do pastors, preachers, and teachers address this issue? Anyway, these are some of the other twenty-six questions that paragraph 2357 of the catechism raises.

But right now, in this chat, I am simply asking: how is a layperson supposed to deal with friends and relatives who are gay or lesbian? Not as an academic moral discussion but as people relating to people? You might add: what would Jesus do? Pick an option.

CHAPTER 53
Sex Abuse and Catholic Culture

March 2010

Who's to blame and for what? The decades-long, sordid details of the priest sex abuse scandal and the extensive cover-up by church authorities continue to spread across the world, with no sign of ending. It is now Ireland, the Netherlands, and Germany, and even the pope is implicated. Who's next?

It is clear to me that pedophile priests and cover-up bishops do not operate in a vacuum. They are part of the Catholic culture, breathing in a set of values, presumptions, thought patterns, behaviors, expectations, and privileges that form that culture. Everyone everywhere absorbs multiple cultures—ethnic, religious, social, political, and economic communities that shape the way people think, feel, and act. The Catholic culture is one of these communities.

What elements in this Catholic culture contribute to the widespread existence of pedophile priests and cover-up bishops? I suggest four; you might add more.

1.   Church law is presumed to be superior to civil law. The mind-set is that the church has policies and procedures that implement the gospel. Love God, love your neighbor, follow canon law and the current catechism, and you don't need civil law, except to regulate traffic and manage other minor social interactions. When someone sins, the church will handle it internally—and better. The inevitable arrogance and protectionism in this mind-set rejects a primary role for the civil justice system to investigate and prosecute criminal behavior, like priest pedophiles. This thought pattern existed for centuries and still lingers even though civil authorities are now supposed to be more involved.

2.   Clerical power dominates. Sanctioned and sanctified by canon law, the priest, bishop, and pope have final authority and decision-making power in all situations. Parish trustees are supposed to oversee

financial matters, but they are appointed by the pastor. Pastoral councils are advisory only, and any decision they try to make can be vetoed by the pastor. Bishops and, of course, the pope have similar and expanded power. While many pastors are wise enough to seek the advice of laypeople, we all know that a new pastor can neutralize the pastoral council immediately. And there is no practical recourse. This system eliminates accountability and promotes a feeling of immunity for some personalities.

3.   Due process is not due. For most of my life, I worked in the church in various parish and diocesan positions, but for eleven years, I was an employee of American Airlines. The policy and procedures manual at AA was a full three-inch binder of small print. It covered almost every conceivable personnel and operational situation with clear, and just, directions. Similar manuals, if they existed, in the three dioceses I worked in are not even close to the thoroughness and fairness of the AA manual. The church preaches justice to employees and even promotes unions, but in practice, church employees work at the whim of the pastor or bishop. There is no due process. It's no wonder priest pedophiles and cover-up bishops felt immune from consequences.

4.   Forced celibacy. There is a debate about the relationship between celibacy and pedophilia. I do not believe that celibacy causes pedophilia. But celibacy is a requirement for priesthood, and for centuries, many priests professed celibacy in order to be ordained because there was no other practical way to be a minister. Today, lay ministry offers a career path in the church for married men who choose to work with and for the church without being a priest. But this wasn't a viable option until the late 1970s. My contention is that some priests who profess, but do not accept, celibacy have serious psychological conflicts regarding sexuality, some of which lead to a variety of deviant behaviors, including pedophilia. Or, in another scenario, the forced celibacy provides a convenient cover for a predator pedophile.

I do not minimize the blame earned by pedophile priests and cover-up bishops. But we must also transform those elements of Catholic culture that nurture these priests and bishops. Otherwise, we grow more pedophiles and more bishops who hide behind their miters.

CHAPTER 54

International Priests

April 2011

The numbers seem to be increasing each week. In our diocese, there were a few of them five years ago; now there must be close to twenty. From what I hear and read, a similar experience is happening in other parts of the country as well.

International priests are priests who come from Africa, India, the Philippines, Sri Lanka, Poland, etc., to minister in the United States for a period of years and who then are supposed to return to their home dioceses. They are needed, presumably, because the number of native priests in the United States is dwindling.

I really don't know any of these international priests personally, but what I hear is that they are generally pretty nice guys and they do the best they can in a foreign culture. My guess is that they are as varied as our own priests. The talk is that some of them have a difficult time dealing with assertive women and collegial decision making is not their long suit, but then again, we have our own chauvinistic, autocratic priests too.

There is one problem, however, that stands out. The language. Over and over again, I hear: "But I can't understand him when he preaches" or "I get maybe 50 percent of what he says." "He speaks English, but his accent is so strong that I don't know what he is saying."

Since communication is a vital part of the pastoral ministry, the language issue is critical. How do you preach a homily when the people can't understand what you are saying? It must be frustrating for them too. How would you like to prepare a homily week after week, knowing your audience can't figure out what you are saying?

Taking English speech lessons should be helpful, but it's not automatic. I tried a couple of languages (Spanish, German, French, etc.), but the main thing I learned is that I am not a linguist. Never could figure out how to think in another language and that includes twelve years of learning and taking classes in Latin. So I sympathize with the international priests and the complicated challenge of the spoken English language.

Why put a priest and the people in such a predictable and inevitably frustrating position? It is blatant disrespect for everyone. And that's not even counting Jesus. The bishops who do this must think that it is better to have a priest who can't communicate than it is to have no priest at all. Ah, there's the rub.

That kind of thinking puts the cart before the horse, the collar before the people, and an abstract theology of priesthood before the obvious needs of any liturgical function. A liturgy doomed to failed communication is a liturgy about to be abandoned. It's no wonder people leave the church in droves. The sterile implication is that it doesn't matter that the celebrant can't communicate with the community because he can validly consecrate. That belief is an insult to everyone involved, a complete disregard for the core purpose of liturgy, and a calloused, contemptuous disrespect for the Word of God proclaimed at every Eucharist.

There are a few options:

- Have someone else preach: a deacon, trained layperson, and/or respected member(s) of the community. Rotate the preaching.

- The international priest could type out the homily, make copies, and distribute them during the homily so the community could follow along.

- Play a recorded copy of a homily for the day.

- After the readings, give the people ten minutes to talk in small groups about how these readings apply to their lives.

- Hand out some written commentaries and homilies, and give people time to read them and reflect.

- And, of course, ordain women and married men, which will eliminate the need for international priests.

- Other ideas?

Any, or all, of these options is better than the current embarrassment. The liturgy is too important to allow known, assured communication failure to undermine the preaching of the Word. Even when the Mass was (and is) in Latin, the homilist spoke in the vernacular—without a troublesome accent.

It's time the people of God demand to be nourished during the liturgy of the Word. So, please, demand away!

CHAPTER 55

Komen

June 2010

My wife, Fran, is a breast cancer survivor. She still battles lymphedema (swelling of the arm and hand related to the removal of lymph nodes), and the chemo weakened her lungs so she needs medication for breathing. But after two and a half years, she is still cancer free and lives a full life. Thank God, and I mean that literally.

We are, predictably, strong supporters of the Susan G. Komen Foundation's campaign to raise awareness and funds for breast cancer research and services. The centerpiece of their excellent work is the annual Race for the Cure, which recently drew seventy-four thousand participants to downtown St. Louis for an enthusiastic rally, race, and fundraiser.

I also admire the Komen Foundation from another perspective. Since we have a foundation also (the Karla Smith Foundation—www.KarlaSmithFoundation.org), I often say that one of my goals for KSF is that we will do for mental illness what Komen does for breast cancer. An ambitious goal, I admit, but Komen has shown the way.

I could hardly believe it, then, when a friend told me that the Catholic Archdiocese of St. Louis issued a statement urging Catholics not to participate in any Komen activities, including the popular Race for the Cure. Who can be against a cure for breast cancer?

Well, I researched it online, and, sure enough, the statement is there, with a latest revision date of June 4, 2010. The archdiocese objects to Komen on three points: 1) Some Komen chapters have apparently funded some Planned Parenthood affiliates, although the archdiocese admits that Missouri is not included; 2) Komen does not believe that there is a proven link between abortion and breast cancer; 3) Komen does support embryonic stem cell research. That's why the archdiocese doesn't want us to support Komen.

Does this add up? Do these three reasons morally trump the immense good that Komen does not only for research but also for public education and emotional support for people with breast cancer and their families? I don't think so.

I consider the archdiocesan reasoning as "derivative morality." Similar to the financial derivatives, which are a major cause of our current economic recession, moral derivatives condemn an organization when there is some connection, however remote and regardless of other benefits and motivations, to abortion and embryonic stem cell research. This morality bundles the condemnation into one package and automatically attaches it to everything related to those two actions. No exceptions, no discussion, no lines drawn.

There is something wrong with that approach. It seems to me that the intensity of the opposition to abortion and embryonic stem cell research should lessen as the connection to that behavior weakens. As the degrees of separation increase, the moral responsibility decreases. In that context, the primary focus of the related organizations takes precedence over their reduced involvement with abortion and embryonic stem cell research. In other words, Komen's primary focus on breast cancer outweighs its secondary and more tenuous connection with the offending actions.

In our complex world, we need some common sense principle like the one I just outlined, or we end up condemning almost everyone and everything because we and our organizations are all so intimately connected. That kind of blanket condemnation sounds more like the Pharisees than Jesus.

There's also the issue of territorial morality. St. Louis condemned Komen, but many neighboring dioceses did not. So, is it a sin if you live in the St. Louis Archdiocese and not a sin if you live in a different diocese? Individual bishops, then, determine what is moral and not moral in their diocese. That, of course, is blatant nonsense.

What are Catholics to do in this kind of situation? What we always must do: rely on our individual conscience. We look to the church and other sources to inform our conscience, but we are responsible for our moral decisions. Statements like the one from the St. Louis Archdiocese regarding Komen muddies the moral water because it does not acknowledge the real complexities incorporated in many moral decisions.

As for Fran and me, we continue to race for the cure and hope we all cross the finish line soon.

Francis Update: It is now well over seven years since Fran had her surgery, chemo, and radiation, and she is still cancer free. We continue to thank Komen for their part in her ongoing recovery and for educating and reducing the stigma related to cancer. While Pope Francis has not entered into this specific debate, the Frances in our house and I persist in supporting Komen without a guilty conscience.

CHAPTER 56

Transition

May 2010

Things change. Times change. The world changes. We change. Change is permanent, a constant in life.

Periodically, it's helpful to look at some long-range changes in order to put the short-term changes in perspective. There is a context for everything. Over time, the context itself also changes.

During the last fifty years, one of these contextual transitions within the Catholic Church warrants a few brief comments. We've gone from a primary emphasis on the universal church to a focus on the local parish. It isn't that every Catholic everywhere has made this transition; in fact, many younger Catholics did not experience the starting point of this major shift, which may be why some of them are moving in the reverse direction. But in the United States and Europe, it's safe to say that, for the most part, the parish now replaces the church universal.

The parish has always been the practical center point for Catholics. But fifty years ago, parishes looked a lot alike. The personalities and talents of the pastors certainly made a difference, but each parish had a stamp of approval from Rome. They were cookie-cutter parishes. The same core theology dominated the pulpits. Parish activities mimicked each other to the point of competition: which parish had the best bingo, picnic, school, Marian devotions? There was no ritual diversity. Each pastor was a local pope, with unquestioned, supreme authority over everything and everyone. From fixing the toilet to the doctrine of the Trinity, he ruled. And he demanded loyalty not only to himself but to the pope, who represented the universal church. Even little kids in the pews knew the line of authority and got out of line at great peril.

No more. Today, most pastors barely mention the universal church or the pope. They deliberately ignore that part of Catholicism, probably out of embarrassment or downright disagreement. This "running from the pope" is more than outrage at the sex abuse / cover-up scandals; it is a deep-seated conviction that the whole structure is misaligned. They gladly focus their energy on the ministerial needs of their parishioners, who increasingly do not turn to Rome for guidance, inspiration, or relevancy.

This switch puts a lot of pressure on pastors. They are on their own, with little backup from the diocese or the universal church. People vote with their feet. When they like a pastor and his style and competence, they will remain and be grateful for his ministry. If they don't get what they feel they need, they will go to a different parish or non-Catholic Church or not attend anywhere.

We now have Catholic Congregationalists, remaining Catholic but choosing their congregation. They have no control over who their pastor is, but they do have control over which parish they will attend. With a discredited universal church and a remote or irrelevant diocesan church, the burden for Catholic teaching, ministry, and leadership falls on the pastor working with his parishioners. In some regards, the Catholic parish is looking more and more like a Protestant congregation.

This megatrend is not destruction; it is a cause for hope. The centuries-long stranglehold on parishes by the universal and diocesan church was doomed from the start. It was too big, too institutional, too reliant on doctrinal teaching, too impersonal to survive the constant, real spiritual and ministerial needs of individual people trying to find God, hope, and love in their daily lives. Force of power, authority, and fear held this form of universal dominance together for hundreds of years, but for many reasons, it is now dying quickly.

The local parish community remains the focal point of Catholic life. That's where the real action is because that's where the people are. That's where the comfort and the challenge of the gospel are real. That's where the search for God, faith, service, community, and hope begins and ends. With less emphasis and a smaller role for the universal and diocesan church, a creative parish is freer to respond to the real needs of Catholics. It is a change worth celebrating.

Francis Follow-Up: Once again, Pope Francis is creating a new kind of universal church, one that is more joyful, inviting, and compassionate. The title of his book, *The Joy of the Gospel*, highlights joy as a central attitude of a Christian. How pastors will tap into that universal church remains to be seen, but the pragmatic relationship between local parishes and the pope is now in transition. Will local parishes and pastors now feel more attached to the pope again? That remains to be seen.

CHAPTER 57

Suicide

January 2013

As a part of his regular routine, Fr. Ron Rolheiser, the noted author, columnist, and lecturer, writes an annual column on suicide. They are insightful, consoling, and helpful articles. He addresses this topic because he knows people who are grieving a suicide. I am one of those people, so I figure I should address it too.

In fact, today, Sunday, January 13, 2013, is the tenth anniversary of the suicide of our twenty-six-year-old daughter, Karla. Yesterday, I put the finishing touches on my next book, *The Unique Grief of Suicide: Questions and Hope*. So, I've been thinking a lot about Karla lately.

Ten years ago, our parish was magnificent in supporting us as we struggled with the shock and loss of our daughter. Our pastor, Fr. Bill Hitpas, led the way with his compassion, skill, and sensitive presence as well as a warm, inviting style of presiding at the funeral liturgy. The rest of the parish was also understanding and sympathetic and expressed these feelings openly and effectively. Since I worked for the diocese at the time, the bishop, Wilton Gregory, also attended and, both publically and privately, extended his empathy and support in human and consoling ways.

We watched the video of the wake service and funeral today and cried again as we relived the unfathomable sadness of those days. There was absolutely nothing but sincere compassion from our church community then, and it continues until this day. There never has been anything even close to a condemnation or negative insinuation about how she died. Everyone knows it was suicide and that she had bipolar disorder. But no one judged her or implied that she might not be in heaven. Jesus clearly was and is present to us through these loving people.

There was a time when the church and society in general automatically condemned suiciders and the family grieving the suicide. Fortunately, those days are mostly gone. But some remnants of that attitude still remain, and I am very sad to report that the condemnatory tone can be found in the wording of our Catholic Catechism's section on suicide (paragraphs 2280–2283). To its credit, it does say that "grave psychological disturbances ... can diminish the responsibility of the one committing suicide." And it also says that "we should not despair of the eternal salvation of persons who have taken their own lives."

As Karla's father, I find the whole section unenlightened, hardhearted, haphazard, and simply missing the point of suicide and suicide grief. It's not that it is totally "wrong"; it's just that it is totally "not right." I can support the teaching from one perspective and condemn it from another.

But it doesn't match the compassion of our parish, family, and friends. Wouldn't it be nice if the official teachings would reflect the unofficial experiences of people?

Suicide raises many questions, many of them unanswerable. The central question is: why? To us, there were options. To them, they saw no options. Their emotional pain overwhelmed their reason, and they could see no way to erase that pain other than erasing their life. Their "reality" at the time did not match reality. Their core intention was not to take their life but to relieve their suffering. They felt like they were alone, that they were a burden to others, and they acquired the ability to counteract their basic drive to preserve their life. When those factors all came together, their illness took their life.

But even after that rationale, the why question remains.

Faith communities should be good at unanswerable questions. We deal in mystery all the time. Maybe that's why our parish community responded so well spontaneously and instinctively. They felt the mystery and stood with us as the grief hunted and haunted our souls, determined to strangle our hope and shrink our spirits. When there is mystery, particularly tragic mystery, faith and community defend against that tragedy. At times, it is the only defense. A parish can be extremely valuable in terms of suicide and its precursor, mental illness, as I know and for which I am continually grateful.

Since Karla is on my mind, I close this chat with her "Gratitude Prayer," which she wrote as a second verse to the popular Serenity Prayer. I believe she is "back home."

Show me the trace of You in everyone I know.
Gently turn my gaze back home, toward simplicity, grace and gratitude.
Remind me that we are all imperfect, holy, and free.
Open me to know and embrace Your peace.

PART 5

Spiritual Tidbits

To be spiritual means to believe that there is more to life than what meets the eye. Catholic spirituality means to interpret personal and societal experiences in the light of a Catholic Christian view of God, the world, and ourselves. Anyway, that's my working definition of Catholic spirituality.

This part of the book breaks open that overall description of spirituality into some bite-sized morsels, beginning with lay spirituality and ending with a plea to find God in the gaps of life. Our spiritual journey is extremely personal, exceptionally delicate, and profoundly significant.

May these tidbits feed you along your way.

CHAPTER 58

Lay Spirituality

June 2009

Here's the problem: almost all the homilies we hear, almost all the spiritual books we read, and almost all the spiritual references we find flow from a spirituality that was originally intended for priests, monks, or nuns. I don't have anything against priests, monks, or nuns—most of them are fine people as far as I know. Some of them are even holy. But they are not laypeople. I know, I know—we're all human at some level or another. But we have to be stupid to think that the life of a celibate priest, monk, or nun isn't considerably different from a layperson's life, married or single.

The point is: the basic principles of all mainline spiritualities were intended originally for clerics. That includes Franciscan, Benedictine, Dominican, Ignatian (with some modifications—it became primarily clerical, if it didn't start that way), and Augustinian, to mention a few. The core principles of these spiritualities are exercises and ways of living designed for monasteries, convents, or religious orders. There are some efforts in recent decades to adapt these spiritualities to laypeople, but they remain essentially clerical.

Your local priests, monks, or nuns are probably very sincere about guiding you spiritually through homilies, teachings, conversations, and personal witness. But their personal spiritual basis and their training come from one of these clerically oriented spiritualities. Maybe that's one reason why so many Christians don't take the official spirituality and teaching seriously. It just doesn't fit their experience of life. So they conclude that their God is outside official religion, and they "leave."

Those of us who remain are faced with trying to translate clerical spirituality into lay spirituality. Tough job! Some laypeople end up feeling inferior because they can't live up to these spiritual exercises when the kids are crying, the car won't start, and the spousal relationship needs some mending. Getting away for a "retreat" looks real attractive, but in the end, the retreat approach reinforces the clerical spiritual style.

So what's a layperson to do? The reality is that family (and/or friends) and work are essential parts of the lay life. Don't listen to any spiritual teaching that doesn't include family and work as positive experiences. It is through family, through work, through the "world" (and not *away from* these experiences) that laypeople find their spiritual foundation. Either politely ignore or not so politely confront anyone who doesn't include family, work, and world as *positive* elements of spirituality. Flock to those preachers and teachers who do understand and express these realities of your life.

Don't expect the institutional church to reward you for growing spiritually or even to recognize the value of genuine lay spirituality. When was the last time a truly holy layperson was beatified, let alone canonized? Martyrdom might work but not daily holiness. Just remember that Jesus was a layman, not a cleric. He knows what we are talking about. Unfortunately and most often unintentionally, the attempt to clericalize laypeople will continue until laypeople say, "Stop it!" So, say it!

CHAPTER 59

Secular Versus Sacred?

September 2011

Some things are so ingrained that they never go away. We assume they are part of human nature or social nature or some nature. It's just the way we think, feel, and act. It's automatic: no reflection, no critique, and no question. It's a mind-set, set in concrete.

One example: secular versus sacred. There are secular places and times. Then there are sacred places and times. Some secular places are: wherever you work; all stores; the Super Bowl and all other sporting events; TV unless you watch "religious programming"; movies; probably your home; certainly your neighborhood, city, state, and nation … in other words, everything else except those places specifically designated as sacred. Secular time is all the time you aren't in a sacred place or praying privately.

Sacred places are: church buildings; shrines; retreat houses; that's about it. Some people try to make their own "sacred place," but that's a private deal, if they really pull it off. Sacred time is most of the time spent in these sacred places and whatever time spent in explicit prayer or spiritual reading.

Conclusion: there's a lot more secular stuff than there is sacred stuff. Bad news for God, right?

Not too fast, O ye of little faith! Here's the truth: the whole distinction between secular and sacred is fundamental nonsense. Do you think God makes this distinction? The Trinity had a meeting and decided that, since Western Civilization divided the world into secular and sacred, They would honor that division and withdraw Their presence from the designated secular areas. Believe it or not, that's the implication in trying to split the world into secular and sacred. It's our division, not God's.

God is everywhere. There is no secular place or time. There are only moments of intensity in our awareness of Godpresence and some "special presence" occasions on God's part (miracles, sacraments, graces, etc.). All time, all space, all places are essentially sacred because God inhabits everything all the time. The secular-versus-sacred thinking turns us into inadvertent but practical atheists most of our lives. Our loss!

There really isn't anyone convenient to blame for this artificial division between secular and sacred, unless we like bashing the Greek philosophers, Plato and Aristotle. That could be fun, but not very helpful. It makes more sense to "desecularize" our own little worlds.

God is with us at work, home, the ball game, movies, shopping, driving, standing on the corner waiting for a bus, eating oatmeal for breakfast, and watching the late news. Did I miss anything? You fill in the blanks.

Get rid of the secular-versus-sacred mind-set. Replace the division between sacred and secular with an awareness of "moments of intensity." All things and all times are sacred, some more than others, but there is nothing that is so far off the sacred scale that it warrants a "secular" label. Eliminate *secular* from your language and thinking. It's a *bad* word. And it's a lie.

CHAPTER 60

The Holy Land

I suspect that some of my friends are not going to like this. So, I hesitate to proceed. I like my friends and don't want to lose any of them. If you don't like this chat, just forget the chat, and let's stay friends. Okay?

Here's the question: what's so holy about the Holy Land? I know, of course, that it is the place where Jesus lived, died, and rose again. I know it is also a primary site for Judaism as well as a major Islamic center. I still ask, what is so holy about the Holy Land?

For the sake of full disclosure, I admit that I have never been to the Holy Land, and I don't plan to go. It would be educational to see the biblical sites, to get a feel for where Jesus lived, but frankly, there are at least ten other places I would rather see before I die.

Is it the danger that keeps me away? Not really, I've been to dangerous places before. No, it's not the danger. I just don't believe that the Holy Land is any holier than any other land. And it certainly isn't worth one Muslim, Jewish, or Christian life. We humans have a tendency to turn some spaces into monuments in order to visualize a belief or memorialize an event. We build shrines and statues, religious, political, athletic, social, to recall past achievements and honor our heroes. Fair enough.

The problem is Jesus. He talked about tearing down the temple, honoring the human person, disregarding presumed sacred places, and establishing the reign of God within and among us. Why would He so forcefully reject spatial memorials only to have His followers reestablish so-called "sacred spaces"? We have allowed our human tendency to negate Jesus's clear intention.

I repeat: the Holy Land is not holy and, by extension, no other land or building or site or place is holy either. That includes our church houses, worship spaces, prayer corners, private chapels, temples, mosques, or the tallest tree in the forest. Only people are holy. We need places to worship together, and some people need specific places to pray well. But the fact that we need these places does not make these places holy. And the fact that Jesus walked on specific roads in Galilee and taught in Jerusalem and died on Mt. Calvary does not make these locations holy either. Jesus insisted that holiness was personal and resided in the hearts and actions of people, not places.

The danger in naming places holy is that it diverts us from real opportunities to grow in holiness. The Good News is that the reign of God is within us, and goes where we go—not just to a designated "holy" place, but wherever we go. There is risk in thinking that we get holy by going to holy places. Ultimately, it is an attempt to control God, to put God into our "sacred spots," and then we don't have to deal with God in our hearts and actions, wherever we are.

As Fr. Richard Rohr suggests, Jesus made time holy, not space. Time is always right now, and God is always present in the right now. That's how and where we get holy—by connecting with the ever-present God. Regardless of space. There is no specific holy land because all land is holy.

CHAPTER 61

Conscience

June 2012

Follow your conscience. Good advice. Even the Catechism of the Catholic Church says "In all he says and does, man is obliged to follow faithfully what he knows to be just and right" (#1778). If you can get past the oppressive, sexist language (and I understand if you can't—I can barely read, let alone type, this deliberate, in-your-face, unnecessary, never-ending, female-bashing verbal assault), it says that all of us must follow what we know to be just and right.

For example, my informed conscience boisterously insists that I publically condemn this infuriating sexist language because I know this opposition is just and right.

When you read paragraphs 1776 through 1802 (just a few pages, actually) of the catechism, you will find a good summary of the church's teaching on conscience. It is pretty radical and worth reading. It also references the famous quote from Vatican II's *Pastoral Constitution on the Church in the Modern World*: "Conscience is man's most secret core, and his sanctuary. There he is alone with God whose voice echoes in his depths" (GS 16). (Again, apologies for the sexist language.)

Anyway, here's my question: what would the Vatican Church be like today if there was a primary emphasis on this teaching about conscience instead of the current preoccupation with antiabortion, antigay, and other sexually related issues?

My guess is that we would have a very different church experience. That switch in emphasis is possible because it is a choice. Everyone is a cafeteria Catholic because there are so many dimensions to Catholicism that no one can give equal attention to all of them. All Catholics, pope and Vaticanistas included, choose their priorities, what they consider to be the most important items among thousands of issues and beliefs that make up Catholicism.

It is destructively bizarre that a presumably celibate hierarchy chooses sex-related issues (contraception, abortion, and homosexuality) as the centerpiece of their public message. Stephen Colbert, on his *Colbert Report*, recently asked Sr. Simone Campbell, "What in the world does a nun know about sex?" She had a great response, but here is another good answer: "Probably a little more than a celibate hierarchy."

If the church focused on its teaching about conscience instead of sex, I believe we would have:

- more Catholics—As people are taught and encouraged to search and develop their conscience, they assume more personal responsibility for their faith journey. They also see the church as a community that helps them form that conscience and make those decisions, without judgment. Now, many of them perceive the church as an institution that tells them what to think, feel, and do and what is right and wrong. They are not welcome if they think, feel, or do what the institution tells them is wrong. So, many of them leave. With an emphasis on conscience, more of them would stay, and many more people in society would be attracted to Catholicism.

- a more pastoral hierarchy—The hierarchy would be more responsive to the personal, pastoral condition of the people of God. There would be less condemnation and more compassion. There would be a very different type of personality selected for bishop. Parish pastoral experience and success would be a primary asset, instead of the current liability, when choosing pastors to become bishops. This "tone" of leadership would change everything about the public perception of popes, bishops, and priests.

- more collegiality—With an emphasis on the primacy of conscience, there would be more inclusiveness because people would be more inclined to respect the conscience of other people and respect the differences that now divide them. There would be no need to resort to a contorted parody of "religious liberty" to deny legitimate health-care insurance coverage for employees of Catholic institutions.

- more ecumenical dialogue with other denominations, faiths, and the unchurched—When the teaching on conscience is center stage, there is more openness to other beliefs, more acceptance of different faith journeys, and less need to insist on personally held belief structures.

- What other consequences do you see? Add your own.

Please note: in this chat, I am not talking about changing any of our teachings about conscience, abortion, homosexuality, contraception, or sex in general. I am merely suggesting a change in emphasis, a restructuring of our priorities.

On the other hand, I am screeching loudly (hear it?) to annihilate the sexist language, once and for all, in all things Catholic. My conscience tells me so.

Francis Follow-Up: The change in emphasis that I called for in 2012 is now in motion with Francis leading the way. It will take more time for that change to impact the whole church and to be the hallmark of the Catholic message, but that change is happening. If we stay on this track, ten years from now, the experience of Catholicism will be considerably different from today.

CHAPTER 62

Feelings

July 2012

Chatting about the church is not my full-time job, even though my family and friends tell me I talk a lot about the church. My official full-time job is retirement, which I claim to have honestly earned.

My semiofficial work during retirement (which means working without pay) is with the Karla Smith Foundation, the organization Fran and I founded, along with our son, Kevin, after our daughter, Karla, Kevin's twin, died by suicide in 2003 following seven years of dealing with bipolar disorder. The mission of KSF is "to provide hope for a balanced life for the family and friends of anyone with a mental illness or who lost a loved one to suicide." It is rewarding work, which often feels like full-time, but who knows with the amorphous daily scheduling that accompanies retirement? If you are interested, check us out at www.KarlaSmithFoundation.org.

In any case, it is inevitable that some of the issues we deal with through KSF overflow into my church chatting. A case in point: feelings.

We encourage people in our support groups to name and claim their feelings, which is not as easy as it sounds. The idea is that if we can identify our emotions accurately and own them, then we have a better chance of coping successfully with our negative feelings and nourishing our positive emotions. It's a crucial process when dealing with the mental illness or suicide of a loved one. It is also a valuable process as we try to figure out our honest stance with the Catholic Church. We can analyze every aspect of faith and church life intellectually and not say anything about our feelings.

So, here are some feelings about the church that may or may not be yours. The purpose of this list is to provide some possible words to the emotions that some people seem to have about the church. What we do with these feelings is the next step. First, we must identify them as clearly as possible.

- Betrayed—This feeling emerges from the ashes of shattered expectations, in many cases stemming from a view of the Second

Vatican Council, which promised to provide pervasive collegiality, creative subsidiarity, hospitable dialogue with the modern world while maintaining basic biblical values, liturgy that is adaptable to various cultures and personalities, and a church easily perceived as a community more than an institution. The feeling of betrayal accompanies the stark reality that none of these expectations have been realized within the official, institutional church. But there are more sources for feeling betrayed: the sex abuse / cover-up scandal, personal affronts, irrelevancy, institutional arrogance, etc.

- Sad—Some of the basis for feeling betrayed may lead others to feel sad. There's less anger in sadness but more depression. As a result, the two different emotions of betrayal and sadness will likely lead to different sets of actions. But the anger fuels both.

- Embarrassed—The pride that was once a hallmark of Catholics is replaced by a humiliating gloom.

- Division—The comforting feeling of church as a community is severed from the heavy-handed authoritarianism of the church as institution. The resulting feeling is a deep-seated internal spiritual division. Some people formalize this emotion and leave the church community. Those who don't leave struggle with this discord.

There are also positive feelings to be identified and owned, some of which may be:

- Acceptance—This emotion coincides with belonging to a community. Being a part of a respected group of people creates a feeling of acceptance. Some people may also feel that they are accepted by God through this connection to community.

- Comfort—Some people feel comforted through their experience in the church. This feeling of comfort comes from many sources: Eucharist, community, shared beliefs, long-term friendships, religious structure, etc.

- Security—Some people feel more secure in their spiritual life by belonging to the Catholic Church. The belief system, the desired code of conduct, and the predictable rituals supply spiritual protection against the whims and impact of a nonspiritual society.

There are many more positive and negative emotions that accompany Catholics as we journey through life. Our challenge here is to identify those feelings as clearly as possible. Label them and own them. No one and nothing can make you feel anything. You own your feelings. Don't lay them on your parents, spouse, children, priests, bishops, popes, or Spiderman. We can argue intellectually about a zillion things, but each of us is accountable for how we feel.

Once you accurately know your feelings, then comes the fun part: what are you going to do with them?

CHAPTER 63

The Real World

February 2012

We are cruising the Caribbean so the ship docks most days at a tourist-prepared island. Nice. Warm. A chance to escape our real world and create a relaxing counterworld, which will eventually mesh with similar alter-worlds to form jumbled memories of times spent "away." Nice and warm indeed.

We cruise as often as our pocketbook and time allow. We like the carefree, entertain-me lifestyle, and the Caribbean is no stranger.

One vacation to these islands anchors all the rest, and my memories of that trip remain clear, persistent, and transforming. It was July 2002, and our then twenty-five-year-old twins, Kevin and Karla, joined us. That cruise was financed by a small inheritance I received from my mother, who died the previous November and who often accompanied us on our family vacations as the twins were growing up—a fitting way to remember and celebrate her life.

It was the last time we experienced the stable Karla. Shortly after that trip, her bipolar disorder drove her to mania, then psychosis, then her deepest depression. It ended, as some mental illnesses do, with her suicide on January 13, 2003.

We are aboard the same ship that we sailed in 2002, the *Explorer of the Seas*. The ship's configuration and some of the islands blend as then and now wrestle.

After time and much grief work, I have assimilated Karla's death into my ongoing life. This cruise reminder of her does not torture me; it brings her to memory, and I can spend time in that memory since I have little else to do. It is mostly a pleasant time; I am able to feel her presence as my living daughter and not get stuck anymore on how she died. Coming here helps me experience her this way better than back in my "real world," and I will take this level of awareness whenever and however I can get it!

There is a spiritual dimension to cruising. The sacraments of blue, horizon-framed seas, and deep, endless skies come alive, and the island cultures awaken innate impulses to unite diverse humans who also reflect God-in-us. Nature and humanity reveal the spark of divinity implanted by the Creator.

In this context, the harsh realities of the institutional church (my usual focus in these chats) shrink to extraneous foibles. When our spiritual core surfaces, when we touch our deepest wounds, strengths, and resurrections, priorities rearrange themselves, and we discover that the God of death and life looks lovingly on our clear-eyed souls.

The most tragic times are often the most fertile times. We proclaim a joyous resurrection, but, sadly, the doorway to that joy is usually pain. My joy will always be shaded by Karla's death, but it is a joy nonetheless. That joy seemed impossible in 2003, but it is now real.

I am convinced that my exposure to multiple versions of the death-resurrection of Jesus conditioned me to get through her death into my resurrected life. Thousands of Eucharists, countless verses of scripture, and repetitive core teachings of Jesus's life, death, and relife shaped me so that I could assimilate Karla's life and death. That's one of the main reasons I remain Catholic when the institutional church provides so many easy reasons to leave. Not even "they" can tear me away from these core spiritual realities that guide my troubled ship to safe harbors.

Theoretically, I don't need a cruise to awaken these central, basic faith convictions. My real world should contain easy enough access to these truths. But generally that world doesn't deliver as well as this counterworld.

On the other hand and more significantly, both worlds, the back home one and this away one, are real. One is not more real than the other. I experience both, and both shape me. In fact, this away vacation may be more "real" than the much longer one back home because this one delivers Karla and my accompanying spiritual impulses in a deeper, truer way than my time at home.

All experiences are real. Our challenge is to integrate all of them into one steady ocean of awareness. I may have to cruise again—soon.

CHAPTER 64

Threat to Faith?

March 2010

There was an AP story a few weeks ago with the headline: "Vatican to Bishops: Admit Blame." Caught my eye! The subheading was "Summit Held to Address Irish Sex Scandal." Now I am definitely reading the whole article.

The news article was very good, and the event it was based on also sounded like a positive step. The story described "an extraordinary Vatican summit with Pope Benedict XVI, which insisted that they (Irish bishops) must admit their own blame in cover-ups of generations of sex abuse of minors, or risk losing the faith of Ireland's Catholics."

I was happy to see this story; it provides some hope that some degree of integrity may emerge. There is, however, one side issue in this fine article that I want to note. Cardinal Tarcisio Bertone, Pope Benedict's secretary of state, is quoted as saying, "this crisis is like a most dangerous storm, that which touches the heart of believers, shaking their faith and threatening their ability to trust in God." Strong words and a fitting image.

My question is this: to what extent does the faith of the people depend on the behavior of the priests, bishops, or anyone else for that matter? The sex abuse scandals in Ireland, the United States, and throughout the world and the cover-up by bishops in Ireland and elsewhere are clearly despicable and worthy of condemnation. Any scandalous behavior by religious leaders in any religion deserves an appropriate, and just, response.

But does my faith depend on their behavior? No, it does not. And neither should yours, or anyone else's. If their behavior, or anyone else's behavior, threatens my "ability to trust in God," then my faith is ill-founded. I cannot give that much control over my faith to anyone else, including popes, bishops, pastors, my wife, friends, or the Buddhists who live in my neighborhood.

My faith is mine; I own it. I am responsible for it. It has been shaped and nurtured by many people: parents, family, friends, priests, bishops, popes, teachers, events, circumstances, etc. But ultimately it is mine—personal, unique, tied to my personality and life experiences, viewed through my eyes, filtered through my heart, expressed through my mind. It is shared with others, but it remains with me. No one else can live it or, in the final analysis, change it. I decide what my authentic faith is. No one else shakes my trust in God unless I allow it.

The experience of faith is complex, and it is dangerous to oversimplify. But somewhere in the core of faith is this insistence that my faith is mine. The unintended, but condescending, paternalism in Cardinal Bertone's comments echoes similar statements and unchallenged assumptions that resonate down the hallways of centuries. Simply put, it insists that the hierarchy must protect the rest of us from our own faith. Here's the way Cardinal Ratzinger (now Pope Benedict XVI) put it in a 1979 homily: "The Christian believer is a simple person: bishops should protect the faith of these little people against the power of intellectuals."

Simple, indeed! The little people! And keep those intellectuals away from us! I am the first to say, "Please don't hold me to everything I said in 1979." I have, fortunately, changed since then. But Cardinal Bertone's 2010 comments are the direct descendants of Pope Benedict's 1979 remarks, and it seems fair to conclude that the basic presumption remains: the hierarchy is responsible for my faith.

I will go to my grave protesting that assumption. But it is so prevalent that I only get riled up about it occasionally, and this article triggered my current reaction. I invite you to tune into this demeaning theme in the next few weeks in what you hear, what you read, and what you see. If you need practice in identifying this message, turn on EWTN where this hierarchy-dominated faith structure is a programming requirement.

My faith is mine, and your faith is yours. The "faith of our fathers" was theirs. Let's simply share all this faith together, and we don't need monitors!

CHAPTER 65

Sacrament Overkill?

January 2011

One of the reasons I remain Catholic is our belief about sacraments. Jesus demonstrated that God communicates with us through material, visible, tangible things and people. I believe the Catholic sacramental system is the best, though imperfect and not the only, way of expressing this God/Jesus presence.

But there can be too much of a good thing. It's not that we believe in seven sacraments and other denominations, in various ways, believe in one, two, or a few more sacraments. It's more like we believe in sacraments so much that sometimes it seems that we do nothing else.

Since we believe that the liturgy of the Eucharist is the source and summit of our worship, we celebrate a lot of Masses. I mean a whole lot of Masses, often and everywhere, for almost every occasion. In recent decades, some of us have used other forms of public prayer for a variety of reasons, but in general, we rely on the Mass as our overwhelmingly favored, ritual prayer.

Too much of a good thing? Yes.

I am not recommending that we abandon the weekend Mass schedule in favor of silent mediation at 8:00 a.m., hymns and homily at 9:30, and an adult religious education class at 11:00. I'm not as radical or congregational as that, although something like that sounds pretty good at times.

But there are consequences to our current reliance on the Eucharist. Here are four of them:

1. The heavy emphasis on the Eucharistic presence of God tends to minimize the presence of God in other areas. The implication is that we go to church, the sacred place, to find God and that other places and occasions for meeting God are ignored or, at least, third best. People who testify that they find God in nature, some events, and other people are correct. And it is entirely possible that these other encounters with God have a much greater impact on their spiritual

journey than multiple Masses. For the most part, Catholics are not expected to pursue these other avenues for spiritual growth. It's okay if they do it, but in many parishes, they are not urged to do so. Just go to Mass; that's the Catholic thing. The Protestants have adult Sunday school and multiple committees with the authority to implement multiple ministries. Catholics don't need all that adult activity because we have multiple Masses.

2. The pastor is required to provide Sunday liturgy but not required to do much else. Okay, funerals, weddings, and baptisms, too—all sacraments. After that, it really depends on the pastor, his theology, commitment, vision, interests, and skills. He can do as little or as much as he chooses. Parish life, ministries, lay involvement, style of parish all depend on the pastor. An active faith community can quickly dissolve into a lifeless gathering of unmotivated adherents because of a pastoral change. It can become a Mass-on-Sunday-only parish. More Masses and nothing else.

3. If you belong to a vibrant faith community, like I do, with lots of activity, a commitment to adult spirituality, pastoral and lay leadership, along with excellent liturgy, you know how good it can be. My question is: why isn't my parish the norm rather than the exception?

4. The Mass can be boring. The repetitious ritual, obscure scripture readings, uninspiring homilies, required prayers from centuries ago, intelligent adults with grade-school theology, and a disconnect with "real life" leads to fewer participants and minimally committed Catholics. It's no wonder preteens tune out, teenagers tweet (mentally if not actually), young adults think about work or football, adults worry about family issues or plan their week or the shopping list, and seniors concentrate on their health or the health of their friends. Not being engaged in the Sunday liturgy, even when people are present, seems to be the standard.

The only way I know to cure a bad case of "too much of a good thing" is to do other things more often. There's more to Catholicism than the Eucharist.

CHAPTER 66

More than a Translation Change

November 2011

Our pastor finally talked about the coming changes in the Mass. I hear that some parishes have been preparing for months, but he didn't even mention it until recently. When he preached about it, he downplayed it, saying the changes weren't all that much anyway, and we will get used to it pretty quickly. Don't let it interfere with our Eucharistic prayer life or your spiritual growth.

His frustration came out about halfway through the sermon: "What else can we do, anyway? Practically speaking, we have no choice." He did a good job explaining the Latin meaning of the changes in the wording. He then went back to his main theme of downplaying the impact of the changes and ended with a smiling reference that he will have to wear his reading glasses for a while until he becomes familiar with the new text.

If I were in his position, I probably would have done the same thing.

But there is more to it than just getting used to some new wording. It is a more literal, accurate translation of the Latin, but why is that important? If you haven't seen it already, here is a link to an excellent analysis of the new text by a young Latin scholar: http://ncronline.org/blogs/ncr-today/16-year-old-latin-whiz-finds-new-liturgy-language-lacking.

I wrote a chat about two years ago in which I claimed that we now know that God speaks Latin because we were being forced to use a stilted Latinized version of English in our worship. Those comments still remain: it is just silly to insist that Latin is a preferred language for prayer.

In any case, there is no doubt that this new, battered-up, Latinized translation will hinder my spiritual life and enthusiasm for the Eucharistic liturgy for a long time. I truly hope that most of you will be able to plough through this nonsense emotionally and spiritually, but I predict that it will dampen my Eucharistic fervor until we get our liturgy back.

Francis Follow-Up: For the most part, my 2011 prediction is still valid. This translation remains a thorn in my liturgical side. But I do attend regularly, even though "consubstantial," "chalice," "and with your spirit," etc., irritate me constantly. I keep telling myself that underneath all that baloney, there is solid spiritual meat. But that's the point ... I *keep* telling myself. I feel confident that if Francis were pope when this hijacked translation was taking place, an appeal to him would have stopped it, and we would now have a much better translation engineered by the English-speaking bishops and liturgists. How about an appeal now, after the fact? That would be better than the current missal we are forced to use.

CHAPTER 67

Beatification

May 2011

I believe Pope John Paul II is in heaven. I likewise believe that my parents, my brother, sister, and my daughter, Karla, who died by suicide due to her bipolar disorder, are also in heaven. They are all doing and being whatever people do and are in heaven—something nice, satisfying, and loving, however that is experienced in our next life. I believe lots of people are in heaven; I have a harder time thinking anyone is in hell, but that is another chat.

Being in heaven is not the same as being beatified or made a saint, declared a model of virtue and worthy of imitation. Here's my observation: this hurry-up march to sainthood for John Paul II seems desperate. I have visions of a secret Vatican sainthood-making agency meeting in a dark room with some deliberately anonymous cardinal giving the staff a pep talk: "We need John Paul II to be declared a saint ASAP. We will take care of the paperwork here. So, get out there and find those miracles—*now!*"

It all seems so contrary to standard operating procedures. Like many things in the Vatican, the mentality and the policy is to slow things down. Take your time; we have centuries. Let's look at all the angles and let history show us something we might be missing. I admit that I am often at odds with this ponderous, change-denying attitude. But when it comes to saint-making, I lean more to the slower approach. The early church rushed so many people with dubious credentials to sainthood, and even some who didn't exist (St. Christopher, for example), that we finally learned to slow things down and validate the qualifications of contenders. Makes sense to me.

Other commentators have extolled the public and private virtues and accomplishments of John Paul II. Still others have catalogued his shortcomings. That debate continues and indicates the wisdom of a more cautious stance toward canonization. My current issue with his beatification revolves around speed.

Why go so fast?

The stock answer is that his saintliness was obvious, his leadership outstanding, and the people are insisting. Over a million showed up for his beatification. All of these factors point to the need to speed up the process and declare him a saint immediately. The usual caution does not apply in this case. But the usual caution should apply. So, I ask: why doesn't it? Who benefits from a quick sainthood for John Paul II?

Among the greatest beneficiaries of a Saint John Paul II is the Vatican itself. Their recent boss gets the highest post-mortem honor possible. That accolade validates and strengthens the current regime headed by Benedict XVI, John Paul II's right-hand man, who continues the policies and priorities of his predecessor. In a political analogy, it's like a vice president succeeding a president, following the same agenda with the same staff and living in the shadow of the previous president. Praise for the departed president equals praise for the current president.

That "honor him, strengthen me" dynamic is clearly a dimension to this rush to sanctity. But there is more: sainthood is a stamp of approval on the style of church John Paul II championed and bullied into being. It's not just his unfortunate and inept stance toward the sex abuse scandal, his unwavering support of Maciel and the Legionaries of Christ, or his selection of loyalist bishops. It is also the authoritarian, Vatican-centered, intimidating style of governing that is solidified and validated by his canonization.

With Saint John Paul II, the coup d'état of Vatican II is complete. The people of God are the new diaspora. I'm not saying that John Paul II should not be declared a saint. He may very well have the qualities that warrant this honor and imitation. What I am saying is that we should slow down the process for quite some time, until the obvious benefit to the current Vatican regime is long gone. The proposed sanctity of John Paul II should stand on its own merits, untainted by the clear benefit his still powerful shadow bestows on his friends and coworkers.

So, at this point, please slam on the brakes!

Francis Follow-Up: Pope Francis, perhaps agreeing with most of what I said in this chat, had a creative response to the issue of John Paul II's canonization. He canonized John XXIII at the same time. Politically, Saint John XXIII neutralizes the impact of Saint John Paul II. Clever! But I know which pope saint I will follow. And Francis sounds, writes, and acts much more like St. John XXIII than Saint John Paul II.

CHAPTER 68

Workfaith

September 2010

Before our daughter, Karla, had bipolar disorder and before she died by suicide in 2003, I had a plan for the rest of my life. I intended to devote my spare time and my retirement to workfaith. Workfaith is the task of integrating work and faith. I even formed a 501(c)3, nonprofit organization called The Workfaith Institute, published a book titled *God on the Job* (Paulist Press, 1995), and wrote about a hundred columns on the topic for the *Eastern Oklahoma Catholic* (newspaper of the Diocese of Tulsa).

Then life, and death, changed my focus, and I now devote most of my time and energy to our foundation. The Workfaith Institute remains a drawer in my file cabinet.

But occasionally something reawakens the passion I had for workfaith. Recently, a conversation with a friend who talked about the difficulty he had trying to live the gospel at work sparked some of those memories.

The church has a long and proud history of teachings about the workplace. Encyclicals (*Rerum Novarum, Quadragesimo Anno*, etc.) and *The Church in the Modern World* (Vatican II) are just some of those teachings. For the most part, these documents deal with justice issues related to our social order and work life. They provide a marvelous, gospel-based vision of what should be and a courageous guide to changing what is.

But I believe that justice issues are only part of the workplace experience. My friend wasn't talking about justice; he was having trouble with some of the people at work and finding significance in what he was doing. These are spiritual questions. And my focus is the spirituality of work.

Church teaching on the spirituality of work is considerably less than the teachings on justice. On the other hand, Pope John Paul II's greatest accomplishment, in my mind, was his 1981 encyclical *On Human Work*. Ever hear of it? Probably not. It too outlines the rights of workers like previous documents, but part 5 introduces "Elements for a Spirituality of Work," which includes a section on "Work as a Sharing in the Work of the Creator." Now, that's what I'm talking about.

Scripture demands the priority and dignity of work. Both Genesis creation accounts have work as our first duty (Genesis 1:26: "Let us make man in our image, after our likeness. Let them have dominion over the fish ...") Having dominion is our work. (Genesis 2:15: "The Lord God then took the man and settled him in the garden of Eden, to cultivate and care for it.") To cultivate and care is the absolute priority and the fundamental purpose of humanity. It even precedes the directive to increase and multiply. We have intelligence and free will in order to have dominion (not domination) and to cultivate and care. An awesome task and opportunity!

When was the last time you heard or read anything along these lines? Probably a long time, if ever. We are not very good at helping people integrate their faith and their work. We address family issues (especially those that emanate from our bedrooms) and some social issues, but we don't hear much about our faith and how we deal with difficult people at work or how we handle a job that doesn't fit us.

A few years ago, I saw the program for the Los Angeles Religious Education Congress, a huge gathering of Catholics, with over two hundred workshops and presentations. Glancing through the program, I got curious and started searching for a title and description of some sessions on the workplace and faith. I found none, not one. And I was generous in my interpretation of workfaith.

If we work for pay for forty-five years (between age twenty and sixty-five), forty hours a week, we spend 93,600 hours on the job, more time than we spend with our spouse, certainly more than with our children, probably more than we sleep. And that doesn't even count the work we do at home that we don't get paid for.

With that much time and energy spent on work, don't you think we could hear more and read more about practical things that might help us join our faith with our work? Ask your preachers, teachers, theologians, and lay leaders to give more attention to what you appropriately do most of the time: work.

CHAPTER 69

People of Good Will

May 2013

Current translation: "… on earth peace to people of good will."

Previous translation: "… peace to His people on earth."

Latin translation: "… in terra pax hominibus bonae voluntatis."

I admit that the current translation is the better literal translation of the Latin.

I also contend that the previous translation of this one verse from the Gloria prayed at Mass is more faithful to the Christian God than the current translation forced on us in 2012. The obvious difference in the wording of this key, liturgical prayer is that the previous translation is more inclusive than our current version. It is one thing to pray for all people on earth. It is very different to pray only for people of good will.

It gets very confusing when we ask about these people of good will and contrast them with the presumed people of bad will. Who are these good will people? Are they people who think well of everyone else, especially you and me? How about people who think well of their own race but think badly of other races? What if you wish your family well, but, to be honest, you basically prefer that some bad things would happen to your neighbor across the street? If you're generally positive about most people but your ongoing conflict with your brother turns into animosity, are you still a person of good will?

You get the point: the line between people of good will and people of bad will is flexible and flimsy.

The problem, of course, is that Jesus wished well of everyone, regardless of good will, including those who killed Him. His harshest words were for the Pharisees, but even there, He left the door open for reconciliation. His whole life, death, and resurrection were about forgiveness and acceptance, good will not required. Not even His apostles had consistent good will.

The relationship between God and each of us is mysterious and unique. No doubt, our faith, attitude, and good will fold into that relationship. But to exclude people of bad will from our prayer implies that God has no relationship or love for them, which contradicts the God Jesus revealed. In other words, Jesus/God loves them, but we can't pray for them. Does that make sense?

Limiting our Gloria prayer to people of good will undermines the more basic message of Jesus as universal Savior. Praying only for people of good will erases the core challenge of "love your enemies" (Matthew 5:44), "turn the other cheek" (Luke 6:29), and "forgive us our sins as we forgive others" (Matthew 6:12). To eliminate this theme of forgiveness from our official prayer of praise puts us in the same category as thousands of other groups who create "insiders" and "outsiders," those people they favor and accept and those they shun and attack. I always figured Christianity was better than that.

This devastating distinction between good-will people and bad-will people is not good news, not the gospel. It's just another group of prejudiced people who discriminate against some other group. And since the people of bad will are so vague as to who they are, each of us can decide who our bad will opponents are, thereby destroying the cross and resurrection.

Wow! All of that in a few words of our solemn song of praise at Mass? Yep. That's what I hear, which is why, when I remember, I don't say them. I believe Jesus wouldn't either. I see Him interrupting the prayer and saying: "Wait a minute! Wait a minute! That's not what I meant."

We finally had it right when we prayed "peace to His people on earth," since His people are all people. The fourth-century Latin text is not the normative translation. It may come as a surprise to some Vaticanistas, but Latin is not God's preferred language. God speaks the language of the human heart, and any words in any language are mere sprinkles on the ocean of God's love.

The Gloria is a magnificent, beautiful prayer and a resounding song of praise, as multiple exquisite musical settings demonstrate. It's a downright shame they messed up one phrase so badly.

CHAPTER 70

The Year of the Priest

September 2011

I've been putting off this chat. I have some things to say, but they may sound contradictory; confusion is fine when we're chatting, but this is a topic that warrants some clear action.

Occasionally, I remember that it is the Year of the Priest. Usually, years of anything designated by the pope, Vatican, diocese, or parish mean nothing to me. I've seen so many theme years go by, from so many organizations that, like the chickenpox, I am immune. I haven't found a theme yet that matched my life, except the slogan of our family foundation: "Hope for a Balanced Life" (www.KarlaSmithFoundation.org).

Despite that immunity, the Year of the Priest gnaws at me once in a while. Some of my best friends are priests—literally. Since I was a priest (laicized many years ago, during the brief period when that reasonable option was rather easily available), I am still friends with many of the guys I grew up with in the seminary. Nice guys drawn to the priesthood by faith, social justice, and the dream of Christian community. A year, and more, for them is fitting, holy, and just.

But our current priesthood is another matter. What a mess. The selection, training, job description, expectations, theology, promotion path, and no-release policy are ineffective, destructive, and dangerous. It's no wonder there are fewer United States ordinations. The criteria today for acceptable candidates is so narrow that it's a miracle a few of the recently ordained actually have a personality and a faith that fits a servant, missionary priesthood. Unfortunately, these few will never become monsignors, let alone bishops, even if they want it.

Priesthood today is about loyalty to the institution and rigidity. My suspicion is that the Year of the Priest is about reinforcing that loyalty and rigidity and to entice as many priests and laity as possible to feel good about it. Even if the Vatican follows this year with the Year of the Laity (no chance), the hierarchical priority has been clearly reestablished.

Does anyone anywhere remember the "People of God," the title of the second chapter of the *Constitution on the Church* from Vatican II, the most authoritative teaching of the church in 150 years? If you do, please raise your hand and say, "Amen." (The title of the first chapter, by the way, is "The Mystery of the Church.")

In my naive youth, I thought it would take fifty years for the church-in-practice to catch up with the clear insights of Vatican II. In fact, it took fifty years for a handful of curial conservatives, augmented by the episcopal appointments of Pope John Paul II, to neutralize the inspired teachings of Vatican II.

Most of my priest friends try to ignore this demoralizing development. They focus on service to their parish community, not to the institutional church. But it is a delicate balance because they, too, represent the institution. Many young people have dreams of a future that never happens. But our youthful dreams were not fantasies; they were clearly described in the documents of Vatican II. The determined, diligent, and deliberate strategy of church leaders to destroy the practical implementation of Vatican II is now complete, with no chance of reversal for at least another fifty years and another John XXIII.

Too pessimistic? Yes, no, and maybe. Take your pick.

So, what do we do during the Year of the Priest? A few suggestions: take your favorite priest to lunch or dinner, or invite him to your home; host a birthday party for him; write him an appreciation letter—better than a card or email; if it applies, give him a round of golf or tickets to a big game; acknowledge his leadership in public, if it doesn't embarrass him; organize a parish celebration in his name; let him use your condo or timeshare for a week, if you have one; pray for him specifically and often.

Here's the hardest part: know your priest well enough to know he will truly value what you do for him. If you're not sure, just tell him you appreciate him and let it go at that. Some priests are genuinely humble enough to be more embarrassed by recognition than honored. Know your priest.

You don't need a Year of the Priest to do any of these things or whatever else you decide. But to offset the heavy-handed institutional, clerical, hierarchical tenor of the official year, this might be a good time to do the more personal and genuine recognition of the man you respect who is also a priest.

Francis Follow-Up: There never was a Year of the Laity. But Pope Francis has changed the model of the priesthood and reintroduced many of the qualities I respect in priesthood. I said it would take fifty years and another John XXIII to recapture the spirit of Vatican II. Pope Francis looks like that

Vatican II pope and the reform may be much less than fifty years. Remarkable. The Holy Spirit breathes again. In *The Joy of the Gospel*, Francis puts heavy emphasis on preaching, emphasizing the preacher's closeness to the people as essential to genuine preaching. See paragraphs 154–155 in particular, but that whole section from 135 to 159 sets the tone for what can reasonably be expected from our priests. It differs significantly from the themes of the Year of the Priest.

CHAPTER 71

Story Versus System

April 2014

In the beginning, we had a story. In time, we created a system. Now, Pope Francis is back to the story. End of chapter.

If I had the courage, I would end right there. It's not that I get paid by the word since I don't. It's just that I can't leave it alone with those few words. I don't know, but it feels like I'm going to gain weight or something if I don't say more. Maybe that's the difference between a poet and a prose guy like me.

Anyway, one way of describing the impact of Francis is to recall that Christianity began with the story of Jesus, His life, teachings, death, and resurrection. Early followers of Jesus retold the story in a number of ways, and the story attracted other followers. Simple. Attractive. Motivating. Inspiring.

Fast-forward a few centuries, after we've analyzed the story, codified the separate elements, interpreted its microscopic meanings, specified its implications, compared detailed theories, chose one interpretation over others, wrote libraries, argued incessantly, killed one another over differing opinions, organized and reorganized the material, established an authority structure to referee the process—after all that, we ended up with a complex system, including a creed, a code, and a ritual. Not as simple, attractive, motivating, and inspiring.

In other words, the original story got buried under the weight of that system. It's not that the story went away or that we forgot it. It was always there, but it was harder to find and respond to, since it was overwhelmed by the system. Some Protestant denominations substituted their system for the Catholic system and called it Reformation. In despair, other Christians supposedly rejected all systems and became fundamentalists.

It isn't that the truth became lies. It's just that sometimes too much truth becomes tedious. A lot of little truths tend to shrink the big truths down to the tiny truth size. That's what systems do to stories.

Francis, a product of the system, sees past the system and has recaptured the story. He relates to the Jesus of the story, and he retells the story in word and deed. That relationship shapes his relationships with people, the world, and all of creation. It is obvious and genuine. That is why he is exciting, attractive, and inspiring. He lives the story even as he dwells within the system.

The challenge is to reinvigorate the system with the story. Can Francis make that happen? Some possibilities are:

- One place where the system dominates the story is the annulment process and the overall stance toward divorced and remarried Catholics. The story says to accept people into the community completely, especially full participation in the Eucharist. The current system says to comply with our humiliating and punishing system and maybe we will grant you some concessions. Of course, there's a whole flawed theology that supports the system. But the story negates the theology and the supposed obstacles to full Communion. Will the Synod on the Family this fall reflect the story or reinforce the current system?

- Another arena of conflict between the story and the system is the lifestyle of the hierarchy. The system supports a lavish, entitled, favored, pampered, and privileged lifestyle for priests, bishops, and certainly cardinals and popes. Francis has clearly pulled their Persian rugs out from under them with his simple, humble, revolutionary lifestyle. Will the hierarchy follow Francis and his adherence to the story of Jesus or defend the style supported by the system? Will they do anything about it or ignore it and continue as is until a new pope— they hope—returns to the lifestyle they have become accustomed to?

- What will become of the renewed emphasis on the needs of the poor? Francis, following Jesus simply and directly, stands for the poor in his teaching and symbolic actions. The system has marginalized the poor. Will, for example, the decades-long persecution of liberation theologians be lifted? Will slogans like "the preferential option for the poor" become policy cornerstones rather than bumper stickers?

Francis has clearly aligned himself with the story. It takes time to remake a system, and it is still debatable whether he can impact the system enough to align it more clearly to the story. But I certainly hope he can.

Now, did I need all those words to say what I said in the first paragraph? Or am I a poet after all?

CHAPTER 72

Gaps

August 2011

You know, sometimes we try to fill in the gaps too quickly. Catholicism is a beautiful religion, with flaws of course, but the core of who we are, what we believe, our code of conduct, and how we worship are intricate, gorgeous, inspiring mosaics of our relationship with God, with each other, and with our world.

But there is a danger in having everything so "buttoned up." We have dogmas, doctrines, codes, policies, and procedures to cover almost every conceivable situation. If you run into any experience in life, whether you're young or old, remember what you have been taught or look up the dogma, doctrine, code, policy, or procedure, and there is your answer! It is a full-service answer system to everything we need. We may have difficulty applying the answers, but the proper response is right there, spelled out in the Catholic catechism.

Those of us who remember the Baltimore catechism know what I mean. Even though the fine city of Baltimore doesn't get the credit anymore, the basic theme of "here are the answers" remains. We even teach our kids these answers and expect them to know them at least for Confirmation.

Centuries of previous Catholics had all our experiences, discovered the correct responses to these experiences, and codified these answers for our benefit. Our role? Learn their answers, and apply them to our lives. Answers for our head before life experiences. Answers for everything. Answers for everyone. Answers. Answers. Answers.

Where is our mystery? Where is our spirituality? Where are our gaps?

Let's be basic. Is there a God? If so, what is God like? Quick now, what's the answer? God is almighty, transcendent, beyond us. God is also imminent, within us, among us. God is Father, Son, and Holy Ghost. Jesus is divine and human. Good answer. Next question?

The problem with this answer is that there is no personal, spiritual mystery. The gaps are ignored, unnamed, and underappreciated. File away your answers for future reference and try this: think about, pray, read, discuss, meditate on this one question, is there a God? For a year. Don't go too fast; don't go to your answer file. Wrestle with the question for one year.

Then, move to the next question: is God transcendent, beyond me? Take another year on this one; it is that big. The next year, deal with the immanence of God, God within you, me, and the world. You better take the next three years on Father, Son, and Holy Spirit. Follow that with the Jesus questions, which could easily be another five years.

Now you are ten years into your spiritual journey. That's about right. The next decade could focus on behavior: how do I live because of what I believe about God and Jesus? After that, it could be another three to five years to consider how you worship in response to what you believe and how you behave. Maybe at this point, you could go back to your answer file and see how your twenty-five years of considering this one question about the existence of God measures up to the answer in the catechism.

Too extreme, you say? Well, maybe. But you get the point: our answers come so quickly that we miss the mystery. We admit that there is a mystery, but we still miss the mystery. Genuine spirituality may reside in the gaps between the questions and the answers. Or, another way to put it, being aware of the gaps between what we experience and what we can describe is a good way to depict spirituality.

It isn't that the catechism answers are wrong, even though many of them are shaped and nuanced by one specific theology. Knowing answers isn't living faith, hope, or love. Never was; never will be. Dogmas, doctrines, codes, policies, and procedures are inevitable after two thousand years, but they don't touch the heart of the spiritual matter.

The gaps give us God.

Francis Follow-Up: *The Joy of the Gospel* demonstrates that Pope Francis clearly understands this approach to core mysteries of our search for God. Paragraphs 35 and 36 are just one place where he emphasizes the priority of the basic relationship with God and Jesus over "the disjointed transmission of a multitude of doctrines to be insistently imposed." He adds: "... all revealed truths derive from the same divine source and are to be believed with the same faith, yet some of them are more important for giving direct expression to the heart of the Gospel." Francis relates to the gaps because he relates well with ordinary people and knows our burdens and doubts. He offers us more than answers; he gives us hope, joy, and empathy.

PART 6

Holydays or Holidays?

All religions have some form of worship, the rituals they use to express their faith. It's one of the things they do when they gather as a community.

Catholic rituals, primarily the sacraments, have centuries of history imbedded in them. As a result, they are not only rituals; they are also ritualized, formatted in a standard flow of actions and words, many of which became solidified centuries ago.

Since they are rituals, they often touch basic human needs so, at one level, they remain relevant throughout the ages and in all cultures. But, on other levels, they do not speak modern, cultural languages and their symbols get lost in a swirl of contrasting images, today's latest fad, social clashes, instant wars, last hour's political crisis, and headline news.

This section takes a glimpse at the personal clash between the Catholic liturgical calendar and our twenty-first century society.

CHAPTER 73

Advent–ually

December 2013

I like the concept of Advent. Waiting, preparing, and longing are deeply ingrained in our human nature, and we draw on these basic emotions often: wedding preparations, births, graduations—even, on a lighter note, Super Bowls, Friday night, and our delightful uncle Harry's visit.

So the Advent waiting, preparing, and longing for Christmas fits right in with a crucial and ongoing experience in life.

The problem with Advent is that we know the ending. Most of the time when we prepare for something, we don't know what it will be like. With Advent, we know we will celebrate, once again, the birth of Jesus over two thousand years ago. We make a big deal out of God-becoming-man in Bethlehem, as we should, but the announcement of the birth of Jesus is not new. Most of us have believed it since we were children. Not being "new" takes the wind out of the waiting, preparing, and longing.

Besides, Santa Claus has stolen most of December.

The other theme that shows up in some of the Advent readings is anticipating the end times, when Jesus is to be glorified as the culmination of world history and Lord of everything. The early church was clearly motivated by this expectation, but as the centuries and millennia have rolled along, I can't get too excited about the possibility of the end times coming before the next calendar year.

The net impact of Advent, then, is undermined by too much history on one hand and too much future on the other hand. So what do we really do with Advent? How does our basic experience of waiting, preparing, and longing for God get activated each December?

My guess is that many of us basically ignore Advent. We prepare for Christmas, but we can do that without much reference to Advent. We go to Mass on the weekend, listen dutifully and sincerely to an advent homily, and sing "O Come, O Come, Emanuel," but after the recessional hymn, we are right back into the holiday planning. When all of the holiday stuff is done, we may get around to the Advent stuff—eventually. Christmas presents, cookies, cards, letters, parties, shopping: there's an urgency about all those things that must be done on a definite time line. Advent has no such urgency.

Does that scenario feel familiar? Do you figure Lent is a better time to be "spiritual" so you plan to get more serious about spiritual practices and devotions then? You don't really "blow off" Advent, but, well, you know, all the Christmas preparations simply take a lot of time and energy. The core themes of waiting, preparing, and longing get buried in more immediate, urgent stuff.

If you want to rescue Advent from Santa Claus, here are a few little suggestions:

- Set aside at least five minutes each day for prayer. If necessary, use one of the many Advent prayer resources or go online to: http://onlineministries.creighton.edu/CollaborativeMinistry/Advent/Daily-prayers.html for some helpful prayers.

- Follow the daily Mass readings. If you don't have a copy of the scripture readings or can't easily access them, use this website: http://www.usccb.org/bible/readings/120513.cfm. Read slowly, and allow your mind to follow any theme or idea that you may have. Close with a prayer of thanksgiving. Don't set a time frame. Just do it as long or as short as you wish.

- Personalize the waiting, preparing, and longing for God. Consciously want a closer relationship with God. The wanting can create the longing.

- Listen to sacred Christmas music periodically. Attend seasonal music concerts that include sacred music. Let the sounds seep into your soul.

- If you are brave enough and if family members are willing, occasionally talk about the spiritual side of Advent and Christmas without bashing Santa Claus or the secular holiday season.

- Make a conscious effort to think about Christ when you say, "Merry Christmas."

- Follow the leadership of Pope Francis and do something extra for the poor this Christmas.

If these techniques, or some others that you may create, don't work for you, don't feel guilty. It's okay. You are not a bad Christian, wayward Catholic, or second-class believer. One thing Christmas doesn't need is more guilt.

The Jesus I know doesn't need your attention and devotion. It's fine if your waiting, preparing, and longing are focused on the holiday of Christmas and not on Jesus Himself. Mary will feed Him and change His diaper. If you are too busy and your mind is elsewhere, He doesn't mind. After all, He too is human now. He knows how it is.

Just enjoy the holidays and try to get into the Lent thing when it comes around next year.

CHAPTER 74

Merry Santa

December 2009

You know, of course, that Santa Claus won. Each year, the gap widens, even though this year, because of the recession, the gap may not increase as much as in previous years. But it doesn't matter; Santa has already won.

The reason for the season is not Jesus; it is commerce, with Mr. Claus as CEO. In the early church, the Christians usurped a cultural holiday celebrating the winter solstice and converted it to the birthday of Jesus. Our society has now returned the favor. Jesus will never again be the center of December 25.

We could continue to be countercultural, insisting on the religious meaning of Christmas, gathering those once-a-year Catholics to our midnight (or is it 10:00 p.m.?) Masses. That's not a bad thing; it just doesn't do much. Besides, we all know that Jesus takes a backseat to family gatherings, green-and-red-wrapped presents, fine food, cheery music, decorated trees, and cutesy cards—all of which looks like a winter solstice holiday to me.

Here's the catch: we better not even try to change Christmas back to being Christ-centered. Think what that would do to our economy. Disaster magnified. For commerce to succeed, consumers must buy things. If we decommercialize Christmas, we deepen the recession, throw more people into the unemployment lines, swell the ranks of poverty, and rob little children of the excitement of Santa, ripping open presents, and learning all those wonderful, nonreligious holiday songs.

Not even Jesus wants all that—especially since December 25 wasn't His birthday to begin with. I doubt if He cares that much in any case. Who really wants another birthday party after 2016 years anyway? (Born in 7 BC, right?)

So, what do we do about Christmas? I have a twofold suggestion. First, we support and contribute to our cultural, commercial Christmas on December 25. The movement toward a "Holiday Season" capturing the holidays of other religions and cultures, then becomes a positive societal development that enhances the winter festivities and commerce. Let's not fight the commercialism of Christmas. Since it is now so central to the season, accept that reality, enjoy the winter holidays, and let's move on. Jesus won't mind, even though the folks who developed our liturgical calendar might.

By the way, the liturgical calendar was made for us; we were not made for the liturgical calendar. But that is another chat.

The second part of my suggestion regarding Christmas is this: we create a moveable feast called "Jesus Day" on which we celebrate the spiritual significance of God with us and within us. We do not focus on the birth of Jesus (let that remain with December 25). We commemorate our core belief that Jesus is divine and human and, for a brief time, lived among us. We celebrate Jesus Day on rotating Sundays probably in June, July, or August to keep it away from Easter. We do it on a Sunday when most people can participate. We promote it within Christian denominations, as a major feast day but not as a cultural holiday, since our culture is not Christian anyway. We could even have an Advent season preceding it. We move it to a different Sunday about every three years, so there is little chance of any momentum for commercializing it. We keep Walmart out of it.

That's the general idea. We could flesh out the details together.

In any case, to continue doing what we are currently doing is foolish. Let's remove the competition between Jesus and Santa by withdrawing from the race. We pushed Jesus into the race to begin with and said, "Now, run." That's not His style.

Santa is not a bad guy. He does good things, has a joyful personality, and bakes tasty fruitcakes. Santa and Jesus are buddies; they just do different things. There is no point in us setting up a false competition between them.

Merry Santa.

CHAPTER 75

Merry Christmas, Church

December 2010

Church Chat wishes you, the church, the people of God, a Merry Christmas and a Happy New Year. I've been talking about you and to you all year, but now, in the spirit of the Christmas season, I want to send you best wishes and many blessings during 2011.

Since the church is so big, I need to be a little more specific about who in the church gets what wish. A convenient way to break down these holiday greetings is to follow Avery Dulles's five models of the church: institution, community, sacrament, herald, and servant. May the Incarnate Word find a welcoming stable in each of you and all of you.

To the church as institution: I know you've been having a hard time lately with the sex abuse and cover-up scandal and being marginalized by society, criticized by many of your own members, and burdened with many of the traditions of the Middle Ages. My wish for you is that you individually and as a body of bishops can truly enjoy the powerful powerlessness of the infant God-Man, the happiness of humble service to the people with physical, social, spiritual, emotional, and intellectual needs, and the pleasure that accompanies honest leadership and inspiring vision. May your ranks grow with pastorally experienced, compassionate men. (I will wait till next Christmas for the women to join you.)

To the church as community: Since the experience of faith community varies so much from parish to parish, I wish you trusting relationships, mutual support, expressed love, shared hope, and relevant faith. Where rivalries divide, conflicts separate, beliefs splinter, and boredom deadens, I wish you passionate unity, reconciliation, and excitement in the gospel. In small faith-sharing groups and in large parishes, may you find spiritual nourishment in each other and in the bewildering yet comforting presence of the Spirit.

To the church as sacrament: Since a priest is central to most of our sacramental life, I wish a pleasant life for all of you who wear a Roman collar. While there is great diversity among you in terms of theology, interests, priorities, and gifts, I hope you can find peace in your ministry, relief in your personal relationships, and a bottle of whatever you like in your Christmas stocking. May all of us let go of some of our doubt that God does in fact relate to us through tangible things like bread, wine, water, and oil because that concrete, visible mode of presence is the heart of sacramentality.

To the church as herald: May any of you who speak out and speak up continue to find the courage to confront mediocrity, challenge hypocrisy, dare conformity, and insist on a better tomorrow. May those who proclaim and live the gospel keep on keeping on, unafraid. May those who evangelize and educate speak the truth clearly and testify to the compassionate God with passion and consistency. May we all kick it up a notch as we tell the world, our friends, family, coworkers, and neighbors that God is love and therefore, we are all little lovers.

To the church as servant: May our institutions of service, our hospitals, schools, social services, and charities, coupled with individual generosity and compassion, serve the poor and needy with dignity and intelligence. My Christmas wish is that the needs of the poor trump the needs of the rich and that each of us finds a niche where we reach out and help others by walking beside them with whatever support and resources we have. May we join hands with all people of good will in all countries and cultures to confront poverty, ignorance, disease, and tyranny.

Lots of wishes for just one Christmas. But then again, it is a big church. To make it more personal and manageable, pick one wish and make it your own. But here's the rub: Wishes are easy. Commit to a wish and you have hope. Add action to hope, and you have change, which becomes a truly Merry Christmas.

Francis Follow-Up: In his *Joy of the Gospel*, Francis exhorts all people to accept the message and joy of the resurrection and to share that joy with others. In terms of a Christmas wish, that acceptance is the heart of a Jesus encounter and becomes the greatest of all Christmas wishes.

CHAPTER 76

New Liturgy Christmas

December 2011

In the spirit of the new liturgy, I want to wish you a Merry Christmas. But to get it closer to Latin, the language we now know that God speaks, I have to translate my greetings into Latin and then transliterate the message back into English. Whew!

The problem is that my Latin is rusty and my translation skills are minimal, if not befuddled. For example, using my method, Merry Christmas comes out Merryisimus Christmicus. I'm not sure if that is the purest English of the Latin greeting, but I am trying to conform to the spirit of our linguistic, liturgical reform. After all, if God speaks Latin, we should do our best to speak it also. I figure getting close, counts.

What better way to wish you a Merry Christmas than with a hymn! And what better hymn than *Silent Night*? Of course, this carol written by Rev. Joseph Mohr in 1816 was originally in German. So, to get it in "most favored linguistic condition," I will have to turn the German into Latin and then into English. I will try. You can supply the melody, even though you may have to scrunch up some of the syllables to fit the tune. But it's worth it in order to have the words more closely match the divine tongue. Here goes:

> Silens nocturnal, sanctified nocturnal,
> Omni is paxified, omni is lucid
> Proximate virgin
> Maternal and kidiker.
> Sanctified babycus, so tendermus and mildiker,
> Somulate in celestial pax,
> Somulate in celestial pax.
>
> Silens nocturnal, sanctified nocturnal,
> Shepherds tremulate at the vista;
> Glories stream from celestial regions,

Celestial populations vocalize alleluia!
Christus liberator is generated
Christus liberator is generated.

Now, isn't that better? I know "consubstantial" fits in there somewhere, but I just can't quite get the translation right. Sorry.

Some of this may sound a little funny right now, but once we get used to it, it will be okay. And remember the payoff: when we pray Latinized English, we are praying in a language that God understands best. I know God has a well-deserved reputation for being a very good linguist but He/She/They think and talk among Him/Her/Themselves in Latin. It is clearly in our own best interest to follow their lead and do our best with the dead language also.

I am also struggling with another part of the reformed liturgical language. It's that simple greeting/prayer: "The Lord be with you." That part is straightforward enough: the celebrant prays that the Lord may be with us. Nice. Thanks. We do say it pretty often during one Mass (once again, the preferred term instead of Eucharist), so I wonder if the Lord sticks around for a while, gets bored, leaves, and needs to be resummoned. A little confusing but manageable. In any case, it is a welcomed prayer/greeting.

It is our response to this greeting that I have the most trouble with. My reflex response is still: "And also with you." If I have that laminated card in my hand, I usually say the Latinized and proper "And with your spirit," which nostalgically harkens back to my youth. But without the cheat sheet, I revert to "And also with you." Good thing that pew card is laminated. It's going to take some time.

Here's my main confusion: the celebrant addresses all of me when he says "you." But I respond to only part of him when I say "spirit." What happens to the other parts of him? Logic forces me to get picky here. Does his "spirit" include his intelligence, consciousness, awareness, emotional life, psyche, intuition, creativity, analytical processes, memory, and those mysterious things that psychics refer to? Or does "spirit" only mean that part of him that channels the God within him? I presume that "spirit" excludes his body, even though our common distinction between body and soul is Greek, not scriptural.

I like to know what I am praying for, so these questions are fair enough.

My Christmas wish for my celebrant (there's a lot less "we" and much more "I" in these reforms) is that the Lord may also be with all those parts of him that are not his "spirit." I don't get to say that in Mass anymore, so I bundle them all together in a Christmas wish.

Merryisimus Christmicus.

CHAPTER 77

Tis Not the Season

December 2012

Here we are right in the middle of the Christmas/New Year/Hanukah/ Kwanza/holiday/winter celebration season (that may or may not cover everyone). How's it going?

The Newtown, Connecticut, tragedy colors everything regardless of your religious affiliation or nonaffiliation. As a Catholic, I was proud of the local pastor who offered the compassion of Jesus, a consoling community, and a practical faith in the midst of the unthinkable.

Our pastor had a similar message and tried to connect the joy of Bethlehem and Advent with the reality of Newtown, and he did a good job—as good as might be expected. But on an emotional level, the sadness, deep frustration, anger, and speechless sorrow are winning out over the anticipated happiness, focused faith, and reinforced hope in the beauty of humanity made visible in the Baby Jesus. I doubt if we have enough time between now and December 25 to drown out the Newtown massacre with three verses of "Joy to the World."

My faith says that the birth of Jesus trumps all evil, including the killing of innocents (both children and adults) in Connecticut. But my mind and my heart need more time to catch up with my faith.

I can't add much to what you have already heard and read. I hope your pastor addressed this tragedy well. If not, tell him he negated his ministry and you will now go to a different parish where at least someone tried to deal with this horror sensibly and compassionately. Not mentioning it or saying something inappropriate is grounds for switching parishes immediately.

Some of us criticize the institutional church regularly. But the killing field in Sandy Hook Elementary School reveals the comforting presence of the local church where compassion, empathy, soothing ritual, and shared sorrow offer arms of support to devastated parents and stricken families.

Because of our family experience with Karla and our work with the Karla Smith Foundation, my reaction to events like Sandy Hook quickly goes to the mental health component. If you have not yet seen this article in the

Huffington Post describing an Adam Lanza-like situation, I encourage you to read it: http://www.huffingtonpost.com/2012/12/16/i-am-adam-lanzas-mother-mental-illness-conversation_n_2311009.html.

The continuing horror of mass killings screams for help and demands greater protection for future victims. Where is the societal Kevlar vest defending us from the attacks of untreated or poorly treated people with mental health problems? One part of that vest must be greater funding for research, more mental health professionals, enlightened family members, and a society comfortable with speaking about and coping with mental illness. Mental illness is manageable, but it takes all of us to manage it.

The evidence from Newtown is still being gathered, and there are thousands of experts analyzing each shred and thousands more media professionals reporting the story every day. Some conclusions will come later. I can't help but think that Adam Lanza was determined to kill himself and, in his twisted mind, wanted to take as many innocent people with him as possible, as innocent and as many as he could find. Sandy Hook then became his perfect target. He went there to die but not before he fulfilled his ghastly and tormented plan. I may be wrong, but this theory, at this time, is my best guess. I have to guess because, like millions of people, I keep asking "why?"

Ultimately, there may be no truly satisfying answer to "why." An unanswerable question. This is where and when a local faith community, in our case, a Catholic parish, can offer its most valuable resource. There, we should find a compassionate, comforting pastor leading a caring community of believers who surround victims and their families with the tangible insistence that God remains close, loving, understanding, and supportive. The church is not about providing answers as much as providing comfort and hope when there are no answers. If a parish can't do that, then what good is it? And that goes for all parishes, not just St. Rose of Lima in Newtown, Connecticut. Terrifying events like this affect all of us deeply, not just the immediate victims.

This year's Christmas season is shadowed by the cruel, cold cloud of the massacre in Connecticut. Jesus, too, was born into a deeply flawed world. Somewhere, somehow, there is a connection between His harsh world and our harsh world, and His peace and our peace. Sometimes those connections are hard to live. May you be so connected this season.

CHAPTER 78

A Christmas Wish

December 2013

This is a Christmas wish, not a New Year's resolution. A Christmas wish is a hope that something will happen that is consistent with a major theme of Christmas. A New Year's resolution is a goal I intend to complete. This is definitely a Christmas wish because there is nothing I can do about it.

My wish, hope, and prayer this Christmas is that some reasonable, doable form of accountability for bishops and pastors will emerge in the near future within the Catholic Church.

I know. I know. That's not a wish; that's a pipe dream, and the pipe is full of stuff that makes you fantasize about things like pink elephants, Rudolf with wings, and an enforceable conduct code for bishops and pastors.

On the other hand, there are some reasons to censure some bishops. Here are two recent examples:

Bishop William Morris was bishop of the Diocese of Toowoomba in Australia from 1992 to 2011 until Pope Benedict XVI forced him into early retirement because he called for a discussion about ordaining married men and women to the priesthood.

In October of 2013, Pope Francis suspended the German bishop of Limburg, Franz-Peter Tebartz-van Elst, popularly known as the Bishop of Bling, because of his lavish, forty-two-million-dollar renovation of his residence and office. Compare these two cases and you see the stark difference between Benedict and Francis—and how arbitrary the accountability nonsystem is now.

The main point here, however, is that any kind of clerical accountability is extremely rare. Ordination to the episcopacy comes with a gold-plated guarantee of immunity and carte-blanche permission to run your diocese however you wish, with extremely unique exceptions. To a lesser degree, pastors have a similar open-ended, do-or-don't-do-as-you-please, free-to-serve-or-not-serve-as-you-see-fit management style.

Fortunately, there are many bishops and priests who minister with selfless dedication, exceptional talent, genuine faith, and a practiced love.

Their ministry reflects the gospel and echoes the best impulses of the Catholic tradition. But even if they feel accountable to the gospel and to the people they serve, they may not be accountable to the institutional church.

Bishops, in particular, are free to exercise their ministry without a boss. I'm not saying they can spend ten months out of the year lounging on a beach on the island of St. Thomas drinking frothy concoctions with little umbrellas in them. They are expected to do churchy things within their diocese. But, frankly, I'm not sure what would happen if they didn't do them. Bishops are directly accountable only to the pope. That's how the theology works out practically. It continues the argument that Peter was the rock, the first among the apostles, and the pope is his successor as the bishops are the successors of the apostles.

Even if you support that whole line of reasoning, there is one enormous difference between Peter and the apostles and the pope and the bishops today. The ratio of Peter to the eleven apostles is 1 to 11. The ratio of the pope to current bishops is 1 to 5000+. In other words, the organizational flowchart for the Catholic Church shows over five thousand direct reports to the pope. That ratio guarantees no accountability. As a result, any bishop who wants to can maneuver the system however he wants.

Where are the checks and balances? An appeals system? Consequences? Nowhere. It is a fertile petri dish for rampant unaccountability, the *Ebola* of our hierarchical system.

I can hear the Holy Spirit now: "Listen, folks, I can and will cover for you occasionally but don't expect me to fill in for your stupidity. Put in place a sensible system of accountability, with appropriate consequences for those who can't or won't comply, and I will fix things when necessary. But for God's sake (and I mean that literally), your current status is all messed up. Straighten it out. That's why We gave you intelligence. 5000+ to 1, that's ridiculous! That's not even remotely what We meant about Peter as rock and leader of the other eleven."

See why I have my Christmas wish?

Pope Francis is obviously and quickly moving the church in the direction of collegiality and subsidiarity, two cornerstones of Vatican II. But without a system of enforceable, clerical accountability, the renewed church will be built on sand.

What do you think? A pipe full of fantasy? Or a Christmas wish worth wishing?

Francis Follow-Up: In March of 2014, Pope Francis accepted the resignation of Franz-Peter Tebartz-van Elst as bishop of Limberg, but I don't know to what extent the diocese must still pay the forty-two million dollars. While this action is encouraging in terms of episcopal accountability, there is obviously a long way to go on many fronts. In his reprimands of bishops regarding lavish lifestyles and in his unwavering insistence on humble, simple service, Francis appears to be heading in the direction of greater accountability. We can only hope that these initial movements in that direction pick up steam and ultimately affect the whole system. I didn't say that my Christmas wish has to be completed by next Christmas, but I would like to live long enough that it would be fulfilled by my last Christmas.

CHAPTER 79

Predictions

December 2010

Wishes are not predictions. In my last column, I sent Christmas wishes to the church. We are now in a New Year and a new decade, and it is time to make a few predictions.

This predicting thing is really dangerous. Who knows what will happen in 2011? And why even try? It gets even more hazardous if I become specific about these predictions. Regardless, I'm going to take a stab at it. I would try to get this chat published in the Catholic version of the *National Enquirer*, but I can't find a Catholic version. Maybe some right-wing, fundamentalist Catholic paper would be interested, but I seriously doubt it.

- Anyway, I will begin with a very safe prediction. There will be hundreds of millions of Catholics around the world who will find spiritual support, inspiration, faith, hope, and love within their Catholic communities. They will experience both comfort and challenge as they walk or run on their journey to God during the next twelve months.

- Here's another safe one: hundreds of millions of people, Catholic and non-Catholic, will be served by our hospitals, schools, charitable organizations, and individuals committed to supporting the poor, responding to basic needs, alleviating suffering in all its forms, and providing comfort to the sick, dying, and grieving.

- Here's where the predicting gets tougher: The pope will experience serious physical or mental illness during the year to the point where his illness will interfere with his pontificating. Unnamed cardinals will position themselves to be electable candidates to succeed Benedict XVI.

- The sex abuse /cover-up scandal will continue with more sex abuse revelations in various parts of the world and more evidence that the cover-up procedures were sanctioned, and perhaps initiated, by the Vatican. The sex abuse incidents will broaden to include more heterosexual abusive relationships. There will be more public awareness of the widespread disregard for celibacy among the clergy. On another level, the scandal will hit new heights in terms of the economic cost incurred through settlements and lawsuits.

- By the end of the year 2011, another spreading scandal will emerge: the financial mismanagement of many parish and diocesan funds. The inadequate accounting practices in many parishes and dioceses and the lack of effective diocesan oversight and auditing practices will gradually become public. "Where has all the money gone?" will get unconvincing answers. There will also be reports of dwindling contributions nationwide and in certain dioceses. While the poor economy will be blamed as the official reason for this decline, there will also be indications that parish, diocesan, and national mismanagement and financial naiveté, ineptitude, and downright embezzlement are also major contributing factors to this downturn.

- The trend toward declining parish attendance by Catholics in the United States will continue. There will be no major effort to discover why Catholics are dropping out (no exit interviews, for example) and barely any interest in the reality itself.

- The reaction to the liturgical changes toward the end of the year will meet with general outrage initially but will be grudgingly accepted as we move into 2012. The impact of these autocratic, top-down, ridiculous changes will not be recorded in the exit interviews that will not be conducted, as in the previous prediction.

- There will be more Latin Masses, a reduced role for lay ecclesial ministers, and fewer ministries as parishes and dioceses move toward a pre-Vatican II style of parish life.

- Vocations to priesthood and religious life will decline some more, and the average age of priests and religious will get still older.

- At least five bishops in the United States will publically break with the conservative majority and support optional celibacy for priests and the ordination of women.

- Add your own:

If these predictions come true, remember them a year from now. If they don't, forget this chat.

CHAPTER 80

Resolutions

December 2012

Christmas is for wishing wonderful things for others. New Year's is for resolving to change some things about ourselves. All things considered, I prefer the Christmas theme. Wishing others well and giving them gifts is much easier than losing weight, eating healthier, exercising more, or accepting my limitations.

But, undaunted, I will follow the lead of the little New Year's guy in the diapers and resolve away.

Okay, I will begin with my annual resolution to lose weight. Enough said.

Since 2012 is a special year (leap year, summer Olympics, and presidential election), I will also make some special resolutions regarding my spiritual life and religious practices. I figure it's about time.

Here are my 2012 resolutions, in no particular order, which will undoubtedly improve my spiritual life:

- I will stop reading and praying the Bible and reverently read and reflect on the Catholic Catechism from cover to cover, as long as it is an approved version. Think how much more spiritually enriched I will be at the end of the year.

- I will memorize that laminated pew card quickly so I can benefit from the new liturgical language for Mass and not fumble over the improved wording of our official prayer. The lyrical flow and spiritually enriching Latinized English will seep into my soul and inspire and elevate my whole being into layers and levels of enlightened mystical prayer I have never before experienced. Can't wait!

- I will watch EWTN every day and absorb their teaching so that I can become a more loyal lay Catholic who knows his place in the hierarchy and who thinks and behaves with sufficient docility to be a forceful and consistent proponent of whatever the Vatican says, thinks, suspects, or mildly insinuates. I will stop watching NBC, MSNBC, and Fox Sports Midwest since their programming is a deliberate effort to undermine the mission of EWTN. And even though FSM broadcasts St. Louis Cardinals (a hierarchical reference) baseball, the game itself dilutes my focus on the essentials of life that Mother Angelica and her friends articulate so clearly.

- I will read only the books that have an imprimatur by a reputable bishop publically endorsed by Mother Angelica. Therefore, I will have to finish the book I am currently reading (*That Used to Be Us* by Thomas Friedman and Michael Mandelbaum) before the New Year because it certainly does not meet the imprimatur criterion.

- I will find a parish that celebrates Eucharist, I mean, says Mass, in Latin as a standard Sunday event, regardless of the distance from my home and the wishes of my wife, and attend that Mass faithfully. Weekdays too, if it is in Latin.

- I will drop most of my friends (and relatives as much as possible) who sometimes criticize the church, and I will find new friends who are courageously loyal to the Vatican. Is the John Birch Society still around? Can anyone take me to a local Opus Dei chapter?

- I will make the Vatican website my new homepage and check the news and Congregational reports daily. I will only pray daily meditations that are recommended by this site.

- I will eat Domino's Pizza often because it was founded by Tom Monaghan, a loyal conservative Catholic.

- I will support my local bishop, even if he is narcissistic and incapable of normal human interactions, as long as he is obviously loyal to the Vatican.

- I will eliminate Vatican II from my vocabulary and burn all my books that reference that misguided, dangerous, and offensive council.

- I will go to Confession weekly to a certified Vatican-loyalist confessor from the parish who promotes Latin Mass on Sunday.

- I will evaluate my progress on these resolutions in June and add more or strengthen these if my confessor assigns them.

That's a start, but you get the idea. In order to swim in the current, hierarchical river, I need to go with the Vatican flow. After all, those old, presumably celibate men in the Vatican certainly know more about my spiritual life and needs than I do. I will do whatever it takes to follow their superior guidance. Thus, my 2012 resolutions.

Oh well, I probably won't lose weight either.

CHAPTER 81

Lent

March 2011

Lent. I always have mixed feelings about Lent and Easter. My left brain (or maybe it's my right brain) tells me that this whole liturgical season thing is so out of touch with my real life that it is all very superficial and irrelevant. And after all these years, Lent is unnecessarily repetitious. My right brain (or maybe it's my left brain) says, "Nonsense! You need this annual season to focus on the central fact of your life as it is reflected in the Lenten and Easter themes."

I sure hope I have a middle brain.

It's easy for me to discount Lent. I've had Lenten experiences in my life when I have lived great suffering: the suicide death of our daughter being the worst, but there are other painful events as well. I have also experienced great joy, hope, and resurrection. I believe in death and resurrection as a basic pattern of life and that Jesus led the way through suffering and death to life and joy. But my life experiences do not follow the liturgical calendar. Life happens when it happens, without consulting the church as to when it should happen. Easter joy didn't follow Lent the year Karla died. In fact, Easter in 2003 was a very difficult day.

Then there's the whole Lenten confusion thing. For example, the gospel for Ash Wednesday is all about praying, fasting, and giving alms in private. Don't let it show. Two minutes later, we receive ashes on our foreheads to let everyone know we are practicing Catholics who went to Mass today. Blatant contradiction. Oh, there's probably some way to rationalize it, some tricky paradox that includes both doing it in secret and doing it publically, but, come on, the gospel message and the ashes on the forehead are obvious opposites.

Here's another confusion: I grew up with the notion that Lent is a time of prayer, giving up things that you like, penitential, ascetical, sacrificial. That was okay and made sense. In more recent years, there is an emphasis on changing some things within me that need changing. And there are certainly plenty of those things. That's okay too. But now I'm hearing that Lent is a joyful season. That one, I don't get. Joyful asceticism? Maybe some people experience whatever that is, but I admit that it doesn't make much sense to me.

On the other hand, my split brain sees Lent as valuable and even necessary yearly. Regardless of whether my personal life is currently in a Lenten cycle, an Easter cycle, or an ordinary time cycle, it is helpful to take six weeks and reflect on how things are going with God and me right now. The Lenten themes force me below the surface and into the undercurrent where suffering transforms into new life, where deaths, and all things dying, flow not only into Jesus's resurrection but also into my continual rising. I can easily drift away from this basic reality and get caught up in less important matters, like conservative bishops and pastors undermining Vatican II, wondering what's in those tea bags at all those Tea Parties, speculating about what is really wrong with Charlie Sheen, and worrying about how the Cardinals are going to win the World Series without Adam Wainwright anchoring our pitching staff.

Lent raises the fundamental questions that the chatter in life can dismiss. Don't get me wrong, chatting is good—that's why I write *Church Chat*. But we also need to face the core issues. And Lent gives me that opportunity, and once a year is not too often.

So, I'm back to my original dilemma. Which side of my brain will win this year? Or will it be a middle-brain year? A little of both sides, maybe. I have tried that middle-of-the-road way a few times, but it is not very satisfying. I meditate for a while in the morning just to be able to tell myself (and sometimes, others) that I meditated in the morning. I doubt if that really works.

So, I think I am writing myself into a more genuine commitment to Lent this year. Thanks for helping. But, if you really do Lent this time, avoid the "joyful asceticism" approach. That just doesn't seem right to either side of my brain.

CHAPTER 82

Holy Week

April 2012

Not all Holy Weeks are created equal. In fact, some Holy Weeks aren't very holy at all, while others are inspiring and faith-molding. The rituals remain the same unless the new re-Latinated missal messes it up big-time. New, by the way, means reused medieval old, like a consignment store pair of 1970s pants that don't fit but you buy them anyway because they are a bargain.

In any case, try as they might, the church cannot destroy the basic message of the death and resurrection of Jesus. We can argue, protest, impugn motives, diagnose personalities, and rant and rave about how the rituals are conducted and who conducts them, but in the end, we must face our belief in the death and resurrection of the Lord. And that's where the rubber meets the road.

Here's the deal: we chat about important but not necessarily essential stuff. I do it all the time. I don't want to minimize the value of those chats; I believe this kind of casual, frank communication is important.

But we don't chat about the death and resurrection of Jesus. At least, I, and the groups I hang with, don't talk about this core belief most of us presumably share. To make matters worse, we are skeptical and suspicious about Christian fundamentalists and evangelicals who are more comfortable chatting about Jesus, His death, and His resurrection.

In our small faith group and our Sunday morning Dialogue with the Word gathering, we discuss our beliefs, but that is not really chatting. We listen to homilies about it, but when was the last time you spoke openly about the death and resurrection (D&R) of Jesus at home, work, on the phone, or informally with friends? Talking about priests, bishops, popes, the latest church-related sex scandal, Lenten fish fries, or women's ordination doesn't count. Do you chat about the D&R of Jesus? I don't.

Why not? His death and resurrection is the core of the matter. Maybe it is so core that we are afraid of it. Talking about it casually may trivialize it. Or maybe we don't chat about it because we're not sure we really believe it, and we don't want to reveal our insecurity about so central a question. Or perhaps we don't want to be labeled a fundamentalist. Or maybe we figure the D&R of Jesus is best left to the theologians and hierarchs who specialize in these kinds of things. Or perhaps we figure it is more beneficial to focus on virtues and techniques to becoming better, more loving people. The net result is that this central tenet of our faith gets little attention in our daily lives and more casual conversations.

Am I right, or is this just me? I have to be careful here. I don't want to homilize, not that I am opposed to homilies, either listening or giving, but not in this chat. Here, we chat. But that's just the point, isn't it? How do you chat about the D&R of Jesus?

Before we can talk about it naturally, comfortably, and without a genuflection in our voice, we have to check our level of belief. Do you really believe that Jesus rose from the dead? If no, that might be the basis of your reluctance to talk about it. If yes, it may be just a matter of practice.

So, practice. Say it out loud. Jesus rose from the dead. Say it over again, a little louder and more convincingly. Say it privately at first. Say it to a mirror with no one around. Say it out loud, in the bathroom at work when no one is there. Say it to yourself. Often. You don't have to tell anyone yet, just say it.

Once that is comfortable, then say it to someone else: family, friend. Go slowly. Say it until you are comfortable hearing yourself say it. Say it until your faith in it is reinforced. Repeat it. Listen for it in the prayers at Mass. While you say it, eventually think about it in greater depth. Think about it not so much as a proof of Jesus's divinity but as a process of redemption. It is the flow of life and death—and life again. It is the pattern of nature. It is the path through suffering and into a greater life.

Say it until you can chat about it with anyone and mean it. That is a truly Holy Week.

Francis Follow-Up: This chat is really the core of *The Joy of the Gospel*. Francis begins his exhortation with these words: "With a tenderness which never disappoints, but is always capable of restoring our joy, he (Christ) makes it possible for us to lift up our heads and to start anew. Let us not flee from the resurrection of Jesus, let us never give up, come what will. May nothing inspire us more than his life, which impels us onwards!" (paragraph 3).

CHAPTER 83

Holy Week Resolutions

March 2013

New Year's resolutions are a weight reduction scheme. Nutrisystem, Weight Watchers, Jenny Craig, and all those body-punishing exercise programs are all over it. In January and February, TV ads promoting weight loss and getting healthy are as frequent as political ads during a presidential election season. They all want to capitalize on our New Year's resolutions. It must work because we get the ads every year. Good. Our country, including me, needs to lose pounds and toughen up.

I have never heard of a similar Holy Week resolution. Generally, Holy Week signals the last stretch of any Lenten resolution we might have made. But Holy Week resolutions are like forever, or, you know, for as long as we can keep them, or at least until Easter Tuesday.

I admit that I might be wrong in this, but I suspect that we progressive Catholics have a harder time expressing our faith outwardly than do conservative Catholics. After all, the conservative Catholics have a huge advantage: they have all those delicious devotions to Jesus, Mary, Joseph, myriads of saints, near saints, and downright frauds (relics of the true cross?) to focus their outward expressions of faith. With clear-eyed, determined conviction, they pray, kneel, attend novenas, say rosaries, recite ancient prayers, talk openly about their devotions, go on pilgrimages, construct their own shrines, and hold prayer services. What did I miss?

And they participate in these devotions with fervor and quiet confidence. They also evangelize, inviting others to join them. I admire their expressions of faith, and I do not judge their sincerity or deny the impact or value of their devotional faith. God bless them. And I mean that literally.

But I do not share their devotional style. I did as a child and a young man but no longer. And I am not alone.

On the other hand, I have never adequately replaced this devotional Catholicism with an updated, theologically based, progressive set of religious practices that nourish my Vatican II view of God, church, the world, and myself. I have tried a variety of things over the decades, but nothing has really stuck with me like the devotions of the conservatives.

Here is an example. I am reluctant to share it because it is personal and, frankly, I am somewhat ashamed of it. But it illustrates my point about the need for a Holy Week resolution. For three or four years after retirement, I attended daily Mass at our parish once or twice a week. The daily Mass crowd numbers about thirty to forty wonderful, faith-filled people, and our pastor celebrates meaningful liturgies with excellent homilies. Attending is spiritually nourishing.

But when the Vaticanistas forcibly usurped our English liturgy and imposed the new, Latinized translation on us, I was (and still am, in many ways) very angry about what they did and how they did it. So, I stopped going to daily Mass. I showed them, right?

Now, of course, I ask myself if my protest is worth my loss of the daily Mass experience. And actually the broader, decades-long question is: how do I replace the fervor, conviction, and pragmatic spiritual nourishment I once received and conservative Catholics still receive from all those delicious devotions? As I said, I suspect that there are other practicing, kinda practicing, and nonpracticing Catholics who have a similar, struggling experience with how they express their faith, kinda faith, or nonpracticing faith. Surely, I am not alone in this? Tell me, please, that I am not alone.

Somewhere in this discussion and personal sharing, there is a place for a Holy Week resolution. I don't know what it is for you, and I have no suggestions. Our Holy Week liturgy and just the basic belief that there is resurrection in life and after life, that even death is not dead, that hope does, after all, exist provides fertile ground for your possible Holy Week resolution. It sure beats turning the calendar on January 1.

For me, I might try going back to daily Mass once in a while. Maybe.

PART 7

The Francis Factor and Other Signs of Hope

Hope did an about-face when Pope Francis stepped out on the papal balcony on March 13, 2013. His papacy breathes personal energy into hope, like blowing up a balloon that lost a lot of air. If hope is the conviction that the future will be better than today, Francis is boldly leading the Catholic Church into that future.

This section describes what hope looked like before Francis, during the selection process, and the surprise and delight that emerged in the first year of his papacy. The future, as always, is open-ended, but for millions of Catholics, and clearly for many non-Catholics as well, the forecast for tomorrow is mostly sunny with temperatures warming.

CHAPTER 84

Pope

February 2013

Do you need a pope to be Catholic? Not does the church need a pope but do *you* need a pope?

The question arises, of course, with the resignation of Pope Benedict XVI. I can't add much to the comments already made and the millions more that will be made in the next two months. But I haven't heard anyone ask the question about whether I, personally, need a pope to be Catholic. So here goes.

There is a brand of Catholicism that insists that the pope makes us Catholic. The pope, and the hierarchical structure that enthrones him, is the most distinctive and normative feature of Catholicism. Without him, according to this theology, we simply lose our Catholicity and become another Protestant denomination. Every dogma, doctrine, practice, and directive stems from this core conviction. Watch EWTN a little and you will see what I mean.

Not surprisingly, the current hierarchy follows this theology. They obviously have a lot to gain from this approach. This "Pope makes us Catholic" belief is all-pervasive. In this view, even our teaching on the Eucharist (real presence) is ultimately valid because it is ratified by the pope. This thinking controls a large segment of the church.

A recent example: did you see the HBO documentary on the sex abuse scandal, which focused on Father Murphy and the deaf children in Wisconsin? The title is *Mea Culpa, Mea Maxima Culpa*. Watch it. My point here: the secrecy demanded of everyone involved, including bishops, reflects this distorted view of the papacy. Breaking the secrecy leads to excommunication. The pope has this power because the papacy makes us Catholic.

It wasn't always this way. In the first three centuries of Christianity, there were multiple theologies, some of which contradicted each other. They were all considered Christian. The pope's influence was limited to Rome, perhaps Italy, while Christians in other countries lived out their beliefs as best they could during a time of persecution.

Even after the fourth century when councils and degrees formalized the Christian creed, papal power was minimized by the lack of instant communication and the inherent inability to enforce doctrine and practices throughout a far-flung region. Most Christians lived their faith without much notice of the pope.

Even today, most Catholics practice their faith and live their lives without significant reference to the pope. I'm not saying that the pope is irrelevant because his positions do affect us, e.g. mandatory celibacy for priesthood, ordination of women, collegiality, birth control, subsidiarity, etc. I am simply stating the obvious: there are many Catholics, like me, who disagree on these and other issues and remain Catholic.

It is my church too.

Many faith-filled people have already left the church for many reasons. Some, I presume, have left because of a pope in particular or the office of the papacy in general. I choose to stay because it is my church too.

So, how does the papacy fit into your expression of Catholicity? Do you accept the office of the papacy but dislike the leadership of recent popes? Or do you really believe in a more democratic structure but remain Catholic because you like other features of Catholicism? On a practical, personal level, does it make any difference?

Fr. Richard McBrien, in his outstanding book *Catholicism* (use it as your primary reference book) maintains that there are three principles that, taken together, make Catholicism distinctive: sacramentality, mediation, and communion. Sacramentality means that God is present and operative in and through the visible, tangible, finite realities of life. Mediation means that God uses signs and instruments to communicate with us through grace. Communion means that our way to God and God's way to us is mediated through community.

His helpful example: the flags of some other countries have red, white, and blue, and some even have stars in their basic design, but the flag of the United States is the only one that is configured in its distinctive way. So too with Catholicism: it is the only Christian church that is configured the way it is with sacramentality, mediation, and communion.

We are also distinctive because of our hierarchical structure centered on the pope. But frankly I get more practical meaning and Catholic spiritual nourishment from sacramentality, mediation, and communion than I do from the papacy, regardless of who the current pope is.

I plan to follow the resignation and selection of our new pope with interest and concern, and I fervently hope for a renewal of Vatican II. But whoever is pope, he will not determine my Catholicity. After all, it is my church too.

Francis Follow-Up: The selection of Francis was not a practical possibility in my mind when I wrote this chat. Francis makes the papacy decidedly more palpable, but my core question remains: Do you need a pope to be Catholic?

CHAPTER 85

Selection of a Pope

March 2013

As I write this, it is three days before the conclave begins, and, in a week, we will likely have a new pope. What a contrast with the multiyear presidential election process in the United States. These cardinal-electors don't know each other well enough to know who is who or how to spell their names, let alone how to pronounce them. But they will select a pope. Wow!

They are having preconclave meetings to "get to know one another and discuss issues." Are they speaking in Latin? Good luck with that. It is the first time all 115 electors are in the same room together, and they are not all proficient in Latin. The Holy Spirit must work overtime to overcome all of those realities. Maybe the Spirit likes red and shows up with greater intensity when all that red is concentrated in the Sistine Chapel. What we do know is that the Spirit in the people of God is locked out of Michelangelo's museum.

Enough sarcasm! Here's my question: what would you do if you were elected pope?

I know, I know. That's impossible. So, why even ask it? My answer: why not ask it? If you were elected pope (women included this time) in this very real, current-day Vatican Catholic Church, what would you do?

Here's what I would do in my first year as pope:

1. I would move the church into greater collegiality and subsidiarity, two major themes of Vatican II. I would mandate that each diocese would have representative diocesan pastoral councils with membership selected by parishes or regions. These councils would have primary consultative powers in the diocese, superseding curia groups and priest councils, though some pastors would also be elected to the pastoral council. I would maintain the hierarchy but with similar representative councils at every level, including regional, national, and Vatican levels. As pope, I would preside over an international

council of clergy, religious, and laity who would advise me on issues that affect the whole church. Other issues would be determined at lower hierarchical levels. Curia members would not be part of this council; their role would be to implement the decisions I make after consultation with the council. I would be inclined to decide with the majority opinion of the council members.

2. Simultaneously, within the first year, I would initiate widespread discussion and seek opinions on many topics. Optional celibacy, ordination of women, and birth control would be some of the initial issues. Using the structure in #1, I would survey the opinions of the people. I would also commission qualified theologians and scripture scholars of all opinions to recommend positions on these topics.

3. I would immediately create a communications department at all levels whose mission would be to report on and present a theological basis for all of the actions of items 1 and 2. Transparency would be their goal and evangelization would be the outcome.

That agenda should keep me busy. And, I maintain, all of that is possible even within our current theological and scriptural framework. The Vatican Catholic Church could look like that and still remain the Vatican Catholic Church. There are no dogmatic teachings that prevent it. In fact, I submit that the church in the first three centuries functioned more like what I described than what we have experienced in the last three centuries.

If I were elected pope next week, I would not call for a third Vatican Council. That would be a male, clergy council and would likely harden both the male part and the clergy part, given the profile of the bishops created in the past forty years.

Will these 115 strangers who are cardinals elect someone who will even get close to what I said I would do? Not a chance. Do I hope that the Holy Spirit does in fact like the cardinal shade of red so much that he or she does show up and move them in the direction I described? There is no realistic hope of that either.

I do believe that, in time, our current hierarchical structure will fail and fall. It may be gradual, but most likely, it will be dramatic. The medieval, secret, clergy-dominated trappings will peel away and give rise to a new form of the church.

That transformation will happen—probably not in my lifetime, but it is coming. I want to be on record now as someone who supports the coming transformation, but I doubt that our next pope will lead us toward that conversion.

The church will remain because Jesus will remain. But the days are numbered for this form of the church, and those days will still be numbered after we have a new pope. I just hope that the number is a little smaller.

Francis Follow-Up: Wow, was I wrong when I wrote this in March 2013. Pope Francis obviously exceeded my pessimistic projections. In fact, he is doing the things I said I would do if I were elected pope, only he is doing them much better than I could even imagine. Along with his public actions, here is one quote from *The Joy of the Gospel* regarding subsidiarity that sounds refreshing: "It is not advisable for the Pope to take the place of local Bishops in the discernment of every issue which arises in their territory. In this sense, I am conscious of the need to promote a sound 'decentralization'" (16).

CHAPTER 86

Trickledown Papacy

April 2013

It's been about a month since Francis was elected bishop of Rome, his preferred title as I understand it. That is not enough time to see what kind of pope he will be; he, and we, need some years to get a genuine sense of how he will lead the church. And he needs to live long enough. It is the right amount of time, however, for a first impression. And he has made an impression.

Many people have already noted his refreshing style: simplicity, apparently authentic humility, extraordinary service to the poor, liturgical flexibility, an international advisory council rather than a curia committee, and a glimpse at a papacy that has different priorities than what we've seen for many decades. We'll see. We'll see.

There are a few things that I have noticed among my friends and in the articles I have read about the impact of Francis on us common folk. There is a renewed vitality, a hopeful interest, an instantaneous expectation that we may have a different experience of church in our future. There is simultaneous relief from the heavy-handed authoritarianism, doctrine-focused leadership of the past forty years.

Whether this relief is justified remains to be seen, but this is the first time in decades I sensed the possibility of real change. Francis's initial impact seems to have accomplished something that our two previous popes were never able to generate: a new kind of hope. John Paul II created a following and some fervor, but it was always couched in his staunch and very personal stance against Communism. Benedict XVI produced a collective yawn.

And each of these popes created a trickledown effect on the church. Their priorities became church priorities. Millions of imitators, clergy and lay, mimicked the popes' interests. Some of them strove to align themselves with the prevailing trend and to curry favor with the pope and his most loyal cardinals, bishops, priests, and laity. Pleasing and obeying not only the pope but his legion of sycophants became the standard for these Catholic insiders.

Popes are able to generate this lockstep reaction because the current church is so hierarchical, structured, and dominated from the top that the whole cumbersome system can rather easily follow the leader. Like a medieval king. Or China. Or North Korea. Things trickle down because there are clear channels for trickling. For example, Latin masses were resurrected because the pope encouraged them.

By contrast, I do not believe in trickledown economics because economic societies are too complex for the trickle to get anywhere. It gets siphoned off to people at the top before it can trickle to people at the bottom. But church structure is so tight, with enough cardinals, bishops, and priests to implement the preferences of the guy at the top, that it can produce imitative effects throughout the system.

If Francis's style prevails, it will be fascinating to see if and how his preferences travel through the structure. Will there be less ermine, fewer Cappa Magnas, more modest clerical housing, more personal service to the poor, greater demonstrated humility among the follow-the-leader cardinals, bishops, priests, and laity? (The nuns, by the way, are already there.) My guess is that many of those guys (and they are guys) are struggling with this issue right now. How do they please their new boss and keep their current lifestyle?

For me, at this early stage, the most exciting possibility surrounding Francis is a deemphasis on the dominating, overpowering focus on doctrine. What we believe is not as important as what we do. I suspect that Francis believes that principle too. If he does and follows through with policies and actions that reflect that emphasis, we are headed for a church that embraces the vision and teachings of Vatican II. Doctrine is important but not nearly as important as service to others, creation of a faith community, and outreach to the modern world.

For many years, I felt like I was blowin' in the wind (thank you, Bob Dylan) about church priorities. I'm not naive enough to think that one month of Francis will reverse the wind or make a substantial difference in the long run. But I do think the wind has died down noticeably.

Francis Follow-Up: After more than a year of the Francis papacy, the early optimism I expressed in this chat has grown and each day seems to solidify and verify a changing Catholic Church. It obviously will take a lot longer, but it is comforting to know that the path we are on is leading back to Vatican II and forward to a reformed church. In terms of the deemphasis on doctrine, here is one relevant quote from *The Joy of the Gospel*: "The second Vatican Council explained, 'in Catholic doctrine there exists an order or a hierarchy of truths, since they vary in their relation to the foundation of the Christian faith.' This holds true as much for the dogmas of faith as for the whole corpus of the Church's teaching, including her moral teaching" (36).

CHAPTER 87

Urgency

May 2013

The urgency is warranted. We need to do something about it very soon.

I hear and read a lot about the style of Francis, bishop of Rome. His initial impact is overwhelmingly positive, hopeful, and encouraging. But I also hear and read a lot about "wait and see," which implies skepticism about the long-term, substantive change he may inspire. I want to make the case that we have already seen enough and waiting may undermine the renewal we need.

Christianity is not a spectator sport. The people of God do not sit in the stands and cheer our team as they march up and down the field, court, rink, or aisle of a cathedral. We, the church, are participants, and as the church, we act. We are players, not watchers.

There are at least four areas where Francis has already led by example. (That type of leadership, by the way, is refreshing: leading by living rather than leading by teaching. We haven't seen that in the Vatican since the early 1960s with John XXIII.)

1. Simplicity. Humility. It is clear that Francis lives simply and humbly. His lifestyle, even within the luxury of the Vatican, retains the character of his slum life in Buenos Aries. He refused the standard living quarters of previous popes. His chosen way of life is authentic and belies his presumed position of honored authority. He has already shattered Vatican pretense and exposed himself as a Franciscan Jesuit, which is a new, ecumenical, clerical species.

   When translated into the people of God, his lifestyle leadership means no more extravagant, medieval church buildings promoting pomposity and power. Simplicity and humility rule our new day, even in our buildings. It means no more mansions for our clerics of whatever rank. It means the end to personal ambition and desires for special treatment.

2. "Preferential option for the poor," remember that phrase? It was formed by the Latin American bishops in the 1980s and enshrined in John Paul II's encyclical, *Centesimus Annus* (1991). Dust it off, folks, because Francis lived it for years, and there is no indication that he will change this focus as bishop of Rome. We were just learning how to apply this gospel message when it abruptly got replaced with abortion, contraception, gay issues, pedophile priests, and attacks on nuns and women in general. The lived commitment of Francis places this core gospel challenge right in the middle of our faces, our hearts, and our pocketbooks.

3. Liturgical minimalism—Evidence of the downgrading of liturgical pomp and ritual scrupulosity dominated Vatican Holy Week. Shortened ceremonies, washing the feet of women prisoners, homilies that focused on central, scriptural themes (not theological treatises), all pointed to liturgical minimalism, where compassion outdoes ritual solemnity. If Francis did this during Holy Week, immediately after his election, he certainly will continue it.

   His example can loosen up liturgies around the world. Can you imagine that impact? And the fear it may lessen among celebrants? One example: my guess is that had Francis been pope two years ago, the Vatican could not have forced the hijacked new English translation onto our liturgies, and Fr. Bill Rowe would still be pastor of St. Mary's parish in Mt. Carmel, Illinois.

4. Doctrinal priorities—This category is not yet as clear as the previous three. He allowed the continuation of the investigation of the nuns in the United States, which is a serious issue, but, on this one, I am willing to "wait and see." There are no final recommendations, and there is no indication of what Francis will ultimately approve.

   His emphasis on foundational Christian beliefs (there is a God, Jesus as a visible expression of God, the church as a community trying to live the love of God) is the key message the world needs, not supposed clarity on secondary doctrinal issues or sermons on sexual, moral matters. Foundational Catholic Christian beliefs and how they offer hope to a troubled world and individual pilgrims: that's the doctrinal message that will resonate.

We can't wait and see. Francis is leading by example, and a leader needs followers as well as local leaders to reinforce the example. So, what must we do now?

Some suggestions:

- Talk it up. How do we implement more simplicity, the preferential option for the poor, and liturgical minimalism in our parishes and dioceses? Grassroots focus on these issues now has clear support from the pope.

- Write letters to the editors of secular and Catholic papers. Blog and send Facebook and Twitter messages.

A new church is emerging. Francis has opened the gates, like John XXIII opened the windows. If we don't rush in now, the gates may close. Remember: John Paul I only lived thirty-three days. So, participate now!

Francis Follow-Up: There is a section in *The Joy of the Gospel* titled: "The Special Place of the Poor in God's People." In these few paragraphs, Francis outlines his understanding of the phrase, *the preferential option for the poor*. Here's what he says, in part: "Our commitment does not consist exclusively in activities or programs of promotion and assistance; what the Holy Spirit mobilizes is not an unruly activism, but above all an attentiveness which considers the other in a certain sense as one with ourselves. This loving attentiveness is the beginning of a true concern for their person which inspires me effectively to seek their good" (199).

CHAPTER 88
The Pope Francis Fan Club

July 2013

I've been trying to contain myself, but being a natural-born optimist, I'm having a hard time holding back my respect, excitement, and surprise with Pope Francis. After forty years of Paul VI, John Paul II, and Benedict XVI, I had become skeptical and, frankly, jaded with our papal leadership.

But Francis is pushing all my buttons. Well, not all of them (e.g. he hasn't found the ordination of women button yet), but he's pushing enough of them to get me genuinely energized. What has happened so far has been astounding. Francis is a direct descendent of St. John XXIII, with less girth and, hopefully, a longer life.

It feels like it's time for the PFFC, the Pope Francis Fan Club. This is not a typical fan club because this one demands that members do more than cheer for a superstar pope. Membership includes participation, doing something gospelish.

Two areas of Francis's leadership stand out:

- Collegiality: he is moving this word and its Vatican II teaching out of the papal-imposed dungeon and into the sunlight where it can flourish and extend its vine-branches into the basilicas, chancery offices, parishes, and hearts of the people of God. He formed an advisory council of eight pastoral cardinals. He is empowering synods of bishops. He is reforming the Vatican bank, and the curia is clearly in his sights.

  So far, his efforts in collegiality are directed at the hierarchy. Makes sense, because they need the most reform. Many bishops, I suspect, are running scared, unable to handle collegiality personally or as an organizational model.

- Emphasis on the poor: this focus of his personal life and papal ministry becomes more evident every day. That emphasis is a key theme of the gospel also. Is it asking too much of our pope to imitate this aspect of Jesus's mission? It should be the first item on the job description for pope. The surprise that Francis actually lives this authentic identification with the poor is an indication of how far from the gospel we've come as an institutional church. Other popes, of course, have talked about it, but Francis is leading by living. No better teacher.

My question here is: how are we following his lived teaching? This chat is not a homily, so I don't want to get preachy. On the other hand, if we are going to join the Pope Francis Fan Club, we need to do something with and/or for the poor. Many of you, I presume, already do service for other people, so what does Francis's leadership add to your service? If you don't serve, it's time to get crackin'.

My particular service niche is with the families and friends of anyone with a mental illness or anyone who lost a loved one to suicide. Like most of us, I chose this ministry because of our personal family experience. The point here is for all of us to have a service niche, since no one can do everything and there are lots of ways to help the poor, however you define that term. Just do something.

I would continue to do what I do with our foundation regardless of who is pope. While we are not officially a ministry of the church, I consider our work gospel-based. Perhaps your service work is similar. If so, what difference does Francis make?

A few thoughts:

- It simply feels better doing our bit for the poor knowing that our church leader is doing his bit for the poor. The operative word is "doing." It feels like we are together doing something central to the gospel. It's like people working side by side filling and delivering sand bags when a flood threatens or dishing out the green beans while the pope is scooping out the mashed potatoes in a soup kitchen. We are together. That is a powerful motivator.

- But it is more than feeling good. It is knowing that doing the gospel is more important than teaching doctrine. Teaching and preaching Catholic faith is important, but the teaching is more credible in the context of the doing.

- In the midst of all the scandals, Francis's commitment to the poor shines a beam of hopeful light into a darkened church, a light that is seen by the world. That's evangelization.

So ... wanna join the Pope Francis Fan Club?

CHAPTER 89

Rio Repeated

July 2013

The pope is at it again. I am reluctant to write about Francis so often, but he gives me no choice. He is dominating Catholic news so completely that other topics must get in line behind him.

His dazzling trip to Brazil exploded with thrilled slum-dwellers mobbing him with their gratitude and hope, with millions packing the white beaches of Copacabana in Rio, with a spirit that out yells "Carnival!", with youth from around the world energized by a pope four times their age.

But perhaps most amazing, and with the greatest consequences, were his frank and challenging speeches to the bishops. Essentially, he told them to get out of their mansions and chancery offices and identify personally with the poor. We have overintellectualized our faith, he said, and missed the simplicity of the love, forgiveness, and mercy of God. Get on with that core gospel testimony. And live it, as you say it.

Whew! Who saw that coming a year ago? Delightfully refreshing, right?

But let's be real. The church is a gigantic ship that has lumbered along a cumbersome course for at least forty years and is incapable of changing directions quickly without a mutiny of some of the crew. They figured they were headed for a pleasant resort port in the Caribbean, but now the new captain wants to steer toward the slums of Rio de Janeiro, San Diego, Barcelona, London, and all points in between. There will be grumbling and rumbling among the crew.

Another reality: the church has been experienced most personally on the local, parish level. A pope with a new direction does not change the personality, history, convictions, style, preferences, work habits, or motivations of a pastor. That kind of transformation takes time, willingness, and effort.

For some pastors, Pope Francis is welcomed with a huge "It's about time someone speaks to my heart and truly represents me." For other pastors, the response is: "What's he talking about? He's too radical and doesn't make practical sense."

Which leads to the question: what qualities do we want in a pastor during the era of Pope Francis? To repeat Rio across the world takes pastors who are willing and capable of leading in the way Francis leads.

Some of the pastoral qualities needed to follow Francis may be the same traits needed in any era but the abrupt change inaugurated by our new pope adds a unique twist. Here are some of those qualities:

- Kindness—In the final analysis, kindness/compassion is essential for a pastor. Kindness and pastor are not synonymous, as many of us can attest. But genuine kindness/care for the people in the parish covers a lot of other possible deficiencies. This kind of kindness does not know arrogance, dominating power, egoism, or privilege. This kindness transcends intellectual capability, liturgical precision, hierarchal position, and influential friends. Kindness translates into authentic service. It is critical for any effective pastor, especially a Francis pastor.

- Leadership—Pastors are public persons who lead parishes. Their effectiveness and style of leadership vary greatly, depending on their native ability, personality development, training, and motivation. Their leadership is most evident when they celebrate Eucharist and especially when they preach. Some pastors are so poor at celebrating and preaching that, frankly, I wonder why they became priests in the first place. To lead a parish, a pastor must, along with the liturgical role, know how to form a faith community, motivate people to serve others, and educate parishioners on the importance and relevance of faith. They perform these tasks well or poorly, but they cannot escape these responsibilities.

- Holiness—Genuine pastors must be personally holy. If they are kind leaders but not holy, they are missing a key requirement for their role. Holiness, of course, is complex, comes in many styles, and includes doubts, dryness, and distractions. But some elements of holiness must be there. Pastors must believe most of what they preach. They must pray, putting themselves in the quiet presence of the God they profess. They must make time for their spiritual and emotional growth. And they must connect their spiritual life with their ministerial life and the needs of their parish. It is not asking too much of a pastor to strive to be holy and to share some of that journey with his parishioners.

Our two previous popes emphasized adherence to Catholic doctrine. Francis leads us to Rio. Will our bishops and pastors also lead us to Rio?

CHAPTER 90

Slow Down?

September 2013

I'm getting ahead of myself. Again. That's dangerous because getting ahead of things raises expectations, and after a generous life span, I finally recognize that expectations can get me in trouble. In other words, I still have a lot to learn about the delicate balance between expectations and hope. Too often, my hope turns into expectations, which can lead to disappointments, regrets, and anger (justified, of course).

Know what I mean?

I am going to blame Francis, bishop of the world, for my hope. And I will add his new secretary of state, Archbishop Pietro Parolin, to my hope-creators list as well. Recently, Parolin said, among other things, that the issue of priestly celibacy is open to question. The latest Francis press conference adds to my hope. But let's stay with one issue right now: priestly celibacy.

Our past two popes never allowed a celibacy discussion. In fact, even John XXIII took priestly celibacy off the agenda at Vatican II (along with birth control). My guess is that he deleted those two items because he needed to offer some concessions to the nonreformers who did not want a "pastoral" discussion about them.

The birth control issue was addressed in 1968, after the council, with worldwide, astonished disagreement and led to Catholics leaving the church in droves.

Priestly celibacy was never addressed and was officially "undiscussable," until Parolin, somewhat casually, said, "It is not a church dogma, and it can be discussed because it is a church tradition." Actually people have been chatting about it for decades, and opinion polls around the world claim the vast majority of Catholics would accept a married clergy.

My hope meter is now very high—not for me because I don't want to be a priest, but for the church because we desperately need a married clergy for many reasons. As I see it today, the question is not should we or shouldn't we have a married clergy. The people of God have already agreed that we should ordain married men. It's the practical "how-tos" that now need attention.

See what I mean about getting ahead of myself?

But while I am out there ahead of things, how about chatting about some of those practical matters just a little?

- How will we pay for a married clergy? Let's start with an analysis of what it is costing us now for a celibate priest. I doubt if the average parishioner knows the cost to the parish for salary plus room and board. It would surely be more with a wife and perhaps children. But how much more?

  The stock, but reasonable answer, is that other faiths and denominations have done it for centuries, so we should be able to figure it out and afford it also. I agree; we can figure it out and reallocate funds to accommodate a married priesthood.

  But some questions remain: Does a married pastor in a large metropolitan parish get paid the same as a married pastor in a small rural parish? When the bishop appoints pastors, does he consider salary level? Or is salary based on seniority, regardless of assignment? Does married or celibate enter into the salary equation at all?

- How would insurance benefits work?

- Are current rectories equipped to handle families? What about parishes with more than one priest? Do those rectories, in effect, become family apartments?

- If a married pastor dies, does the family have to move out to make room for the new married pastor? Does the church have any financial obligations to the surviving family members?

- Would adding a married priestly clergy create a two-tiered priesthood? If so, would this be a benefit or hindrance?

- Add your own questions/issues. There are clearly many more.

Are any of these practical considerations "show stoppers"? I don't think so, but they must all be addressed. And there must be a period of flexibility and adjustments before we get too rigid with the rules regarding a married priesthood.

I know, I know. This is all speculation, perhaps useless chatting. But this is the first time in centuries that a married priesthood is even remotely possible. The signals are not strong enough yet to get too hopeful, but the faint signs seem real. And it wouldn't surprise me if the signals get considerably stronger quickly.

See how my hope turns into expectations? Am I headed for more disappointment, regret, and justified anger? Or …?

CHAPTER 91

Choices

September 2011

The only hope left for a vigorous Vatican II church in my lifetime is a new pope with the spirit of Pope John XXIII. Soon. I assume that is not going to happen.

That would be fun to see, though: collegiality at all levels; subsidiarity throughout the church; de-Latinized liturgy, led by ordained men and women, with meaningful local adaptations; courageous champions of social justice all over the world; the church greeting the modern world with open arms and intelligent dialogue; vocations to priesthood, religious life, lay ministry everywhere; ecumenical and interfaith collaboration on multiple fronts; and evangelization thriving because of all of the above.

What could have been … What could have been.

But it's not going to happen. Nostalgic, wishful thinking. But one fun side effect of another John XXIII would be to see how the current crop of bishops would respond to this new pope. Most of them have been selected because of their loyalty to the pope. Would that loyalty transfer to a very different pope? Do they do an immediate about-face on core issues and follow their new leader, or do they fight back to preserve their pre-Vatican II power and privilege? Intriguing to watch. An HBO miniseries, at least.

But since it isn't going to happen, what choices do we have, those of us who will never see our leadership adopt the vision of Vatican II? I think they can be narrowed down to three:

1.   Leave. Like so many before us, we can say "the hell with it" and just leave the church. For most of us, that simply means stop going to Mass. Maybe keep enough of a tie for weddings and funerals. Or we could join another denomination or no faith community. This is a viable option, not only out of anger at church leadership, but because the official, hierarchical Catholic Church no longer provides spiritual meaning or anything resembling faith, hope, and love—just doctrine and more doctrine.

2. Stay and ignore. This option is also viable. Concentrate on your local parish. Find a pastor you can relate to and respect. Become active in whatever ministry you find attractive and where you are needed. Nurture your spiritual life through whatever means works for you. But ignore whatever the hierarchy says or does. Their credibility is shot, and you need to take care of your own spiritual journey; you can do it without them, even within the Catholic Church. We have rich and varied spiritual traditions you could follow.

3. Become prophets. Stay and confront. This option generally takes some real thought and practice, unless you already are a prophet. But many of us are peace-preferring people, and we know what prophets are. Scary! We read the scriptures; we know what happened to the Hebrew prophets, Jesus, and His apostles. If our times call for more prophets, we would rather it be other people—maybe more outspoken priests and perhaps a bishop here and there. But we laypeople who know things are seriously wrong; we too can be prophets.

   We can speak up boldly on local and national issues. It's okay. Do it your way, on the problems you care about. Not every issue is worth a picket sign, but some are. Do it alone or with others. Join Call to Action, Faithful of Southern Illinois, Voice of the Faithful, or a similar group. Confront without expecting change. Confront because it is the right thing to do. Passive resistance. An active, passive resistance. Study Gandhi, Martin Luther King Jr., and, of course, Jesus. Sign petitions. Make statements. Protest.

In any case, stick to your belief in God, Jesus, the church, and Vatican II, and when you die, you will die with dignity and integrity, a life well-lived and a death well died.

And when you enter into paradise, it will likely be Pope St. John XXIII who will greet you with open arms because the first pope, Peter, will be too busy explaining to some bewildered bishops and popes why their entry into heaven has been delayed.

Francis Follow-Up: Well, with Pope Francis, this chat is now obsolete and depressing. But it does show what our very recent options were and demonstrates how far we have come in so little time.

CHAPTER 92

Remaining Catholic

July 2010

This is the twenty-fifth Church Chat. That's not much of a milestone, but I must admit that when I started this project, I wasn't sure I had twenty-five ideas that could or would become chats. Anyway, twenty-five gives me a convenient excuse to look back over the chats to see if I can detect any trends. I expected when I began that I would be critical of some aspects of the Catholic Church, and I have been. From my perspective, there are many opportunities for criticism. There's a lot of low-hanging fruit, ripe for easy pickings.

But I have been more critical than I thought I would be when I began. I thought I would be a little more balanced since I am not a cynic by nature or choice. A little sarcasm here or there is, in my opinion, warranted and needed. But a steady diet of it becomes tiresome, even for me.

In this chat, then, I want to list some reasons why I remain Catholic. It has been suggested that if I don't like stuff about the church, then I should leave it. Take my cynicism elsewhere. Actually, I am not going anywhere with my faith; I will die a practicing Catholic.

I remain Catholic because of the many institutions we have established over the years: hospitals, schools, Catholic relief services, Catholic charities and social services, etc. These are institutions that for centuries have done the gospel. I am proud to be part of an institution that serves people in need in the name of Jesus.

I remain Catholic because, all things considered, I experience faith community in my parish. We have prayerful weekday and weekend liturgies that are both comforting and challenging, with a pastoral pastor who preaches well, responds compassionately to individual and community needs, and provides collegial leadership. I am also part of a small faith community within our parish, which nourishes me in my faith journey.

I remain Catholic because the Eucharist and our sacramental system provide a believable understanding of God in Jesus, accessibility to the divine, and a spirituality that is rooted in our human nature while it pushes us beyond our presumed limitations.

I remain Catholic because, despite all our frailties and flaws as an institution and as individuals, the core message proclaims the love of God through Jesus and for others, the reality of hope, and a faith that surpasses doctrine.

I remain Catholic because this religion does, in fact, motivate millions of Catholics around the world to serve others in multiple ways. Regardless of the competence, relevancy, or integrity of some of the professed leadership and members, these Catholics know and do the gospel daily in ways only God can acknowledge.

I remain Catholic because this church houses people of varying views, faith experiences, and visions of the future. Even in an era when there are mighty efforts to corral everyone into one way of thinking and acting, there are many voices, some prophetic, who shout that one way is not God's way.

I remain a Catholic because I still receive the spiritual energy and intellectual foundation to face each day with hope in this life, faith in my resurrection after my death, and the absolute conviction that humankind is a community in search of the Trinity.

I remain a Catholic not because I was born and raised a Catholic but because my personal, practicing Catholic history infuses my current me with the water and oxygen I need to love spiritually.

I'm sure there are other reasons why I choose to remain a Catholic. I just can't think of them this week. For me, some of the above, and certainly all of them taken together, are sufficient to keep me Catholic until I die. I have serious issues with some of the official policies, current teachings, leadership styles and priorities, personalities, and direction of the institutional church, but none of those issues alone, or taken together, will negate my reasons for remaining Catholic. And while I respect other denominations, I am simply not interested.

I envision a future church that doesn't copy the past because we can do better than that. We glance at the past, but we don't stare. For me, moving into the future means remaining Catholic.

CHAPTER 93

Staying Catholic

March 2011

Each Lent, our parish invites us to use *The Little Black Book: Six Minute Meditations*, published by the Diocese of Saginaw and based on the writings of Bishop Ken Untener, for our private prayer. I'm not sure about the six minutes, but the format and content is very helpful, and I have my prayer chair (actually a recliner—dangerous on some mornings) where I read the text for the day and spend some quiet time, sometimes with God and sometimes inside my own head where God may or may not be present.

But so far this year, the Little Black Book just sits unattended on the end table by my chair. That's because Michael Leach, a classmate of mine from the seminary, sent me a copy of his new book, *Why Stay Catholic?* (Loyola Press). The title alone got me, but since I know Mike and his remarkable accomplishments as an author, editor, and publisher (now publisher emeritus and editor-at-large of Orbis Books), I figured his book would be insightful, conversational, researched, enthusiastic, and hopeful like he is. I got what I expected in spades.

I'm not trying to recommend this book because I know Mike and quite a few of the people in the book, including myself. That would be nice and loyal, but that is not why I endorse the book. I encourage you to read it because of what it says and how it is said.

As regular readers of these chats know, I have addressed the "Why Stay Catholic?" question a number of times. It's not that I am planning to leave; I'm not going anywhere. But I am publically critical of the church on a number of fronts, and some people have told me to "love it or leave it." *Why Stay Catholic?* insists that I don't have to "love it or leave it" but that I can love it, criticize it, and stay. It's my church too.

The book has fifty short chapters divided into three sections: ideas, people, and places. Ideas include, for example, the sacramental imagination, the Bethlehem principle, and the seamless garment of life. Some of the people profiled are: Dorothy Day, Sister Thea Bowman, Pat Reardon, and Fr. Andrew

Greeley. This section reminded me of a little book written by the Gallup organization titled *The Saints among Us*, based on their survey, which reported that approximately 13 percent of the people in the United States are considered saints by their family, friends, and neighbors. Mike identifies fifteen of them. In the section on places, he lists Catholic schools, hospitals, relief services, and Vatican II.

All fifty chapters are reasons why he stays Catholic. You may have more or different ones. Gloria Steinem famously said: "The truth will set you free, but first it will piss you off." There is plenty in the history and current life of the Catholic Church to piss us off, and a lot of it is low-hanging fruit, rotten, easy to identify, pick, and toss. Much of it grows right back, and some of it is more than a piece of fruit, it is a whole limb. But the pruning must be done, some of it individually and some of it systemically. There are ideas, people, and places that need pruning. Any tree that isn't pruned, naturally or artificially, will eventually kill itself.

But trees do live, some of them a very long time. So it is with the Catholic Church. And we shouldn't miss the tree because of the rotten branches and some of the diseased fruit. We can be so consumed by the negative stuff that we miss the point of faith. We can also be naively blind to the negative and, then too, miss the point of faith. It isn't that we need to balance the negative and the positive; it is misleading to make those kinds of lists. We need the ability to see through the negative into the positive, not denying the rotten fruit, but seeing beyond the rot, seeing the whole living tree and grafting ourselves to the vibrant branches and eating that nourishing and tasty fruit.

Why Stay Catholic? points out some of those thriving branches and lush fruits, perhaps on the other side of the tree. Taste and see. It gives us reason to be more than pissed off.

Now, where did I put that *Little Black Book*?

CHAPTER 94

No Going Back?

October 2010

In the September/October 2010 issue of *Corpus Reports*, Anthony Padovano reminds us that Vatican II was and is a remarkable success. In an era of obvious attempts to turn the clock back to 1960, Padovano clearly insists that core changes initiated by Vatican II are here to stay. For his full article, go to http://www.corpus.org/index.cfm?fuseaction=feature. display&feature_id=1340&CFID=1535116&CFTOKEN=28572593.

Here is a brief summary of some of these permanent changes:

- The liturgy is now in the vernacular, and we will never go back.

- We are now the people of God, and we will never go back.

- We no longer support the pope's every word, and we will never go back.

- The church is in the world, not against it, and we will never go back.

- Birth control, for example, is now accepted by progressive and conservative Catholics alike, and we will never go back.

- Mixed and interfaith marriages are commonplace, and we will never go back.

- There is widespread indifference to church teaching on multiple issues, and we will never go back.

In other words, the council has held.

Padovano's insightful article is refreshing and needed. For those of us who are impatient, frustrated, and angry at some of the current issues facing the church, it is valuable to look where we came from fifty years ago and celebrate where we are today. He ends his article with a rousing and courageous litany of witness statements that outline a vision and hope for the future as well as a powerful testimony to what we believe and stand for today.

There are a few "buts" and "howevers" that necessarily emerge in this optimistic snapshot of where we were, where we are, and where we will be. For some of us, the "never go back" refrain sounds right and is probably correct, but there is still a lingering suspicion that some people who want to negate Vatican II completely will eventually get their way. That total reversal is not likely, but it could be miserable trying to prevent it.

For many progressive Catholics, the concern is not about not going back but the slow pace of going forward. Catching up with Vatican II is one thing; going beyond Vatican II is another. The issues tabled at the council or which emerged since then (celibacy, birth control, ordination of women, homosexuality, sexuality in general, genetics, ecology, relation with Islam, technological advances, etc.) are all waiting for substantive, mutual, and respectful dialogue with the gospel and with the world. Many progressive Catholics are weary of the ridiculous in-house, petty priorities (rubrics, hierarchical maneuvering, nostalgia for the past, etc.) and the disastrous sex-abuse and cover-up scandals that they have given up on the church and have confidently joined the swelling ranks of secular humanists. The Sunday edition of the *New York Times* is now their Bible.

It's likely that this flow to humanism will continue and probably increase as the church becomes more engulfed by its scandals and its inability and unwillingness to address real issues among the people of God and the world. Besides, there is no indication that the official church even cares if these progressive Catholics leave; in fact, the impression is that the institutional church prefers a leaner and meaner church. So, why bother to hang around?

Another problem with the "we cannot go back to a pre-Vatican II church" theme is that many younger Catholics have no idea what that church was like. The twenty- to forty-year-olds probably will not recognize elements of that church when they are reintroduced. Red flags go up when we older progressives see signs of the pre-Vatican II church emerge, but the younger folks may not see them as red flags. If that gradual reversal takes place, young progressives may wake up one Sunday morning and find themselves in a church that runs contrary to all their basic instincts. The exodus to secular humanism then continues.

None of my negative comments undermine the value of Padovano's article. He provides a clear reminder that all the work that went into and flowed from Vatican II has not been wasted. An articulated vision of what we could be is always a morale booster and a blueprint for constructive action.

But beware: the Vatican II haters are alive and well, and they're on a roll.

Francis Follow-Up: With Pope Francis, the comments of Padovano remain valid but now within a more positive context and boost.

CHAPTER 95

Step by Step

January 2014

It's not all going to happen at once. In terms of tone and emphasis, things are moving so rapidly with Pope Francis that it is hard to keep up. With newsworthy statements, gestures, and events every day, this superstar pope continues to get headlines.

The novelty is wearing off, but the pundits, columnists, and reporters are going beyond daily stories, and they are now analyzing, predicting, and supposing. It is exciting and promising. Stay tuned.

We progressives are delighted, of course. Just one year ago, no one even dreamed we would have a pope and a church like we are currently experiencing. And with new Francis-made Cardinals coming soon, the possibility for long term Vatican II reform becomes even more realistic.

But (there is always a But, isn't there?) doctrinal change is another matter. I argue that the change in tone and emphasis, the living testimony of Francis, his compassion, style, and infectious love is substantive change, not superficial, but the core of the gospel.

On the other hand, what do we do with centuries of teaching on specific topics? Surround them with love? Yes, and that is what is happening now. But when the teaching itself is problematic, what do we do? Ordination of women, for example.

I do not believe that women's ordination is a litmus test for Francis, although it appears that some other progressives do take this position. I do not subscribe to the "ordination of women or nothing significant has happened" approach.

I have said often in these chats that I support and promote women's ordination. In my opinion, the most likely scenario for this change will be a step-by-step progression, not a full-scale, immediate transformation of the policy.

Here are the steps I see:

1. The ordination to the priesthood of married men will come first. There is obvious and widespread historical precedent for a married clergy, and obligatory celibacy is a clear cultural issue. Current married permanent deacons are likely first-step candidates for a married clergy. Since theological and pastoral formation is practically in place for these deacons, the transition to a pastoral priesthood can be smooth and quick. Practical issues like salary, living arrangements, etc. will be determined and implemented.

    This first step need not be limited to current deacons. Qualified married men could be identified, trained, and ordained. Former priests, married or unmarried, fit here too.

2. My second step could actually be implemented along side step 1. Some parishes are currently being led by parish life coordinators—deacons, religious sisters, or laypersons, male and female, who lead a Catholic faith community. There is even a provision for these PLCs in canon law, and there have been decades of positive experience with this model of parish life. Promoting and expanding this model of parish leadership through to their ordination to priesthood is a natural progression. This development would include the ordination of women who, for all practical purposes, have already been pastoral leaders for many years.

3. Increased roles for women in positions of leadership in all levels of the church. While there are women in many key positions right now, they often report to a priest. It is time priests report to some of them. Ordination does not confer leadership. Priests celebrate sacraments but that does not mean that they are qualified to assume other positions of leadership. They can, and some should, have female bosses. We now assume that priesthood means positional authority that extends to all areas of parish life. That assumption is a fatal flaw. An ordained liturgical celebrant could report to an unordained, qualified lay or religious pastor, male or female.

4. The training and ordination of women will follow developments in steps 1 through 3. While these steps generate practical experience and experimental adjustments, theologians and bishops need to deal with the academic basis for ordaining women. They need to spell out the theological, cultural, doctrinal, scriptural, and historical foundations for including women in ordination. In the recent past, they couldn't

even talk about these issues. Francis needs to open the doors to these discussions. Once that happens, I am confident a solid, positive basis will be established for the ordination of women to priesthood. Implementing steps 1 through 3 will provide the pastoral experience and readiness for a smooth transition to women priests.

One caution: some women can be as clerical as some men, ordained or not. Avoid clericalism everywhere. Having clericalized women as priests only gets us anatomically different tyrants. That's not progress. That's stupid.

But any movement in any of these areas is a movement in the direction of women's ordination. So let's get moving, even if it is step by step.

CHAPTER 96

Big Stuff, Little Stuff

January 2012

You know, when you get right down to it, there's big stuff and then there's little stuff. Mountains and molehills. But what is big and what is little can be very relative. Someone's big may be someone else's little. Lots of people spend lots of money and time trying to get other people to agree with their list of what is big and what is little. In a formal setting, we call this process "prioritizing" and companies, governments, and groups do it all the time to establish goals and objectives. They then allocate resources to achieve those goals and objectives. It's how the world works.

But it's not how the institutional Catholic Church works.

The last time the Catholic Church did the big stuff was the Second Vatican Council fifty years ago. When dealing with the Catholic Church, fifty years is not very long. When dealing with our lives, fifty years is a very long time. And while I am interested in the long-term direction of the church, my primary focus is my lifetime. Call me selfish, but after fifty years, I want the results of Vatican II *now*.

Here is some of the big stuff from Vatican II:

- *Dogmatic Constitution on the Church*: reestablished a collegial form of governance, which included regular papal consultations with bishops, usually through synods. This constitution initiated similar collegial structures throughout the church: episcopal councils, diocesan pastoral councils, and parish councils. The primary image of the church as outlined in this document is the people of God.

- *Pastoral Constitution on the Church in the Modern World*: acknowledged "the signs of the times" and pledged to engage in dialogue and action on the major issues that face the human race.

- *Dogmatic Constitution on Divine Revelation*: reinforced modern insights and methods of interpreting sacred scripture.

- *Constitution on the Sacred Liturgy*: reestablished vernacular languages for the liturgy and encouraged the people of God to take active and leadership roles in our rituals.

And what has become of the big stuff initiated at Vatican II? It has been undermined, rejected, deliberately neglected, ignored, crushed, and ridiculed by a small minority of Vatican insiders, sniveling loyalists, two backward-looking popes, and a host of conservative bishops who left their courage in their cradles.

How did they do it? They snuffed out the big stuff by overemphasizing the little stuff. Some examples:

- There hasn't been a genuine episcopal synod in decades, and with good reason. They couldn't decide or recommend anything anyway. The Vatican inside-raiders (rhymes with Wall Street inside-traders) would do whatever they wanted anyway. These raiders use little stuff like bureaucratic procedures and governing policies to undermine the big stuff and install their little stuff. Effective diocesan pastoral councils and parish councils are headed to the same fate as the genuinely pastoral bishops and pastors retire or die to be replaced by pre-Vatican II hierarchs.

- Dialogue with the world? Don't make me laugh. All they want to talk about is abortion and sex. Simple message: don't do either one. More little stuff.

- Dynamic emphasis on scripture? Not a chance. Doctrine, as spelled out in the catechism, is their one and only tune, with the lyrics from the sixteenth century and the melody from the 1940s. Little, small, tiny …

- Liturgy? Well, we've just been hit with the euphemistic "reform of the reform," which is a callused, transparent power play to put the people of God back into their pews and elevate the role of the male presider.

That's the status of the four key constitutions of Vatican II, promulgated with such hope and enthusiasm fifty years ago. My prediction: We will pay. We will pay.

Actually, we already are paying, but it will get worse. We are the diaspora within the church, not counting the millions who have left. The scriptural theme of "the remnant" sounds prophetically contemporary.

I ask myself: Am I becoming a cynic in my elder years? And I answer: Nah, this analysis is simply the truth. The big stuff is too much for the raiders. They can't comprehend it, and they certainly don't want to promote it because it changes their status. That's not cynicism; that's reality. Find your faith, nurture your hope, and always love joyfully in your smaller faith communities, hopefully even in your parish. That's where these harsh realities become the small stuff, and that's where you can deal with the genuine big stuff.

Francis Follow-Up: The seismic change and rapid reversal initiated by Pope Francis puts the big stuff immediately on center stage and relegates the little stuff to the back room. It will take more time, of course, for the big stuff to filter through the system and be implemented, but it could go more quickly than we think.

CHAPTER 97

Hope

June 2011

Is there any hope left for us progressive Catholics? There are multiple and obvious reasons for us to be discouraged to the point of exiting the Catholic interstate superhighway and continuing our spiritual journey by some other more scenic route. Do I need to list some of those recent reasons? No, you already know them.

The hope question, however, remains. Hope is more than a wish, a dream, a vision. Hope is the conviction that the future will be better than today. Where in the world does that kind of conviction come from in these dreary days?

Hope differs from its cousin, optimism. An optimist, with that half-full glass (is that water or gin?), sees the more favorable side of events, interpreting current conditions in ways that reflect desired outcomes. Hope believes that what is wanted can be had; events will eventually turn out for the best. Hope emphasizes the future; an optimist sees the best of the present.

If you buy that distinction, a person of hope can also be a short-term pessimist, which is my reluctant and uncharacteristic status these days. I am, by nature and by nurture, an enthusiastic optimist and a hopeful guy. But reality has forced me into unaccustomed, short-term pessimism in terms of the institutional church. If that, more or less, describes your present state of mind, what is the basis for your hope?

Here's mine: hope is personal; it travels from person to person. I know people who are genuine believers in God, Jesus, the Holy Spirit, and in being Catholic. Their faith inspires me. I also know people who love well. Faith and love give birth to hope. I know people who remain hopeful during extreme personal tragedies and overwhelming circumstances and remain absolutely convinced that the future will be much brighter than today. Hope is real because these people are real. My guess is that you know people like this too. Take a few minutes and name them.

That's where we find hope: in the people we know or know about.

Do you believe in the presence and activity, the fire and the wind of the Holy Spirit? If you do, that's a basis for hope despite the disappointing behavior that leads to short-term pessimism. Remember when you memorized the twelve fruits of the Holy Spirit for your Confirmation? Recall them now. (Just in case they don't pop into your head immediately, here's a cheat sheet: charity, generosity, joy, gentleness, peace, faithfulness, patience, modesty, kindness, self-control, goodness, chastity.)

To me, some of these virtues overlap (I'm glad the bishop didn't ask me to distinguish between kindness and goodness when I was confirmed.), but it remains a pretty reliable list of what to look for when we are trying to figure out where the Holy Spirit is showing up these days. They are not splashy, spectacular gifts, but they still reflect my kind of God.

Put the name of a person to each virtue or cluster of virtues. Those are some of the people through whom the Holy Spirit is working. And those people, with their beliefs, attitudes, and actions, are the ones who exude hope and are the basis of hope for others.

But that list of virtues does not encompass the whole Spirit. Where are the fire and the wind in this list? It looks pretty docile to me.

This hopeful voice must harmonize with the prophetic voices, the calls for reform from the confrontational folks who point out the weaknesses, inconsistencies, and sins of the church. The Holy Spirit I know is hopeful and prophetic, not either/or but both/and. And that is the real challenge of being hopeful: accepting the critical, justice-demanding shouts of the prophets *while* living the traditional fruits of the Holy Spirit.

If you are a gentle soul, try using your prophetic voice occasionally. If you are a comfortable critic, try some docility occasionally. We don't all need to be in the middle, but we do need to recognize, accept, and support both sides of this spectrum. That's where realistic hope always resides.

Now, what was that list of recent events that make you most discouraged?

Francis Follow-Up: Since Pope Francis, my hope is heightened, but I still stand by the main theme of this chat. His emphasis on joy is intriguing because he addresses it, not as a periodic, fleeting moment of contentment, but as a foundational, persistent, overarching, full-bodied stance of a fully integrated Christian believer. Joy comes first.

CHAPTER 98

Hope 2

July 2011

This chat is a sequel to my previous chat on hope. I received quite a few responses to that one, ranging from "Thanks, I needed that," to a reminder that hope is a transcendental virtue. I suspect that the large response is at least partially due to how bleak the Catholic landscape looks to many people. Hope in that context is a very bright light.

Hope is naive to the hopeless. When there is no hope, the heart dies, the spirit shrivels, and the mind tilts to anger and cynicism. It's not a fun place to be.

So, here are a few more reasons for Catholics to be hopeful:

- The disconnect between progressive Catholics and papal/episcopal leadership is profound, but many of these faithful Catholics are finding what they need for their spiritual journeys. Whether its small faith groups, selective reading, nourishing liturgies, favorite websites, beautiful stubbornness, or friends sharing their lives and their faith, these folks are growing in faith, hope, and love despite the out-of-it interests and concerns of their designated leaders. This disregard for their official leaders is often without anger or even disrespect; it is simple awareness that the hierarchy has nothing relevant to say about real life. These believers gravitate to compassionate, knowledgeable pastors. These progressives are mature and intelligent adults who know how to seek and find God in their lives. And they are doing it. That is hope.

- History exudes hope. A superficial look through church history easily shows how terrible the church and its leaders have been through the centuries. The Crusades, the Inquisition, papal atrocities (did you see the HBO series on the Borgias?), greed, power, lust, etc.—it's all there to shame us into misery. But look deeper—inspiring saints, outstanding and courageous spiritual leaders, martyrs, brilliant holy thinkers, unmentioned millions of faith-filled believers, all following the way of Jesus. How can so many flowers grow among so many weeds? The Holy Spirit. No one, no church policy or hierarch, can take our holiness away from any of us. How do I know? History tells me so. Hope thrives on this kind of history.

- Speaking of history, they can't take Vatican II away from me either. Try as they might (and they are trying.), that outburst of the Holy Spirit remains and will remain, standing tall and immoveable. It is a mountain range, with towering peaks, that erupted out of a desert. That serendipitous gathering of old mitered men from 1962 to 1965 rode that range as it exploded out of the flat, dry land. Today, they turn away because they can't climb the foothills, let alone the mountaintops with their majestic panoramas, clear vision in all directions, and crisp, healthy air. And we know who "they" are. But those mountains are made of boulders of hope and rocks of courage, and, sing along now, "they can't take that away from me."

- Balance. Catholicism offers balance. It is a faith of both/and rather than either/or. Core dogmas are both/and: God is transcendent and imminent, beyond us and within us. God is both Three Persons and one nature. Jesus is fully divine and fully human. There is grace and free will. Lay spirituality is both in the church and in the world. We are called to prayer and to action. Some other faiths and other Christian denominations emphasize one or the other side of each of these both/ands. We sometimes lose our balance also and need some correction, but then that correction eventually comes and we regain the creative tension and mysterious beauty of all our both/ands. Hope is the child of balance.

- I have said it before in these chats, but it bears repeating: our major Catholic institutions, schools at all levels, hospitals, social service agencies, and relief organizations do the gospel extremely well. Hope explodes through the work of the dedicated people in these service institutions.

The pool of hope is cool and refreshing. Jump in. Or, if it is more your style, tiptoe into the shallow end and gradually enjoy its soothing waters.

CHAPTER 99
Prophets with a Smile

October 2011

I recently spent a day with three prophets: a sister, a father, and a movie. The sister is Sr. Jeannine Gramick, the father is Fr. Roy Bourgeois, and the movie is *Pink Smoke over the Vatican*. The event was sponsored by the Faithful of Southern Illinois, a lay group dedicated to education and advocacy in the spirit of Vatican II.

First, the movie: *PSOV* is a powerful, compelling, straightforward, hour-long documentary about women priests in the Catholic Church. Ordinations and excommunications follow the lives of courageous Catholic women who acknowledge and answer the call to priesthood. The movie is not yet in wide distribution because negotiations with HBO are still underway. Once that is resolved, it will either be on HBO or more widely distributed, or both. See it.

Sr. Jeannine Gramick is and has been for decades a clear, brave voice for the Catholic gay and lesbian community. Her story of maintaining that voice through Vatican investigations and profound pressure on her and her religious communities earns her the distinguished title of public prophet.

Fr. Roy Bourgeois, the Maryknoll priest who was the subject of a Church Chat recently and whom the Vaticanistas are now trying to excommunicate because of his public stance promoting the ordination of women, demonstrated his bold commitment to the primacy of his conscience in refusing to recant.

Here's one permanent takeaway for me: these are not angry people. I see clear, courageous, consistent, almost mild-mannered resolve, but not anger. The predictable, hierarchical response to these prophetic voices does not silence them, nor does it seem to infuriate them. I had the pleasure of spending some social time with them and three of the women priests after the presentation, and the sense of outrage was once again noticeably absent. They all appeared to be strong and composed. I had just seen the movie *Invictus* on TV, and these folks reminded me of Nelson Mandela.

There are many issues in the church and in the world that scream for gospel scrutiny. But it's not the people who scream their response who get the best results. It is the intelligent, informed, smiling prophets who persist and persuade.

If we are in the protest and prophetic business, how do we manage our anger? There is, of course, basis for anger. But unmanaged, uncontrolled anger runs amuck and ultimately destroys us, while the external cause of our anger goes merrily on its way. Though I don't know them well enough to say, here's my guess on how Roy, Jeannine, and the women priests (and Nelson Mandela) dealt with their anger:

- They separated their personal experience and hurt from the policy that caused the injustice and the people who implemented that policy;

- Through prayer, personal reflection, and/or the help of some trusted counselors or friends, they named, owned, and resolved their personal anger;

- They focused their attention on other people who are affected by the same policy and attempted to speak for them because they do not have the opportunity, talent, or courage to speak for themselves;

- They accepted the inevitable pushback and criticism from the policy makers and implementers with the perspective of the William Ernest Henley poem, "Invictus": "I am the master of my fate: I am the captain of my soul."

The many world issues and church issues that cause or contribute to injustice must be challenged. Some issues are minor; some are major. How they are ranked in order of importance is usually the prerogative of the person who does the ranking. My suggestion is to pick the issue that affects you the most, that you are most passionate about, and stick with it. Acknowledge that it is not the only issue, but make it your issue.

In this process, take a lesson from these three prophets: deal with your personal anger, perhaps something like I think they did. Then, your credentials as a prophet will improve immensely. And, God knows (literally), we need many more prophets, in and out of the church.

CHAPTER 100
Small Christian Community

September 2011

I've been part of one for over forty years. In the 1970s, they were called adult education classes. In the 1980s and '90s, they became faith discussion groups or Renew groups. More recently, they are called small faith groups, small Christian communities, or small Eucharistic communities.

Each version has a little different emphasis, and they vary somewhat because of the people involved and the leadership. But the good ones have some common features: prayer, faith sharing, community, education, and service. Some may focus on the service component, or the education piece, or the faith sharing, community, or prayer experience, but they are most mature and most beneficial when all five dimensions are present at least to some degree.

For me, the small faith communities I have been a part of in Iowa, Oklahoma, and Illinois were, and still are, a source of inspiration as well as growth in faith. They provide a setting for adult-level searching for God in our lives—and finding some assurance that our personal faith journeys are okay. The groups are a safe place to express our doubts and our convictions. Often, the experience of community becomes the clearest expression of the value of the group. Personal joys and sorrows are shared at an explicit faith level and the social support system is a comfort. Personal faith is refined and clarified. The faith witness of other members is truly inspiring.

The benefits multiply. Some people, of course, do not like the small group experience and do not join or leave after some time. But many believers rely on these small communities as a primary source of faith growth. And there are hundreds of thousands of people who experience these communities in the United States and around the world. The small faith community movement is arguably the most hopeful, wide-ranging Catholic expression of faith in our era.

The official, hierarchical response to this movement is mixed. Some papal writings offer some encouragement. Some bishops and priests openly support the small communities. Other bishops and priests try to ignore them in the hope that they will go away. And some bishops and priests condemn, outlaw, or castigate them with direct opposition.

The main opposition seems to be that these groups are not clerically controlled, and there is fear that the leaders do not know and promote orthodox teaching sufficiently. In these criticisms, the Holy Spirit is not mentioned.

But it appears that most groups are simply not intimidated by these criticisms. Group members sense the value of the faith-sharing experience and have discovered that doctrinal purity does not lead to genuine faith growth anyway. Faith, they know, is more personal and experiential than intellectual adherence to creedal or magisterial statements. It isn't that these people are categorically opposed to hierarchical authority or official teachings. They simply, and wisely, discovered that the small groups offer practical, personal support as believing Catholics living in this very real world.

In my experience, the issues in the small groups do not usually revolve around conservative versus progressive perspectives. The central issue is how to discover, nurture, and respond to the presence of God in our lives.

I encourage everyone to participate in a small Christian community of some kind at some point. Check locally through your parish, diocese, or by word of mouth for what is available. Look for the five components of a healthy group: prayer, faith sharing, mutual support (community), service to others, and education. Join or begin a group (many resources are available), give it some time, and see what happens to you. If it isn't your cup of latte, there's no harm. If it is, you have found a valuable way to know and grow your faith.

Francis Follow-Up: In case you didn't notice, I dedicated this book to my small faith community. I did so because I want to thank my friends in our group for their faith, friendship, and support as we share our life experiences and seek to find and follow our God in the midst of our very real lives. Francis would be a welcomed and comfortable member of our group.

PART 8

Bishop Schneider's Dilemma

A JOURNAL

I can't tell you how I got a copy of his journal, but I will say that the computer hacking Edward Snowden had nothing to do with it. On the other hand, I do have some related advice: don't keep a journal on your computer. Write it out the old-fashioned way.

In any case, I have access to the almost-real Bishop Herman Schneider's ongoing personal journal. He is the bishop of the fictional Mt. Vernon, Illinois, diocese, in his late fifties, personally connected with archbishops and cardinals both in the United States and in Rome, an articulate defender of the faith, pleasant enough publically but devious privately, very conservative, and, as his journal shows, willing to accept a higher ranking position in the church immediately.

In other words, Bishop Schneider lives somewhere near my frontal lobe, a very dangerous neighborhood. While he doesn't represent any particular bishop, he does inhabit many bishops. At least in my frontal lobe neighborhood, he does.

Here's the problem: since Francis became pope, Bishop Schneider has lost some of his confidence and direction. Some selected journal entries paint the picture:

3/13/13: They elected a guy from Argentina as pope, Bergoglio. Never heard of him. But something didn't seem right. He came out in a plain white cassock, smiled a lot, and then asked the people to bless him. That's strange. It should be the other way around. Everyone is trying to figure out who he is and what he's like. Jesuit, of all things. Picked the name of Francis; the first one who dared to do that. Called Bernie and even though he is my vicar general and has lots of connections, he didn't know anything about this Bergoglio either. Wait and see, is all he could say. Anyway, I have a new boss and I guess the Holy Spirit is involved, but something doesn't seem right.

3/15/13: Janice called and insisted I should fly to Rome and meet with Francis. Since she divorced Bill, she has turned her formidable focus on the family. That usually means she has a great idea on what we should do. Are all older sisters like this? Mom and Dad can handle her pretty well, but, though we love her, Dan and I have to draw our boundaries. I am not flying to Rome to meet Francis. That would jeopardize my chances of making a good impression. I have to be more subtle than that. I will watch and look for opportunities, but I have to be careful.

3/18/13: At our monthly staff meeting today, we all reported on what we learned about Francis before we got down to business. Bernie is still saying "wait and see." Caution is his middle name, but it's good to have someone like that around. Mike spoke up for a change. As the only layman at these meetings, he is usually more reserved. Then again, that might be the way he is. He did the most research on Francis and had details about his life as a Jesuit and how he botched some things as a superior in Argentina. But he too said wait and learn. I guess that makes sense since it's only been a few days, but I'm beginning to think I will not fit in with the Francis papacy.

3/28/13: Holy Thursday and Francis washed the feet of some young Muslim woman in a prison. What am I supposed to do with that? His living, his dress, his whole style—it's not appropriate for the pope. I call it "commonizing" the papacy. I admire his commitment, in a sense, and the people seem to be with him all the way, but there is a certain decorum that goes with the papacy and he is undermining that. The image is extremely important. And I am not able to do what he does. I'm not moving into an apartment, and I need a driver so I can keep up with my correspondence and grab a nap. I never thought I would have these kinds of issues.

4/6/13: This journal is a good project for me. I've been doing it for about a year now, and I wish I had done it years ago. Our retreat master suggested it, so I tried it, and after I got used to the discipline, I like it. Tonight I had a little time so I read the last six months or so, and it helped me see some patterns I would not have noticed. I don't get to it every night, but most of the time, I do. I am also glad I am not writing it out because who knows who might eventually find it and read it. I am confident that I buried it in the files of my computer so that I feel secure no one will ever see this. I have to be so careful about my bishop image that it is sometimes hard to know what I really think and feel. This journal gives me a chance to try to sort out the real me from the public me, if there is a difference. That's not easy.

4/9/13: If it were up to me, I would not have John Conroy as pastor of the cathedral. But I inherited him, and it would be complicated to move him. The people love him because he never says "no" to anyone. He lacks decorum—dresses like a layman most of the time, talks in church like it is a coffee shop, too interested in sports. He and I are not on the same page with liturgy either. He's low church; I'm high church. He's the pastor, but the cathedral is the bishop's church. So we clash on style and content. Very frustrating. He preaches love all the time when the people need some guidance and clarity. I would transfer him to Red Bud, but he is so popular that I would look bad. I have to get him to want to leave and admit that in public. I feel stymied, and there is no way out. Unless I just move him and hope it works out. I'm not sure yet. Delicate and maddening.

4/25/13: Thank God for Denise. I couldn't ask for a better secretary. She is organized, efficient, and very loyal. There are some administrative things that I just hate and wouldn't do them well, but she picks up all those pieces and makes me look good. Today she got out a complicated mailing from Mike about finances, and she even made great suggestions to the cover letter he wrote. She is a little rigid at times, but in the long run, she presents a good picture of the diocese, particularly to the parishes. God bless, Denise.

5/14/13: Had Confirmation in Marion tonight and an eighth-grader asked me what I thought of the new pope. Caught me off-guard, actually. I was tempted to say, "No comment," but knew I couldn't get away with that. Said the right things: different approach, humble, speaks for the poor, teachings haven't changed, etc. But what do I really think of Francis? Honestly? Serious reservations. Not enough emphasis on church teachings. A key role of bishops, and the pope, is to teach authentic doctrine. We must stick with that as our foundation. Without changing doctrine, he is changing everything. I fear what's coming. I'm sticking to my agenda, and I will try to smile more and learn some jokes. But I'm not sure where I stand anymore. I can't talk about this in public, not even to Bernie, especially not to Bernie or other bishops. I have to work this out myself.

5/22/13: Got a call from Janice about Mom and Dad's fiftieth wedding anniversary. She is organizing it, of course. God bless her, I couldn't do it. Since August 14 is a Wednesday, she wants to move the celebration to a weekend. Needs to know a good date for me. Told her I wasn't sure yet, but I will check my calendar. While I am in Cleveland for the anniversary, I want to meet with Bishop Harrison and talk with him about Francis. Harrison is also a friend with Cardinal O'Malley from Boston, since Harrison is also from Boston. It looks like O'Malley will be on the inner-circle council for Francis. So, one of my channels to the pope and the Vatican could be through Harrison to O'Malley and then to Rome. I want to make sure Harrison is in town when I go for the anniversary.

6/3/13: I had my annual meeting with women religious superiors today. Why do I bother? They smile nicely and say cordial things, but I can't get them to do what I want them to do. It isn't that they don't do good work, but they need to get behind the bishops more on issues like abortion, gay ministry, contraception, and women's ordination. Since they have a lot of credibility, they could sway people on these issues. In any case, many of them are social workers, not nuns, anyway. And some of them think they are priests. I hope the Vatican investigation on them recommends some strong action to get them back in line. But, there again, Francis doesn't seem to put much priority on this problem. So, I can't take them to task. Another unaddressed problem.

6/17/13: At the staff meeting today, I told them of my plan to restructure the diocese. I've been working on this for a while and have it pretty well worked out. It is time to bring others on board, starting with the staff. There are too many parishes in the diocese, and we are certainly running short of pastors. I brought in many international priests, but that is not the overall solution. The only logical thing is to close parishes. But that is very tricky. My plan involves the parishes making decisions themselves to close. No one will voluntarily close their own parish, so I decided to partner all the parishes in various ways and have the partnerships decide which parish will close. The masterstroke with this approach is to force each partnership to decide how they will operate when only one priest can serve two or more parishes. It will take a whole process, but in the end, parishes will close. And most important, they will decide which ones will close, not me. I am covered. Staff, of course, asked some questions, but they all agreed. It was easier than I thought. Now we will work out the details. I like projects like this.

7/9/13: I assigned two more Nigerian priests to parishes today. They seem like nice priests, and they will fill some gaps. It doesn't take as long as some people say to get used to their accents, and it sure beats laypeople running the parish. What I like best about these international priests is that they are loyal to the church and to me. I can rely on them. They come from a culture where the clergy are respected, like it used to be here seventy-five years ago and still is today in Nigeria. It's a good thing I have personal connections with bishops in other countries so I can recruit these priests. As long as they say Mass on weekends, I don't expect much more from them, and they keep the parish going by being there.

7/24/13: One of my classmates, Steve Norton, was accused of sexual abuse of a twelve-year-old boy years ago. I'm not close to Steve so I don't know how credible the accusation is, but I am glad he's not in my diocese. I hate these cases. It is a no-win situation, and frankly, I think bishops are getting a bad rap. They are often accused of covering up, but I know some of these guys, and I think the only thing they can be accused of is forgiving too much. Can't say that, of course. SNAP would crucify me. And a lot of other people would be cheering at the cross. But an abuser who confesses should be forgiven, just like other sinners. That's the heart of our faith—forgiveness. Even Francis preaches that regularly. I don't know what will happen with Steve, but he is probably ruined, especially if it is true. I remember him as being pretty fragile to begin with. I wonder who the boy is.

8/18/13: The anniversary celebration was yesterday, and it was great being with the family. Janice ran a good show, and Dan and I caught up. His daughter Michele just got out of rehab for drug abuse and with a probable diagnosis of bipolar. Difficult times ahead, I suspect.

The nephews and nieces, cousins, and friends of the folks appreciated having a bishop say the Mass and socializing with them. I don't get to see the family often anymore. I think my homily did the folks justice. They are good people.

I did see Bishop Harrison this afternoon, and we had a nice visit. When we talked about O'Malley and Francis, Harrison seemed guarded, almost protective. I still think I could cultivate a closer relationship with Harrison in hopes of getting some access to O'Malley and therefore a step closer to Francis. Maybe get on some committee that O'Malley heads or as an independent advisor on the media, which I have experience with from my days in the Chancery in Cleveland. But I got the impression from Harrison that he was angling for some role with O'Malley himself and not too interested in representing me. But it is still worth the effort. These kinds of things take time.

8/27/13: I introduced my restructuring plan to the presbyterial council today, and frankly, I feel like I need to appoint all those members instead of having some of them selected by the priests. There was some opposition to the whole idea and various parts of it. Not from everyone, of course, and Bernie defended it well. But Conroy objected and said it would destroy some wonderful small but active and financially sound parishes. People will leave the church. Then he and Fr. Boswell both said that the root problem is limiting the priesthood to celibate males. Those are issues beyond my control, and I don't want to be a bishop of married men and certainly not ordained women. Besides, John Paul II had decided, infallibly, that women cannot be ordained. And a married clergy would disrupt everything. I can't control some of my priests now. Can you imagine how hard that would be if they had wives and children?

Anyway, we are moving ahead with the plan. I anticipated the objections, but today helped me sharpen my responses to those objections. Actually, I plan to write an article in the *Southern Illinois Catholic* about this parish "renewal" project, and I will start with the objections and answer them right up front. That will take the wind out of their sails.

9/12/13: I keep getting letters and emails from people complaining that they can't understand the international priests I brought into the diocese. Sometimes they say the sound system in the church makes it even harder, and sometimes they say they can't understand them even in normal conversation. There are even some complaints that a few of these priests don't fit into our culture.

Makes me mad. Damn! Don't these people realize that there are no other priests? They should be grateful, not complaining. The Mass, the sacraments are available. Everything else is secondary. Why don't they see that? The people are spoiled, and it is time they appreciate what they have because before long, they won't have anything. If they are so upset, why aren't their sons becoming priests? It's their fault we are in this predicament. The church had a formula for centuries for providing priests, but the people stopped having enough children and then discouraged the boys from becoming priests. I dare not say that though. Cardinal Burke probably would, but he doesn't say much of anything either during this Francis reign. I'm not going to say it in public, and it's one reason I limit myself to one scotch when I am out.

It's time for bed. I better calm down, or I will never get to sleep. Maybe a nightcap will help.

9/13/13: I glanced at last night's entry and my mention of scotch reminds me of Bernie. Fortunately, I don't have a problem with alcohol, but I am beginning to wonder about Bernie. When I was a priest back in Cleveland, I had some parishioners who were alcoholics and who convinced me to attend some open AA meetings with them. A few of the priests here are also dealing with it. So, I know something about alcoholism and I am quite sure I smelled alcohol a number of times with Bernie. He also seems less enthusiastic than before, and he is obsessed with Francis. I can't have any issues with my vicar general. I better talk to him.

9/16/13: I talked to Bernie about his possible problem with drinking. He denied he had a problem and seemed insulted with my question. But he said he would watch it. I still wonder. I will watch it too.

10/10/13: Every day, I get comments or questions about Francis. Everyone seems so eager to praise him. I have my stock answers now: remarkable and admirable style but the teachings remain the same. What disturbs me the most is that Francis doesn't seem to care about church teachings too much, even though he hasn't denied anything. He seems to think that other things are more important. I don't get it, and I am convinced he is making some big mistakes. Frankly, he is making my job harder. People are beginning to expect me to be more like him. Well, I am not moving out of my house and I am not changing my style or teaching. Pretty soon, people will lose interest in him and we'll be back to the way things used to be.

10/13/13: I just don't understand why some of my diocesan pastors became priests. They dress how they want. They think how they want. They do what they want. They don't seem very reverent. And they clearly don't respect me. They claim to be Vatican II priests, whatever that means. Vatican II didn't change things nearly as much as they think it did. We need to emphasize how that council continues the long-standing traditions and teachings of the church. Continuity is much more valuable than change, despite the different style of Francis. Some of my priests are terrible representatives of the church. I don't know what to do with them, but I am determined to maintain my course.

11/6/13: Today was very frustrating. We had a meeting of the Priests' Personnel Board, and a few of my pastors on the board always question my assignments. They claim they know some of my pastors better than I do, and they said Fr. Schilling would not be a good fit for Vienna. Nonsense. I talked with Fr. Schilling, and he said he would go, so I am sending him to Vienna. Just because these priests know one another from seminary days doesn't mean that they know better than the bishop. When will they accept that?

12/16/13: I got another anonymous letter today about Fr. Boswell changing some of the wording at Mass. When I ask about him and a few others, I never get too many specifics although it seems he recites the Eucharistic prayer pretty much intact. But he keeps adding his comments and prayers like his homily extends to other parts of the liturgy. We can be "personal" but only within the approved ritual. After all, it is the church's prayer, not his. I'm not sure what I will do about this, but it is not right to let it go. I have to come up with something.

1/8/14: Pope Francis is remarkable. I will give him that. But his impact on my priests is a problem. He is encouraging the ones who have criticized me, and I feel some pressure to imitate his style. I can hear it in the comments of people when I go to a parish and they ask about Francis and my reaction. One lady in Waterloo had the gall to ask if I was going to move out of my house. I even sense a change in some of my pastors who have been loyal to me, including Bernie, my vicar general. They're switching some of their personal loyalty to Francis. I can feel the tension when I talk with some of the other bishops too. We don't know where we stand anymore. The wheels are coming off my career, and I may end up here in Mt. Vernon for a very long time. Francis is taking things away from me. I deserve honor and respect as a bishop, and he is downplaying everything I believe should accompany this position. Here's the worst part: I know some of my priests want me gone, and they think Francis is giving them a reason to get rid of me. Little do they know! I hate that I have to defend what I deserve.

1/15/14: This guy is a disaster. Every day, it's something else. His popularity keeps growing, and he keeps insisting on helping the poor. It's not that I disagree; I read the gospel too. But my whole career is going backward. I studied canon law, worked in the chancery back in Cleveland, met the right bishops and two cardinals who assured me I was on the right path, became the youngest auxiliary bishop in the country, was made bishop of Mt. Vernon, and now I'm ready for a bigger diocese. Then Francis changes things so that now I am an outsider instead of an insider. Depressing. And I am still young. How can I handle this? I don't want to be bishop here for the rest of my life. What can I do?

2/3/14: Fr. Schilling called me today, and he now wants out of Vienna. The people are nice, but it is too small and there's not enough for him to do. I told him absolutely not!

2/18/14: That silly survey from last fall about the family is beginning to haunt me. It was so long and involved and asked questions that only a bishop or loyal theologian could adequately answer that I didn't encourage it here. I had a deacon send it out, but he tells me the responses were predictably hard to tabulate and had a variety of uninformed opinions. Waste of time. I answered the questions based on church teaching and sent it in as our official diocesan response.

But now other countries are reporting their results, and they consistently show that many people either do not know or do not follow official teaching. After all the time, energy, and money spent on Catholic education, we end up with adults who don't believe in or follow our teaching. We obviously have to teach better because they are influenced by our secular culture more than by our teaching. I have spent a large part of my life, as a priest and a bishop, promoting Catholic education. I am very discouraged by these results.

Now the local media wants my response to the reports and a statement on how people voted here in the diocese. I will put them off for now, but I fear this ill-conceived synod this fall. What will I say then?

2/23/14: I don't feel like writing much tonight. Too tired and getting depressed. Just one thing: Francis is not prolife enough. I spent years emphasizing antiabortion and fighting *Roe v. Wade* and the prochoice crowd. I wanted Cardinal Burke as pope; he would take a strong stance against abortion.

On the other hand, I don't disagree with Francis. He stresses the basics of the gospels and who can argue with compassion, mercy, and love? I just thought we were beyond that—that the basics were covered and we had to stand up for the implications of those virtues, like opposing abortion, gay marriage, contraception. Francis is back to basics when we are past the basics. It is frustrating.

3/5/14: I am becoming more intrigued and appalled by Francis, all at the same time. I cannot oppose him publically, not only because he is so popular but mainly because he is the vicar of Christ. Burke would have been better, but it is as it is. To be honest, I also admire Francis and yet he remains the greatest personal challenge to my ministry. Many of my retreats in the seminary, and as priest and bishop, emphasized the centrality of love, and I believe that. But Francis's way of showing it is not the way I thought popes and bishops were supposed to show it. We have to guide and direct people. That's our role. Besides, we are the princes of the church. But he wants us to love directly. I see what he does, but I have never done it that way, and I doubt if I can at this point. It is a personal and difficult struggle for me. I talked with my spiritual director the other day, and he wasn't too helpful. I sometimes wish I weren't a bishop anymore. I used to enjoy it, but I am losing my footing.

3/9/14: It is the First Sunday of Lent, and I met with the catechumens and candidates for baptism this afternoon. About the same number of converts this year as last. If you believe the statistics, more people left the church this past year than joined us. The Hispanics help keep the numbers up nationwide, but in Southern Illinois, the movement is clearly downward.

Along with that, I know that many of these converts don't really know the Catholic faith very well. There's not enough discipline, and our expectations are way too low. These people need to study more and do more service. My guess is that half of them will not be coming to church a year from now. I keep telling the pastors and RCIA leaders that they need to strengthen the instruction part of the program and stress that being a Catholic has serious obligations. But they don't comply with my orders. I didn't see evidence of much knowledge on anything when I questioned them today. Distressing.

3/11/14: Tomorrow, we have a provincial meeting of bishops in Chicago. Perhaps this will be Cardinal George's last meeting with us. His cancer has come back, and he handed in his resignation letter a few years ago. The agenda is typical, but I wonder how much I should say about my struggles with Francis. If I say something, will it impact my career? I'm not sure how much I can say with these bishops. We also have to report on our survey results, and I am not sure how I want to do that either.

I will not initiate any comments on Francis, but if the others do, maybe I will say something. This job is getting harder by the day. I would just as soon stay home.

3/20/14: I had the thought today that maybe the problem with Francis is that he is not managing the media very well. He is too much off-the-cuff, spontaneous. The media is always right there, and anything he says or does leads to endless speculation and analysis. And people follow the media. Other popes taught love, compassion, and mercy too, but they controlled their message better. It was part of documents, encyclicals, prepared homilies. Francis just says and does what he wants at the moment. That's no way to be a world leader in this age of instant communication. He has to control his message better.

4/8/14: That whole thing with Wilton Gregory in Atlanta about his new residence really upsets me. That's not too extravagant. It's about right in my opinion. We have to entertain and much of that entertaining is about raising money. The people with the bigger checkbooks expect that kind of residence. If Gregory moves out, I bet his contributions go down. Besides the money really came from a donation from Margaret Mitchell, but now the money will be gone with the wind. He is a good man but way too progressive for me.

It messes up things for me. I was planning to build a new residence here in Mt. Vernon. My hopes for getting a bigger diocese are dwindling since Francis has changed the formula. If I stay here longer, I want a better place. Bigger and updated. Besides, I deserve it. I am equivalent to a CEO and should be compensated much better than I now am. Two years ago, I probably could have pulled off a new residence without too much opposition. But today, with Francis and this Gregory incident, I don't dare even suggest it. Besides, the diocesan restructuring plan makes it harder to spend a few million on my home. It is very depressing.

4/18/14: I always liked the Good Friday liturgy, but today it seemed almost too real. It occurred to me that my life at this time is an extended Good Friday. And I don't see Easter Sunday in three days. It may be like this until Francis dies and we get a regular pope again. I see Francis continuing on the same path he started a year ago. In fact, that path may become a superhighway, and then I will really be lost. Then again, he keeps preaching and doing the basic message of the gospel. You can't argue with him because what he says and does is so obvious and, in a sense, correct. But it's too simplistic. He is my dilemma.

I really don't know what I am going to do. My frustration in being stuck here in Southern Illinois grows deeper each day. And yet, I don't see any way out, and I have burned a lot of bridges here, especially with the clergy. Good Friday isn't so good. And like the movie *Groundhog Day*, it keeps repeating itself. Where is my resurrection?

4/22/14: Now that Holy Week is over, I plan to get away for a few weeks.

Vacation followed by retreat. I am headed for the South of France with Archbishop Chanute from Philadelphia. We made these plans when I thought he was in favor with the Vatican, but now I wonder about his influence. And I'm not sure I can talk with him about Francis too personally, but maybe I will.

In any case, I am very depressed about my life right now, and I definitely need a break. Maybe vacation and retreat can get back my old enthusiasm and direction. But I doubt it. The church under Francis just doesn't fit with me like it used to. I don't know what I am going to do or can do.

This will be my last entry in this journal for a while. Not sure if I will pick it up again in three weeks, but I know I will read it. I will see then if I want to continue. It does take some commitment and time. And, like I said, I am losing my enthusiasm.

CONCLUSION

The past does not always predict the future. Unexpected events and unforeseen people reverse trends, establish new priorities, create fresh hope, or smash us with heart-splitting despair. Will New Orleans ever be the same after Katrina slashed and pounded the Big Easy into tons of rubble and mountains of water? How many lives have been transformed by the courage and vision of Gandhi, Martin Luther King Jr., and, of course, Jesus?

Some people and some events have that kind of impact. They defy predictions, emerge, and leave behind a changed world. The same dynamic erupts on smaller scales too. Sometimes there are reconciliations after longstanding feuds between family members, neighbors, races, or countries made possible by the wisdom and strength of one person.

The Catholic Church is now experiencing a time of rapid transformation due to the papacy of Pope Francis I. Is it an exaggeration to shout boldly that we Catholics are part of an extraordinary period of history, a period that will be recorded as exceptional and will change the direction and impact of Catholicism for centuries? Nope, I don't think that prediction is an exaggeration. Pope Francis is that kind of leader.

Many people are less certain and advise us to wait and see. The least we can say right now is that Francis and his style of leadership were not predicted or expected. Recent history gave us no indication that this Argentinean cardinal would become pope in the first place, let alone the kind of pope he turned out to be.

Church Chat records some of that remarkable transformation as it is happening. The contrast between the previous two popes and Francis is dramatic and profound. From a heavy emphasis on doctrine to a priority on service; from clerical privilege and preference to collaborative discipleship; from preoccupation with sexual issues to a focused attention on the poor; from medieval liturgical pomposity to a simplified ritual flow that emphasizes the core message of the gospel; from an elegant, aristocratic, advantaged, hierarchical lifestyle to a simple, humble, compassionate shepherd; from an intellectualized, theological defender of the Catholic faith to a wise grandfather who insists on the centrality of practical, demonstrated love, Pope Francis has reversed the image and the substance of papal leadership.

We do not know where the Francis path will take us. Will he continue in the direction of reform or be stopped by counterforces within the church? Will he live long enough to effect permanent and substantive change? Will he go so far but hold back in some areas like ordination of women? Will the people of God follow his lead or give verbal support but do nothing to help implement his vision? Will the hierarchy give public adherence but inwardly, like the fictional Bishop Schneider, long for the day when Francis dies and the papacy can return to its old normal? We do not know.

What we do know and what these chapters demonstrate is that Francis is making a qualitative difference. The five years between 2009 and 2014 are pivotal because they represent the end of one era and the beginning of a new one.

The millions of us who chat about the church have much to talk about as the Francis era unfolds. It is refreshing that we can smile more than we did a few short years ago and that our hopes for a church renewed in the vision of Vatican II seem more possible now. Today cannot predict a better tomorrow. But it sure feels better today and, maybe, that's as good as it gets.

ACKNOWLEDGMENTS

While many people have influenced the development of this book, I want to recognize and thank those who had a direct impact on this effort. The Southern Illinois Association of Priests (SIAP) is mostly a group of priests from the Diocese of Belleville, Illinois. Some are pastors, some retired, while others are married and have left active priestly ministry, but all are still committed to the vision of Vatican II. I was one of the founding members over forty years ago, and, though aging, we continue to meet regularly for support, fellowship, and doing our part to promote that vision. They are not only my friends, but they keep me focused on the dreams we had as young priests. Thanks, guys.

Bob Stewart remains in the forefront of promoting progressive activities within the Catholic Church and, among other things, identifies and distributes articles to his list of *Voice of the Faithful* members. Bob was an early supporter of my *Church Chat* columns and forwarded them to his extensive network. I am very grateful for his dedication, savvy, sound suggestions, and friendship.

Mike Leach is the noted author of the book *Why Stay Catholic? Unexpected Answers to a Life-Changing Question* and writes an inspiring column (*Soul Seeing*) for the *National Catholic Reporter*. He has also been a consistent and encouraging commenter on *Church Chat* columns and provided a back cover endorsement for this book. Thank you, Mike, for your insight, guidance, friendship, courage, and humor.

Dan and Sheila Daley also endorsed this book. In 1978, they cofounded *Call to Action*, a Catholic organization dedicated to progressive and justice-oriented issues within the Catholic community and in our society. I have valued their work for decades and truly appreciate their endorsement of this book.

The staff of iUniverse has been, as always, friendly, professional, and extremely helpful in shaping these columns into this book. In particular, Traci Anderson has been invaluable in guiding this project through the iUniverse publishing process and Sarah Disbrow offered insightful and expert direction during the editing phase. I appreciate their commitment to publishing a first-rate product and their patience as I incorporated their suggestions into the text.

I also am affectionately grateful to my wife, Fran, for forty years of marriage and specifically for being my first reader for all my columns and this book. She finds things that I miss, and her findings improve the text. Thanks, now and always.

INDEX

W

Y